MEN AND IDEAS

An Informal History of
Chinese Political Thought

By LIN MOUSHENG

Developing independently for three thousand years, the political conceptions and philosophies of the West and of China did not come into close contact until the last century. Yet, as Dr. Lin Mousheng shows in this book, there is throughout a striking parallel between European and Chinese thought not only in the initial assumptions about man and society, but also in the evolution of those premises towards many identical conclusions.

There is the Idealist School of Confucius and Mencius, who assume with Plato and Aristotle that man is by nature a social being and that only through a code of moral laws can society be organized harmoniously. There is the Naturalist School of Laotzu and his followers, who with Rousseau argue that man is born free but everywhere is in chains. There is the Utilitarian School of Mocius, who with Bentham advances the theory of the greatest happiness of the greatest number of people. There is Huang Tsunghsi, the philosopher of democracy, who formulated the basic democratic assumption that man is not made for the state, but the state for man. In short, Chinese thinkers as well as Western have confronted all the various problems of feudalism, monarchy, democracy, progress, and reform. Though widely separated in time and space, these men meet on a common human situation. Laotzu preceded Rousseau by two thousand years; Wang Anshih antedated the Roosevelt New Deal by nearly a thousand; K'ang Yuwei's world commonwealth is prophetic of Vice-President Wallace's Free World speech.

With this book, Dr. Lin has filled in an important section of political literature, for his, we believe, is the first concise history of Chinese political thought available to the general reader in English.

Men and Ideas

MEN and IDEAS

An Informal History
of Chinese Political Thought

LIN MOUSHENG

Introduction by
PEARL S. BUCK

The John Day Company
New York

MANUFACTURED IN THE UNITED STATES OF AMERICA

INTRODUCTION

THE Chinese are the most modern-minded of all the peoples of Asia, not because they are westernized in the usual sense of that word, but because they have kept through the centuries a mind so fluid, so unbound by social and political traditions, that they have been ready at all times for change. So they were ready mentally and spiritually even for this strange day in which we live.

In this, as in everything, apparently, China and Japan are almost the complete opposites in Asia—Japan, seeming so modern in her acquirement of western mechanical techniques, has shown herself to have a mind almost entirely medieval in its working. China, careless of the techniques, apparently slow to acquire the skills which the West values so highly, has shown herself to have a mind so modern, so lively, so comprehending of the times, that actually she is further ahead in her readiness for international conceptions than any of us.

One may ask why there is this difference. Why has Japan kept the stiff traditional medieval mind almost unchanged and why has China, far older than Japan, this young vigorous adaptable mind which gives her such energy in the long war she has been waging against her superior in arms? I believe the answer is to be found in one fact—China has always believed that her great men were her thinkers and her philosophers, and she has followed these rather than bureaucrats or militarists, while Japan has held bureaucrats and militarists to be of the first importance in the nation.

The inevitable consequence of this has been that in Japan there have been few if any great original thinkers while China has been rich in such men. The rulers of Japan did not encourage great thinking, for only free thinking can be great. But the Chinese encouraged all such thinking as the source of their wisdom and their strength, and emperors and people alike respected the thinkers. Thought, in a word, has always been free in China. There have been moments in her long history, of course, when tyrants strove to suppress free thought. China had her period of dictatorship, too, centuries ago. There have been other partial suppressions from time to time, even in modern times, but they were never successful. The Chinese mind is accustomed to freedom and it will be free. The fruit of such freedom has been the illustrious roll of the Chinese philosophers.

I know that philosophy is a word to frighten many persons in the West, and I think we have a right to be afraid. The sole touch with philosophy that most of us have had was in college when with nothing but bewilderment we were enmeshed in the winding coils of European philosophical thinking. Abstraction piled upon abstraction was the chief impression it left upon us. For if the West did not follow exclusively the Japanese military-ruler pattern of complete suppression of thought, nevertheless the western peoples have segregated the philosopher, at least from their ordinary living. They have not had time for these coils, these twistings and turnings of the soul, these examinations into the primary being of man and matter. Life was too short a span between the first gaze of the opening eyes and the last closing. I cannot tell where the fault was, or who did the segregating, whether the practical people in impatience pushed aside the dreaming philosophers and gave them no honor, so that, being without honor they retreated still further into dreams, or whether the philosophers themselves made the first retreat before the hard facts of life.

But in China the philosophers were not allowed to retreat. Some of them tried it, being there, as everywhere, proud and sensitive men, but the people would not have it. They believed that these thinkers had the secrets of life and they forced them to reveal what they knew. The Chinese were really far more practical than we were; they said in effect to their philosophers, "If there is anything to what you are thinking, then put it to some use for us—go and tell our emperor how he ought to govern us, and tell the landlord how to change his evil ways, and tell us, too, what we ought to be."

In short, they demanded of their thinkers practical values. These were essentially moral values, but the Chinese wisely believe that moral values pay a good deal more than their price in direct returns of peace and prosperity. Good will among men is valuable not as a religious asset but as an excellent atmosphere for trade. A good man as emperor, they reasoned, was the best surety for good government, and good citizens insured good business. Tyranny in the palace and crime on the streets simply made life a nuisance for all concerned. For above all else the Chinese love life, its pleasures and pastimes, its work and play. Virtue, they reasoned, made for the abundant life, not in heaven but on earth. "Therefore," they told their thinkers, "teach us all, high and low, what is the superior man, not for some future state, but here and now."

With such demands upon them, it was impossible for the Chinese philosophers to retreat into abstraction. The people held them grimly to earth and made them think to the point of their practical need. The result is a great body of the finest political-philosophical-ethical thinking in the world. It was political thinking, too, for political thinking is essentially philosophy in the practical terms of the people's life.

This body of thought and thinkers Lin Mousheng has put into compact form in a book. I am glad to introduce both the book and the author because I consider what he has done of the highest importance for this moment in the world and in our relations with China. For the western reader as he reads these quiet, clearly expressed pages will realize that the great thinkers who have been China's leaders in the past are still China's leaders today. Here is modern thinking, not ancient. The road which we travel now, the road which seems to us so new, so difficult, has been traveled before—but by Chinese feet. Perhaps that is why China meets her present disaster with such unyielding courage and such unpuzzled calm. She has lived through a flurry of lesser men before in her own history and has come through to freedom and the realities of her own life, and so she will again. Such courage, such calm ought to be a tower of strength to us now and a fountain of wisdom to us at the peace table, when the tangled human relations of our world must somehow be untangled.

There is another reason why I am glad to introduce this book. The author not only reveals the thinkers who have shaped the thoughts of the Chinese, but he reveals most interesting and significant parallels to western philosophical thinking. Our philosophers, East and West, in the span of human history, though unknowingly and at different times, have thought alike. Human beings, it seems, are only human beings still, wherever they are in time and space, and whatever the color of the skin. We need today to have practical proof of our likeness to each other and here it is. Not only is there nothing alien to us now in the thought of the Chinese great men, but actually ours have done the same sort of thinking, East and West, separately, independently. Our differences in thought have been superficial and our likenesses profound. It is time we knew it.

PEARL S. BUCK.

PREFACE

IN THIS volume I have discussed the lives and works of fifteen outstanding political thinkers in Chinese history, eight of the feudal age and seven of the monarchical age.

Such eminent philosophers as Wang Ch'ung of the Han dynasty, Chu Hsi and Lu Chiuyüan of the Sung, and Wang Yangming of the Ming have not been included, for they did not make much original contribution to the philosophy of politics. A few lesser known thinkers—Pao Chingyen of the Chin, Ch'en Liang of the Sung, and Wang Fuchih of the Ming and Ch'ing—have been selected, for each of them fathered a new trend of political thought.

Both in translation and in interpretation I have taken great liberties. Of passages difficult to translate I have rendered free versions in English; of those doubtful in authorship or obscure in meaning I have given interpretations to the best of my knowledge.

In preparing the manuscript I have consulted the works of competent translators and interpreters, which are listed in the bibliography. To those authors I owe a great intellectual debt.

Finally I wish to express my profound gratitude to Pearl S. Buck, who has kindly written the introduction; to Mr. Richard J. Walsh, who has graciously read the entire manuscript and offered many valuable suggestions; and to Lin Tanp'ing, who has assisted me in the preparation of this book.

LIN MOUSHENG.

September 10, 1942
New York, N. Y.

CONTENTS

Contents

xiv Contents

Men and Ideas

PROLOGUE

PROLOGUE

Nature of Chinese Philosophy

CHINESE philosophy is essentially social and political philosophy and contains little metaphysical speculation or logical inquiry. This does not mean that the Chinese are not at all interested in the meaning of existence or the process of knowledge, but rather that they are primarily concerned with the human situation, with the problems of interpersonal, interfamily, intergroup, and interstate relations. Throughout the ages the Chinese philosophers have seldom entered deeply into the first principles of being or knowing; they have devoted themselves almost exclusively to the exploration of the best possible social and political order. In this sense the Chinese are social and political beings par excellence.

Indeed so socially and politically minded are the Chinese philosophers that they have translated virtually every metaphysical concept into a moral concept and every logical theory into a social or political theory. To them it seems that pure reason and practical reason are a unity and cognition and conation are one. Every concept or theory they have ever formulated is never a concept or theory as such pure and simple, but invariably a concept or theory of human behavior or of social and political action. In the history of Chinese philosophy, therefore, metaphysical doctrines are *ipso facto* moral doctrines and logical problems are *ipso facto* social and political problems.

The Confucian doctrine of the rectification of names (the defining of terms), for instance, theoretically falls within the sphere of logic. As all students of philosophy know only too well, the greatest difficulty in the universe of philosophic discourse lies in the fact that philosophers—sophists and dialecticians in particular—often do not take the trouble to define the terms they use and, as Thomas Hobbes put it, they enjoy the "privilege of absurdity." The rectification of names is, therefore, a first step toward sensible philosophic discourse. Confucius, however, is not interested in the rectification of names as such, but as a means to establishing a moral order. To him names are essentially definitions of social and political roles. If names are not correct, human relations cannot be properly denominated and the moral order cannot be established.

Take the concept of tao as another example. When Laotzu speaks of tao as meaning the first principle of, or the ultimate reason in, the universe, he indeed appears to be in the realm of pure metaphysics. And in his mind this thing-in-itself is neither human nor divine, but a natural principle. Yet despite his pure reason Laotzu advises man to follow the way of the tao by returning to the state of nature. This very advice itself suggests that tao is perhaps less a pure concept in the realm of metaphysics than a practical concept in the art of living.

It should occasion no surprise that throughout the ages China has not produced a Francis Bacon or an Immanuel Kant. No works of the Chinese philosophers are comparable to the *Novum Organum* or the *Critique of Pure Reason*. The Chinese philosophers are so homocentric that they cannot ascend to the high realm of abstract thought without looking down at this earthly abode of man. To put it figuratively, they must feel that the "starry heavens above" are less awe-inspiring than the "moral law within." So completely earth-bound are the patterns and contents of Chinese philosophy.

In the annals of Chinese history we find a long roster of moral philosophers, that is to say, social and political philosophers. In manifold ways they are comparable to Plato and Aristotle, to Machiavelli, Bodin, Hobbes, Locke, Montesquieu, Rousseau,

Hegel, Marx, Proudhon. Chinese philosophy is fundamentally an expression of the collective experience of the Chinese race—the largest aggregate of human beings on earth—in the art of social intercourse and political organization. What little metaphysical speculation or logical inquiry there is in Chinese philosophy is never pursued for its own sake. Practically all metaphysical and logical concepts and theories are "socialized" or "politicized" in terms of human relations. This seems to be the outstanding characteristic of Chinese philosophy as a whole.

Cycles in Chinese History

To the average westerner—as to the average Chinese—the history of China must be a formidable record of dynasties and kingdoms, of dry bones, forgotten names, and remote events.

In order to make this informal history of political thought intelligible, we present herewith a simple outline of Chinese political history, to serve as a frame of reference within which men and ideas may be properly located and understood.

We may conveniently divide Chinese history into four cycles (beginning with the twelfth century B.C.). The first cycle covers about 900 years, the second and third about 800 years each, and the fourth about 600 years. Each cycle, strangely enough, falls into two periods, equal in length, a period of peace and unity and a period of war and disorder.

FIRST CYCLE (1122-222 B.C.)

1. Formation and Expansion of the Feudal System
   Chou Dynasty (first half, 1122-771 B.C.)
2. Decline and Fall of the Feudal System
   Period of Spring and Autumn (770-481 B.C.)
   Period of the Contending States (480-222 B.C.)

Second Cycle (221 b.c.-a.d. 588)

1. Peace and Expansion
   Ch'in Dynasty (221-207 b.c.)
   Han Dynasty (206 b.c.-a.d. 219)
2. Internal War and Foreign Domination
   Three Kingdoms (220-264)
   Chin Dynasty (265-419)
   Northern and Southern Dynasties (420-588)

Third Cycle (589-1367)

1. Peace and Expansion
   Sui Dynasty (589-617)
   T'ang Dynasty (618-906)
2. Internal War and Foreign Domination
   Five Dynasties (907-959)
   Northern and Southern Sung Dynasties (960-1276)
   Yüan Dynasty (1277-1367)

Fourth Cycle (1368-1911)

1. National Revival
   Ming Dynasty (1368-1643)
2. Foreign Domination
   Ch'ing Dynasty (1644-1911)

Fifth Cycle (1912—?)

The Chou dynasty constituted the first cycle, during which the feudal system arose and expanded and then declined and fell. Significantly, while the feudal system was growing, there were great statesmen but no systematic political theorists. It was not until the system began to disintegrate that political thinkers arose either to moralize and rationalize the feudal *status quo* or to advocate some new social and political arrangements.

The Han dynasty covered the first half of the second cycle, the T'ang that of the third, and the Ming that of the fourth. During these great periods of peace and expansion China produced many literary writers and classical commentators but few original or radical philosophers of politics. It was during the second halves of these cycles, when the Chinese were divided against themselves on the one hand and invigorated by the infusion of new blood and culture on the other, that great political thinkers were born.

From this cyclical phenomenon we may draw a tentative conclusion that in times of political tranquillity man passes the day more or less leisurely and tends to accept or idealize the existing *status quo,* while in times of storm and stress he seeks constantly to reorientate himself to the perpetual crisis in society and tries to blaze new trails of thought and action.

In dividing Chinese history into four cycles, let it be inserted parenthetically, we are by no means suggesting a deterministic theory—whether it is of the Hegelian, the Marxian, or the Spenglerian variety—nor a fatalistic prophecy that the future history of China will repeat the past in the same cyclical manner. Although it can hardly be accidental that Chinese history falls into four cycles, we are unable to explain satisfactorily the cause or causes underlying the cyclical movement. The present state of human knowledge does not permit any historical scientist or philosopher to venture a sweeping interpretation of the course that China has thus far traversed, much less her unknown future. For a long time to come we must stand humble before the stage of the great drama of history.

Social Analysis

The natural history of a political theory—that is to say, the seeding, flowering, and withering away of a political theory—presumably follows a series of laws, which unfortunately at present we are unable to define. We can only assume that no political theory ever originates in a social vacuum and disseminates through the cross-section of society by a series of chances and accidents. The first task of the interpreter of a political theory obviously is to analyze the nature of social existence or the social milieu out of which it rises and which it permeates.

Human thought is necessarily limited by the horizon of human experience. He is a rare thinker indeed who can transcend the scope of the general consciousness of the times and grasp problems of political life that are timeless and spaceless. Plato and Aristotle, whose systems of political philosophy are amongst the most universal and comprehensive in the West, were essentially Hellenic. The city-state was the limit of the Platonic as well as of the Aristotelean political philosophy. The ideal of Plato was but an Atticized Sparta, that of Aristotle a Spartanized Athens. Likewise the Chinese philosophers were largely confined within the horizon of Chinese experience.

The early philosophers in China, living in the time when the feudal system was in process of dissolution, could not but assume certain postulates and categories of thought that were prevalent in the general consciousness of feudal society. The political thinkers in the long monarchical age (with the exception of the anarchist) never questioned the soundness of the monarchical system, although they thought that the monarch should act in accordance with the voice of the people.

It may be stated as a general principle that political theory is by nature a product of political experience and that no theory ever rises beyond the range of societal perception and cognizance.

We may go a step further. In the history of political thought few phenomena are more conspicuous than the simultaneous existence of conflicting and antagonistic schools of thought. This was particularly true in the feudal age when four major and five or six minor schools were advancing different panaceas for the ills of mankind. The explanation, it seems, lies in the fact that these schools represented the patterns of thought and behavior of dif-

or later personality types?

ferent classes in feudal society. The Confucian school apparently was the school of gentlemen—princes and dukes. The Taoist school was made up of disillusioned intellectuals. The Mocian school represented the lower middle class—free artisans and free farmers. The Legalist school stood for the interests of the upper middle class—plutocrats and landlords. An understanding of the structure of feudal society and the changes it went through is a key to ancient political thought.

When the feudal system finally disappeared and the monarchical system came into being, Chinese society underwent a profound transformation. Hereditary classes ceased to exist. Henceforth there was free and rapid social mobility. Under the monarchical system any man could rise from the humblest station to the highest post of the state. The political thinkers of the monarchical age belonged to that large and unique intelligentsia class. The members came from all social classes, peasant as well as landlord, artisan as well as plutocrat, officialdom, and the intelligentsia itself. It was a large class, for it included all scholars of the nation; it was unique because it was an unattached, unorganized, floating class which might defend or attack the interests of any established estate or any suppressed group. Most political thinkers were conservative in outlook because they themselves were either in power or on the road to political prominence, while some were liberal and even radical, believing that social values, whether incomes or deferences, should be more or less equally divided.

Psychological Analysis *of whole school?*

The second task of the interpreter of a political theory is to understand the personality of the theorist. To some extent a political theory is an externalization of the autobiography of the theorist. The state without is a mirror of the life within. Whether the state is regarded as a paradise or an inferno, the symbol of an indulgent mother or that of a tyrannical father, the *summum bonum* of society or the very negation of humanity, is in a certain degree a reflection of the life of the theorist himself. A political theory, being the creature of a theorist, is necessarily an image of his own. It cannot be entirely free from the shadow of his sentiments and attitudes, his hopes and fears, his ambitions and frustrations, his pride and prejudice. In order to understand a theory, therefore, we must look into the life of the theorist.

In the feudal age, for instance, there was an interesting pair of trios: the illustrious trio of Confucius, Mencius, and Hsüntzu, and the obscure trio of Laotzu, Yangtzu, and Chuangtzu. The former were extraverted world reformers, while the latter were introverted fugitives from the prison of humanity. The former had a very high level of political aspiration but were time and again frustrated; they were compelled to retire into teaching and writing. The latter had an extremely delicate sense of self-pride, or self-esteem, disdained to associate with the powers that were, and escaped from the world of coarse and brutal realities into the blissful state of nature and the dreamland of speculation.

These two trios set up two patterns of life, the classic and the romantic, which have profoundly influenced the life of the Chinese people. An understanding of the inner recesses in the minds of these pioneer thinkers will throw light not only upon the history of political philosophy but also upon the development of the nation as a whole.

In addition to these there was Mocius, that prototype of the ascetic, puritanical, humorless, authoritarian character, who represented the artisan class; there was Hantzu, the worldly, practical, realistic, cold-blooded, tough-minded thinker, who represented the plutocrat-landlord class. The theories of these men were excellent ideational photographs of their intimate lives.

Of the outstanding political thinkers in the monarchical age, none save Wang Anshih was successful in politics. It is an almost universal phenomenon that political philosophers are masters in dialectics but amateurs in political engineering. Plato could not make a philosopher-king of Dionysius II, nor could Aristotle tame the wild Alexander. For political philosophers in general are eloquent in speech and writing, but unskillful or diffident in real politics; they are men of ideas, not of deeds.

Let us glance at the panel of political thinkers in the monarchical age.

Tung Chungshu, the metaphysical monarchist, was obsessively systematic in thought but nervous and awkward in action, and died a disappointed and frustrated old man.

Pao Chingyen, the sociological anarchist, was an escapist of the Taoist persuasion.

Wang Anshih, the new dealer, was a rare political genius with a strong will to power and endowed with a great literary gift.

Ch'en Liang, the political synthesist, was a very original and courageous thinker, who suffered repeated political blockades and died an untimely death—a victim of ego-inflation and social inertia.

Huang Tsunghsi, the philosopher of democracy, was a wholesome personality, lucid in thought, kindly in temperament, scrupulous in conduct.

Wang Fuchih, the philosopher of nationalism, was a man of strong emotions, a great creative mind, uncompromising in action, completely free from earthly temptations.

K'ang Yuwei, the last of the Confucians, was a willful, dogmatic, obstinate character, but a great literary genius and an extremely imaginative thinker.

The political theories of these men were in a sense the true confessions of the lives they had lived. No man, not even a political philosopher, can get away from himself.

Comparative Analysis

To study political thought as a phenomenon—that is to say, to study why certain men in certain countries think of certain ideas at certain junctures of history—we venture to suggest the method of comparative analysis. Only through comparative analysis may we perhaps eventually arrive at some working hypotheses regarding the nature of political thought as a whole.

First of all, we should compare the political theories of different lands and classify them, if possible, into certain basic patterns. Second, we should study the common factors, if any, in diverse historical situations which occasion the emergence and propagation of certain patterns of political thought. Finally, we should pay attention to certain temperamental or psychological affinities between thinkers of like minds. In this way we may perhaps formulate a "science of political thought."

Obviously at the present state of human knowledge we are unable to draw any sweeping generalization concerning the phenomenon of political thought. The "laws" of political thought are not yet known; they are intricately related to the complex nature of society and deeply rooted in the psychological recesses of man.

It is not within the scope of this informal history to enter into a comparative analysis of political thought. Nevertheless we shall make a few perhaps obvious comparative observations, as we tell the story of Chinese political thought, with a view to stimulating popular interest in comparative analysis.

The illustrious trio of Confucius, Mencius, and Hsüntzu, for instance, may be likened to the equally illustrious trio of Socrates, Plato, and Aristotle. Both trios are aristocratic in temperament and in outlook. Confucius and Socrates are the world's first philosophers of politics. Mencius and Hsüntzu are molders of Confucianism much as Plato and Aristotle are interpreters of the Socratic doctrine. These two trios have exercised the greatest influence upon the course of political thinking in the East and the West respectively.

Standing in opposition to the Confucian trio is the Taoist trio of Laotzu, Yangtzu, and Chuangtzu. The role of the Taoist school in Chinese thought may be likened to that of the Epicurean and the Stoic in Greek thought. The Taoist school is a protest against the dominant Confucian school, while the Epicurean and the Stoic constitute "a rebellion against the central Socratic philosophy." As a person Laotzu the inscrutable is unique, while Yangtzu the egoist may be called the "Max Stirner of antiquity" and Chuangtzu the mystic the "Rousseau of antiquity."

The Mocian and Legalist schools of political thought are really the forerunners of the Hobbesian and the Machiavellian respectively. Both Mocius and Hobbes begin with the contractual origin of the state and end in the creation of the monstrous Leviathan. Both Hantzu and Machiavelli teach the science and art of power politics.

The Chinese political thinkers in the monarchical age, like those in the feudal age, lack no comrades-in-ideas in the West. We shall here briefly indicate some of the kindred spirits among the Chinese and western thinkers.

Tung Chungshu and Hegel are both metaphysical philosophers of politics, considering the fabric of the state and society as analogous to the structure of the universe.

Pao Chingyen advances a sociological concept of the state—a concept which is developed more fully by modern communists and anarchists.

Wang Anshih, the new dealer, is a precursor of modern social legislators.

Ch'en Liang, the political synthesist, anticipates some modern thinkers who find the dichotomy of idealism and realism in politics unessential or unnecessary.

Huang Tsunghsi, the philosopher of democracy, and Wang Fuchih, the philosopher of nationalism, both living in the seventeenth century, are the first ideological fathers of the modern Chinese democratic and nationalistic movements. The former is akin to Locke and J. S. Mill in spirit, while the latter shares certain ideas with Montesquieu, Hegel, and Herder.

Finally, K'ang Yuwei, the last of the Confucians, conceives of a great commonwealth, a global utopia, that is at once democratic and socialistic in organization.

A comparative study of the comrades-in-ideas of the East and West would reaffirm the view that men are more or less alike and similar ideas arise from similar circumstances.

Before closing this prologue the author wishes to express the thought that, while he endeavors to be objective in the preparation of this informal history of Chinese political thought, he realizes most keenly that he is prisoner of his own experience and must necessarily interpret political thought in a circumscribed way, perhaps projecting quite unaware his own maxims of thought and action into categorical imperatives. No philosopher can transcend the horizon of his experience, much less a novice at philosophy.

Part One

THE FEUDAL AGE

1. FEUDAL INSTITUTIONS AND CONVENTIONS

The Establishment of the Feudal System

THE golden era of Chinese philosophy is the second half of the first cycle, the periods of Spring and Autumn and of the Contending States which saw the decline and fall of the feudal system.

In this golden era there were "a hundred schools" of philosophy which rivaled one another in intellectual brilliance and social eminence. The most influential of these schools were the Confucian, the Taoist, the Mocian, and the Legalist. They established the patterns and created the symbols and illustrations of Chinese political thought.

Before going into the story of this philosophical galaxy, let us turn for a moment to the salient institutions and conventions of the feudal regime. For the early systems of political thought were largely determined by conditions within the feudal order, and the early thinkers, conservative and radical alike, were necessarily children of the feudal age—whether they were filial or not.

The beginnings of Chinese history are shrouded in the seven veils of mystery. After P'an Ku created heaven and earth, there were thirteen Celestial Sovereigns, eleven Terrestrial Sovereigns, and nine Human Sovereigns, who reigned for a total of 81,000 years. Then came the Nest-Dweller and the Fire-Driller who taught people how to build shelters and cook foods. In the twenty-seventh century B.C. appeared the Yellow Emperor who was the first to set up some civil government and from whom Chinese history is traditionally dated.

The most significant political legends of antiquity are the voluntary abdications of the model kings, Yao and Shun, who lived in the twenty-third century B. C. It is said that Yao offered the throne, not to his own son, but to Shun, a wise and virtuous minister, and that Shun likewise chose as his successor an able hydraulic engineer by the name of Yü, who had drained the waters of a great flood. Yü, it is said, was the first king to establish a hereditary dynasty, the Hsia, which lasted for more than four centuries *(circa* 2205-1766 B.C.).

Authentic history began with the Shang dynasty, founded in the eighteenth century B.C. by T'ang Wang, originally a ruler of a principality. He staged a political revolution which overthrew the Hsia dynasty, then under the tyrant Chieh. Toward the end of the twelfth century Wu Wang, also the ruler of a principality, started another revolution which vanquished the Shang, then under the tyrant Chow, and set up the Chou dynasty.

While we are here chiefly concerned with the feudal system of the Chou dynasty, we must bear in mind the legends of the two voluntary abdications and the stories of the two political revolutions, which have figured significantly in all discourses on Chinese politics. The voluntary abdications are invariably cited as examples of government by the wise and virtuous, and the political revolutions as precedents for the right to overthrow tyrannical government.

When Wu Wang became the Son of Heaven, he appointed as his prime minister the Duke of Chou who, more than anyone else, was responsible for the organization of the great feudal empire. Upon the advice of the prime minister the Son of Heaven established a royal domain where the central authority resided, and created many vassal states by apportioning territories to the members of the royal family, to several deserving ministers and generals, to the descendants of certain ancient rulers, and to the son of the last king of the fallen dynasty. These feudal lords were divided into five grades: duke, marquis, earl, viscount, and baron. According to Mencius, the Son of Heaven had a territory one thousand li in length and in width; every duke or marquis a hundred li; every earl seventy li; and every viscount or baron fifty li.

Every vassal state, whether a dukedom, a marquisdom, an earldom, a viscountcy, or a barony, was itself a feudal regime. The vassal lord generally subinfeudated parts of the territory, which he had received from the Son of Heaven, to his subordinates or subvassals, who were ranked as follows: chief minister, great officer, upper scholar, middle scholar, and lower scholar.

The vassals and subvassals either cultivated their own estates directly through the services of their slaves or servants, or distributed their lands to serfs or tenants. It is said that the lands were portioned into well-farm units, each of which had nine square farms. The central farm, similar to the demesne, was a public farm, while the surrounding eight farms were private.* The serfs tilled both the public farm for the vassal or subvassal and their own private farms.

The great feudal empire was therefore a highly organized hierarchy. At the summit was the Son of Heaven, under whom were dukes, marquises, earls, viscounts, and barons. Subordinate to each of these again were chief ministers, great officers, upper, middle, and lower scholars. All these constituted the ruling class of the empire. On the broad foundation of the hierarchy were the masses of the people, serfs and slaves, who constituted the ruled class. The entire empire was in perfect pyramidic formation.

The fundamental principle of the feudal system was that the king was the ultimate owner of all the territory of the empire and the highest sovereign of all the people.

> Under the wide heaven,
> All is the king's land;
> Within the four seas,
> All are the king's subjects.

---

* The configuration of nine square farms is similar to the shape of the tick-tack-toe, which is exactly the Chinese character *ching,* meaning a well. Hence the term well-farm system.

Furthermore, by virtue of his position as Son of Heaven, the king was the highest priest of the empire. He controlled not only the temporal but also the spiritual affairs of the empire, not only the present but also the future life of the people.

In medieval Europe, the emperor was the temporal leader, while the Pope was the spiritual leader. The authority of the Chou king twice exceeded that of the Holy Roman Emperor.

An important principle of feudalism was that of heredity. The Son of Heaven gave his throne to his eldest surviving prince. The vassals and the subvassals could not transfer their titles freely but must pass them on to their eldest male children. Even slavery and serfdom were hereditary: slaves were owned by their masters and serfs were attached to their farms. A corollary principle was that of public ownership of land, which was not a commodity of exchange. The vassal who received territory from the king, the subvassal who received a fief from the vassal, or the serf who received a farm from the subvassal, while enjoying the right of usufruct, did not own the land and could not alienate it.

When the Son of Heaven created the vassal states, he stipulated a number of conventions governing feudal relationships. Such relations were personal in character. The vassal lord was personally bound to the king and personally obliged to observe the feudal conventions. In the first place, when a vassal lord died, his eldest son, though by the principle of heredity the legitimate heir, must seek the recognition of the king. He became the new vassal only after formal appointment by the king. In the second place, the vassal lord must periodically pay homage to the king and presumably report on the state of the vassalage. Thirdly, the vassal lord was under obligation to pay annually in spring a fixed tribute to the king. Finally, the vassal lord had to render military service to the king. Whenever the empire was in danger of invasion the king might order the vassal lord to raise a contingent of troops for national defense.

It appears that these conventions governing feudal relations did not constitute a legal contract between the sovereign and the vassal, but were rather a series of obligations, stipulated by the sovereign, which must be fulfilled by the vassal. The obligations were not reciprocal as were those in European feudalism.

The Decline and Fall of the Feudal System

Theoretically, the feudal age lasted for nine centuries (1122-221 B.C.). During the first half of this period the king was more or less able to maintain and exercise his sovereignty; but during the latter half, which was subdivided into the period of Spring and Autumn (770-481 B.C.) and the period of the Contending States (480-221 B.C.), the feudal system gradually declined and finally collapsed. By degrees the king lost his sovereign authority and the vassal states assumed increasingly independent powers. Except in a few rare cases, the vassal lords no longer sought the recognition and appointment by the king and ceased paying homage and tribute to the royal domain. Though the king was the nominal head of the empire, the royal domain for all practical purposes became itself an insignificant feudal state in the midst of several rising and growing states.

At the beginning of the feudal age there were about 1,800 feudal states, but by the beginning of the period of Spring and Autumn the number had dwindled to only 124, a little more than one-fourteenth of the original. Certain states, such as Ch'i, Chin, Sung, Ch'in, and Ch'u, having conquered and absorbed many small feudatories, became far more powerful than the royal domain. As the central authority declined, strong states arose to assume the leadership in the empire. The first of these was Ch'i, which in 681 B.C. organized a league of feudal states, aiming to uphold the royal house and to resist the invader, the semi-barbarian state of Ch'u on the southern border. The duke of Ch'i was appointed head of the feudatories by the king. Later, the states of Sung, Chin, and Ch'in successively achieved hegemony in the league. At the beginning of the sixth century Ch'u, the very state against which the league was organized, threatened to bid for the command of the league.

While the central authority was formally respected by the league of feudal states in the period of Spring and Autumn, the king lost all semblance of sovereignty in the period of the Contending States. The empire was then literally divided into seven states, the rulers of which had each assumed the title of king and were in perpetual warfare with one another During the fourth century the state of Ch'in, which arose from the western border, made frequent incursions into the central and eastern states. The other six states, under the organizing genius of Su Ch'in, an adventurous diplomat-scholar, formed a "vertical alliance" against Ch'in. The alliance was short-lived, for the six member states were individually and severally defeated by Ch'in time and again. Finally under the premiership of Chang I, another adventurous diplomat-scholar, the state of Ch'in succeeded in forming a "horizontal coalition," whereby the six states were brought under its hegemony. By 221 B.C., after having conquered one by one the six states, Ch'in unified the empire and established the first monarchical regime in the history of China.

Thus, after a career of nine centuries, the feudal system was finally destroyed, and in its place the monarchical system was instituted. The passing of feudalism and the appearance of monarchy marked probably the greatest political transformation in Chinese history. For the next twenty-one centuries China was to remain under monarchical rule.

Economic and Social Structure of Feudal Society

While this chapter deals mainly with the political institutions and conventions of feudalism, it is important to inquire into the economic and social structure of feudal society. In the earlier centuries of the feudal age every feudatory was a self-sufficient rural community. Life was simple. There was little exchange and communication between the feudatories and no metallic currency. The basic occupation was agriculture, and the chief products were millet, rice, wheat, barley, silk, cloth, pigs, and chickens.

In the later centuries, however, the capitals of the royal domain and the feudal states became important centers of business and handicraft, where urban civilization fast spread. These capitals grew from small market places to big cities, surrounded by walls and moats, to which people of neighboring communities came to exchange their products. The self-sufficient rural community, which was the cellular basis of feudalism, dimmed out of existence.

The iron age dawned, succeeding the bronze age. Labor was increasingly differentiated.

In the following celebrated passage Mencius discussed the necessity of the division of labor with Ch'en Hsiang, a disciple of Hsü Hsing.

Mencius said, "I suppose that Hsü Hsing sows grain and eats the produce. Is it not so?"

"It is so," was the answer.

"I suppose also he weaves cloth and wears his own manufacture. Is it not so?"

"No, Hsü wears clothes of haircloth."

"Does he wear a cap?"

"He wears a cap."

"What kind of cap?"

"A plain cap."

"Is it woven by himself?"

"No, he gets it in exchange for grain."

"Why does Hsü not weave it himself?"

"That would injure his husbandry."

"Does Hsü cook his food in boilers and earthenware pans, and does he plow with an iron share?"

"Yes."

"Does he make those articles himself?"

"No. He gets them in exchange for his grain."

With the introduction of iron and with the use of oxen for plowing and of animal manure as fertilizer, the productivity of agriculture was increased. Cities thrived on manufacture of iron and bronze articles, earthenwares, chariots, carvings, and embroideries. Intercity and interstate commerce developed. Business houses became as powerful as noble families; iron mines and salt fields were as important as feudal estates. There emerged a new class of business entrepreneurs, a new bourgeoisie, the rise of which signalized the decline and fall of the feudal order.

In the earlier centuries of the feudal age the chief form of the wealth of the empire, land, was under public ownership. But in the later centuries the increase in the productivity of agriculture and the progress of industry swept large numbers of serfs off the land and drove them to urban centers where they became industrial laborers. The well-farm system was gradually abolished and, with it, the institution of public landownership. In the sixth century, several feudal states began to levy land taxes according to acreage—a fact which signified the breakdown of the fief system and the rise of the institution of private landownership. There arose a new class of independent landowners and free farmers, a new middle class, which, while required to pay taxes, owed no personal bonds or obligations to the nobility.

As indicated above, every feudal lord, whether a duke, a marquis, an earl, a viscount, or a baron, created a number of subvassals, who were divided into five grades, chief minister, great officer, upper scholar, middle scholar, and lower scholar. Since the eldest male children inherited the titles and fiefs of their fathers, the younger children were frequently left title-less and fief-less and had to secure their own means of living. Being the ruling class, the nobles were trained from childhood in the art of government and in military and humanistic sciences. Sons of nobles who were not of the first-born but who nevertheless were well educated frequently fell outside of the circle of the ruling class. It was they who formed a new intellectual class, a class of noble origin but without the privileges of nobility. There were of course members of the intelligentsia who were not of noble origin but came from the urban bourgeois and the independent landowning classes. This new intelligentsia became a powerful political force in shaping the body politic in the latter part of the feudal age. It was largely from the intelligentsia that the early systems of political thought originated, systems that either challenged or idealized the existing feudal institutions and conventions and the established right of government by the nobility.

The Rise of Political Philosophers

There was no systematic political thought during the early centuries of the feudal age. It was not until the feudal regime began to disintegrate that political thinkers arose to rationalize the feudal institutions and conventions or to challenge the very reason of the feudal state. As "there arose the ethical and political philosophy of Plato and Aristotle, the successors of Socrates, just at the time when the distinctive political life of Greece was beginning to decay," * so there evolved the social and political philosophy of Confucius and Laotzu when the pyramid of the feudal regime was starting to crumble. Just as "it was in the midst of the widespread conflict between aristocracy and democracy that the most brilliant contributions of Greek thought to political theory began to appear," ** so it was in the midst of the struggle between the rising middle classes and the traditional feudal nobility that the "one hundred schools" of philosophy explored and examined the whole scope of political life.

The Confucian school was unquestionably the most influential

---

* Bernard Bosanquet, *The Philosophical Theory of the State* (London: Macmillan and Co., 1899), page 5.

** William Archibald Dunning, *A History of Political Theories, Ancient and Mediaeval* (New York: The Macmillan Co., 1936), page 5.

in the feudal age. In this conservative school the feudal regime found its first systematic rationalization. Alarmed by numerous instances of "ministers who murdered rulers and of sons who murdered fathers," Confucius, the first and greatest intellectual of noble origin, launched an energetic campaign for the restoration and stabilization of the traditional feudal hierarchy. Putting it tersely, Confucianism was really a *post facto* rationalization of a social and political order that was rapidly disintegrating. "For such a purpose"—to borrow from Hegel—"philosophy, at least, always comes too late. . . . The owl of Minerva takes its flight only when the shades of night are gathering." * The economic and social basis of feudal society was fast corroding, and the political structure could no longer be maintained. Not even Confucius and his brilliant disciples, Mencius and Hsüntzu, could have turned the tide of history. *Did they want to?*

Disillusioned by the chaos and disorder that reigned, a group of sensitive romantic individuals chose to live in splendid isolation and longed to return to nature, to the simple childhood of humanity. Laotzu was the first original thinker of this Taoist school, and Chuangtzu and Yangtzu were its most eloquent exponents and propagandists. This school was anarchistic, defying all authority and denying the very reason of the historic state. In essence Taoism was a postmortem idyllization of a social life, an imaginary paradise that had been lost in the remotest antiquity (if ever it existed). Again to paraphrase Hegel, Taoist philosophy came altogether too late. The nightingale began to sing her most eloquent love song as the darkness of night deepened.

There was another school which opposed the hereditary feudal nobility and expressed apparently the sentiments and ideals of the lower middle classes, the artisan and farmer classes. This school preached the principles of universal love and mutual aid, the bases

* G. W. F. Hegel, *Philosophy of Right,* trans. by S. W. Dyke (London: G. Bell and Sons, 1896), page xxx. The quotation is from the famous final paragraph of the preface.

of which, it frankly acknowledged, were enlightened self-love and self-interest—a most typical philosophy of the lower middle classes. Mocius was the founder of this school, which wanted to reorganize the tottering feudal empire into a unified theocratic monarchy, the ruling class of which, instead of being the hereditary nobility, was to be elected from among the capable and virtuous of the populace. This influential school, however, was destined to pass away, for it failed to recognize that the order of the day was military power rather than universal love and mutual aid. Even though it anticipated a unified monarchy, it did not realize that the coming state was to be founded upon military conquest rather than popular election.

It remained for the Legalist school to anticipate a universal absolute monarchy based upon law and maintained by military power. By the time of Hantzu, the greatest Legalist, the feudal states had already become independent political entities, owing no allegiance to the king. This school represented the most revolutionary force in the decaying feudal society, a force springing from the co-operation between the rulers on the one hand and wealthy merchants and landowners on the other. The theory of government by man—a theory that was rooted in the personal character of feudal relations and advocated by the Confucian and by the Mocian—was fundamentally rejected by the Legalist, who advocated the theory of government by law. In contrast with the Confucian and the Mocian, who emphasized moral influence and divine authority respectively, the Legalist was a frank champion of military power. By adopting the philosophy of the Legalist school the state of Ch'in was able to unify the empire and to establish the first absolute monarchy in the history of China.

An understanding of the growth and decay of the feudal system is a key to the comprehension of the early political thought. Men, even creative thinkers, are prisoners of their experiences and cannot fathom realms of thought which are beyond their kens. The early Chinese political philosophers are no exception. They breathed, moved, and had their being in a feudal order that was in process of disintegration, and faced social and political problems that required immediate solutions. It was the chaotic but dynamic conditions prevailing in the periods of Spring and Autumn and of the Contending States that produced the early schools of philosophy and determined the scopes, as well as the methods, of their political inquiries.

There are, however, problems that the early philosophers dealt with, which are not purely Chinese but are more or less universal, transcending the limitations of time and space. These problems concern the evolution of the historic state, the art of government, and the nature of man as a social and political being, problems which challenge the great minds of all ages and nations. A comparative study of these universal problems will reveal similar strains of thought and even modes of expression between certain Chinese and western political philosophers. The Confucian is an idealistic school, for it assumes that politics is ethics, that political problems are fundamentally ethical problems. In this respect, the Confucian political philosophy is strikingly parallel to the Socratic, as expounded by Plato and in an attenuated form by Aristotle. The Taoist is a naturalistic school, for it denies the moral basis, and rejects the moral justification, of the historic state. This school, individualistic and anarchistic, is akin to the Cynic, the Stoic, and the Epicurean in ancient times, and to Rousseau in modern times. The Mocian is a utilitarian school, expounding a theocratic theory of the absolute state, a state which seems a strange union of the Augustinian City of God and the Hobbesian Leviathan. The Legalist is a realistic school, which makes politics an independent art and science, divorced from ethics and religion altogether, and which is a worthy predecessor of the Machiavellian prince, the great master of real politics.

2. THE IDEALISTIC SCHOOL: CONFUCIUS

Confucius the Man

THE place of Confucius in Chinese history is so eminent and important that no writer can legitimately entertain the thought of interpreting this great man in any adequate manner in a brief space. He was the first and greatest philosopher (lover of wisdom), in whom the accumulated, collective experience of ancient China found its most systematic expression. Throughout the ages he has been revered as the supreme teacher and even worshiped as a divinity. He has remained up to this time the greatest moral and rational personality that the Chinese race has ever produced. No other thinkers or statesmen have exercised such a profound influence upon the Chinese for such a long duration as has Confucius.

The life of Confucius is so well known that a mere sketch would seem superfluous. We are here interested in the growth of his mind and character in relation to the political conditions prevailing in the period of Spring and Autumn. Born in 551 B.C., Confucius lived to the age of seventy-two. Of noble origin but without the privileges of a title or a fief, he was the first of the rising intelligentsia that stood between the feudal ruling class on the one hand and the serf and slave class on the other. As a young man, he studied feudal institutions and conventions, thereby preparing himself for governmental service. In his mature years he visited many a feudal state, interviewing dukes and marquises, looking for an opportunity to restore the decaying feudal order. At the age of sixty-eight, after many years of wandering, disappointed though not disillusioned, Confucius returned to the state of Lu, where he devoted the remaining years of his life to teaching and editing, and to working out a systematic philosophy.

Of the childhood and youth of Confucius little is known for certain. It is said that he was born out of an extra-marital union between Shuliang Ho, who was more than sixty years old, and a young girl of the Yen family. Soon after he was born, his father died. He was in doubt as to the place of his father's tomb because his mother for some reason had concealed the truth from him. If this story were true, Confucius as a child and youth must have suffered from a great deal of anxiety as to his own origin and must have searched for the unknown father. This might partly account for his life-long quest for intellectual certainty and moral authority.*

The picture of Confucius the man was best drawn by the master himself.

"At fifteen I set my mind upon learning.
At thirty I stood firm.
At forty I was free from doubts.
At fifty I understood the law of heaven.
At sixty nothing that I heard disturbed me.
At seventy I could follow the desires of my heart without transgressing the right."

This is an excellent autobiographical outline, showing the growth of his intellectual and moral stature. It seems that there were two significant stages. At forty he was a wise man—having no doubts. But not until he was seventy did he become a truly good man—who could follow the desires of his heart without transgressing the right. In modern psychiatric language, he was free from mental

---

* John C. H. Wu, "The Real Confucius," *T'ien Hsia Monthly,* I (1935), 11-20 and 180-89. On page 14, the author says: "But in whatever forms the search for the father might be clothed, the main idea remained the same: to have an infallible guide, to arrive at a stable *point d'appui,* to attain the highest, the completest, and the most ideal." Wu's account of Confucius the man is probably the best ever written.

uncertainties and anxieties at the age of forty; and at seventy he was free from moral conflicts arising from the exactions of the superego and the impulses of the id.

Undoubtedly, Confucius was one of the most rational and balanced personalities of all ages. He could apparently enter into and withdraw from political life at will. Yet one cannot but observe that the mental citadel of Confucius was constantly the battleground between the will to reform the world and the desire to withdraw from it. Seeing many instances of regicides and patricides which were undermining the foundation of the social order, Confucius set out to restore the moral basis of the feudal body politic. An escapist contemporary of his remarked that Confucius was the fellow who knew it was impossible, but who nevertheless tried, to reform the world. He firmly believed that, were he to administer a state, he would succeed in putting the political house in order within a period of three years. Yet this same optimistic Confucius advised his disciples to retire from the world: "Do not enter a tottering state, nor live in one that is rent with disorder. When righteousness prevails in the world, show your heads; but when wickedness has its way, retire into a hermitage." This same politically-minded Confucius admired and even envied those who had escaped from the world altogether.

In the last years of his life, Confucius apparently lived a quiet, contemplative life. As he described himself, "I am simply a man who in his eagerness for knowledge forgets his food, who in the joy of its attainment forgets his sorrow, and who does not perceive that old age is coming on." Yet one cannot be certain that even in these last days Confucius was completely peaceful and resigned. The failure of his political mission weighed too heavily upon his mind for him to forget and forgive the world. Just before his death, early one morning after he had dreamed that he was about to die—to die without having fulfilled his mission—Confucius sang the following verse:

> The great mountain must crumble;
> The mighty pillar must fall;
> The wise man must wither away like a plant.

Referring to this dream, the gifted emperor of the T'ang dynasty, Hsüantsung, wrote these lines:

> O my Master! What was it that agitated your mighty soul?
> Why such storm and stress, why such endless ferment and
> fluctuation?

The General Character of the Confucian System

Much as the Socratic and Platonic, the Confucian political thought, comprehensive and profound as it is, never assumes the systematic form of an independent science or art. To Confucius, as to Socrates and Plato, politics and ethics are identical. Confucianism, both as a theory of the state and as an art of government, is essentially a morally idealistic discipline. The Confucian utopia, known as the great commonwealth (tat'ung), is a state of moral perfection. The Confucian art of government consists in "putting things right." Throughout the entire body of the Confucian classics, politics and ethics are completely blended.

The word for the Confucian ethical ideal is jen, which etymologically, it is significant to observe, consists of two parts, two and man, which therefore is best rendered into English as goodness, meaning goodness in interpersonal relations. According to Confucius, man is never a mere individual, but is always an interpersonal entity. With Aristotle, Confucius believes that only in association with fellow beings does a man realize his goodness and that in isolation he can be neither good nor bad. *morality*

Before achieving goodness, Confucius thinks, a man must acquire knowledge. If to Socrates knowledge is virtue, to Confucius knowledge is the basis of goodness. The following famous passage

only exists in association with other people.

in *Higher Education* is the best exposition of the general character *when?*
of the Confucian political and ethical thought.

"The ancients who wished to preserve the clear character of the people of the world would first order their national life. Those who wished to order their national life would first regulate their family life. Those who wished to regulate their family life would first cultivate their personal lives. Those who wished to cultivate their personal lives would first set their hearts right. Those who wished to set their hearts right would first make their wills sincere. Those who wished to make their wills sincere would first achieve true knowledge. The achieving of true knowledge depended upon the investigation of things.

"When things are investigated, then true knowledge is achieved; when true knowledge is achieved, then the will becomes sincere; when the will is sincere, then the heart is set right; when the heart is set right, then the personal life is cultivated; when the personal life is cultivated, then the family life is regulated; when the family life is regulated, then the national life is orderly; when the national life is orderly, then there is peace in this world."

In this Confucian system the ruler must be a man of knowledge and virtue, for only such a ruler can regulate the family life, order the national life, and bring about peace throughout the world. He can accomplish all these, not through military power or legislative and judicial authority, but through personal moral influence. There is little difference between the state and the family in the Confucian system. The state is but a big family, the government of a state is but the government of a family writ large. The relation of the ruler to his subjects is similar to that of the father to his sons. The good ruler is a good father, the good subject a good son. The principles governing political relations are substantially the same as those governing familial relations. Politics and ethics are essentially identical.

In the time of Confucius there were two main classes, the ruling noble class and the serf and slave class, the gentleman and the commoner. The Chinese characters for gentleman and commoner are *chüntzu* and *hsiaojen,* the former meaning lord's son, the latter small or mean man. The middle classes, the merchant, the free landowner, and the intellectual, were just beginning to arise. Apparently Confucius expressed the view of the gentleman class. As an ethical doctrine, Confucianism taught how to become a gentleman; as a political discipline, it was essentially a body of principles concerning the method of governing the commoner. Such being the case, there is little wonder that Confucianism has been the official doctrine of the ruling class in China, long after the feudal regime passed out of existence.

The Theory of the State

In the Confucian system society is a configuration of interpersonal relations, which are classified into five categories: ruler-subject, father-son, husband-wife, brother-brother, and friend-friend. The state refers to only one phase of these manifold relations, namely, the relation between the ruler and the subject, and is therefore only a part of society.

Even though Confucius never attempts a formal definition of the state, he indicates in his discourses certain essential elements of the state, namely, people, territory, and government. The Confucian might define the state formally as a people in a territory with a government.

The state is a product of social evolution, according to Confucius. The prepolitical stage of human existence is neither the Rousseauan paradise of nature nor the Hobbesian condition of war in which every man is against every man; it is simply a primitive circumstance in which human savages, noble and otherwise, first live in isolation and then establish families and clans, and presumably may fight against as well as co-operate with one another as necessity dictates. The historic state comes into being in the gradual process of social evolution from simplicity to complexity; it does not come as a consequence of a contract between *rex* and *populus* or among all sovereign individuals.

The following passage in the *Book of Change* is a simple and clear statement concerning the stages of social evolution leading to the appearance of the historic state.

"Heaven and earth existing, all material things then got their existence. All material things having existence, afterward there came male and female. From the existence of male and female there came afterward husband and wife. From husband and wife there came father and son. From father and son there came sovereign and subject. From sovereign and subject there came high and low. Following the distinction between high and low came the arrangements of propriety and righteousness."

not mother & son(?)

This theory of social evolution, which seems naturalistic (objective and descriptive), is really on a high idealistic plane in the sense that society is conceived as progressing from a simple, natural existence to a complex, moral hierarchy. Assuming an idealistic point of view, Confucius regards the state as a moral product of social evolution, and justifies the distinction between high and low, the ruling and the ruled, as a natural phenomenon in society.

The state then, as Confucius sees it, is a moral institution that comes into being as an end-product of long social evolution from time immemorial. He does not conceive of the state as the realization of a transcendental ethical idea or the image of an absolute will, as does Hegel. The German philosopher is metaphysically idealistic, the Chinese philosopher morally idealistic. Hegel gives a metaphysical justification of the Prussian absolute state, Confucius a moral justification of the Chinese feudal regime.

Sociologically, Confucius regards the historic state as a hierarchy of the ruling and ruled classes. He does not, however, view the

高下等差.
天經地义

state as the official form of class antagonism, as do Marx and Engels. To the Communists the state is "an organization of the particular class which is *pro tempore* the exploiting class." In ancient times, it is "the state of slave-owning citizens; in the middle ages, the feudal lords; and in our own, the bourgeoisie." To Confucius the state is an expression of social harmony between the ruling and the ruled, between the morally superior and the morally inferior. Marxism is materialistic, while Confucianism is idealistic. The former starts from the point of view of the ruled, the latter from that of the ruling.

The idea of social hierarchy, of which the feudal order is a concrete embodiment, is based upon the law of nature, according to Confucius. "The heaven is high; the earth is low; hence the order of the cosmos. There is distinction between high and low, hence the organization of all existents," including men and things. Society follows nature, and is therefore naturally divided into the high and the low, the ruling and the ruled.

Not only upon the law of nature, but also upon human nature is based the idea of social hierarchy. According to Confucius, men are not born equal in intelligence or identical in temperament, although they all can become moral men. Some are endowed with superior intelligence, others with inferior. Some are tough-minded, others tender-minded. Some are aristocratic by nature, others tend to be mean and vulgar. While "education knows no class," nature and environment do produce gentlemen and commoners. The former are to administer public affairs, the latter to be private citizens. Confucius does not indicate clearly whether human nature is good or evil. This problem, as will be seen in the following chapter, is the main bone of contention between his most prominent disciples, Mencius and Hsüntzu.

If the organizing genius of the Duke of Chou was largely responsible for the establishment of the feudal system, the philosophic genius of Confucius made for the first time the most perfect rationalization and moralization of the system. Confucius was living at the time when, as Mencius described it, "the world fell into decay, and principles faded away. Perverse ideas and oppressive deeds waxed rife. There were ministers who murdered sovereigns and sons who murdered fathers." Essentially conservative in outlook, Confucius chose to tread upon the beaten path of history. He was anxious to restore the feudal order, which he considered as the best possible order.

It would be inaccurate, however, to assume that the philosophic vista of Confucius was strictly confined to the feudal order. Whether it was a flight from reality or an enduring vision, Confucius did envisage a utopia that was radically different from the feudal order. Once while taking a walk with a disciple to the city gate, overlooking the suburb, Confucius heaved a deep sigh over the state of world affairs. In an andante mood, Confucius the Penseroso revealed his vision of the great commonwealth to his disciple as follows:

"When the great way prevails, the world is a common state. Officers are elected according to their wisdom and ability, and mutual confidence and peace reign. Therefore people regard not only their own parents as parents and not only their own children as children. The old are able to enjoy their old age; the young are able to employ their talents; the juniors are free to grow; the helpless widows and widowers, the lonely orphans, and the crippled and deformed are provided for. Men have their proper occupations and women have their homes. While not to be thrown away, wealth is not to be kept as personal property. While not to be idle, labor is not to be used for personal advantage. In this way, selfish schemes cease to exist, and banditry and rebellion do not rise. As a result, outer doors always remain open. This is the age of the great commonwealth (tat'ung)."

This utopia of moral perfection, a communist and anarchist utopia, is rather Taoistic than Confucianistic in outlook. Though entertaining such a vision, Confucius felt that it was not humanly practical. He was willing to work for the best possible state, the feudal state, which was only the state of the minor peace *(hsiao-k'ang)*. In the same meditative mood, Confucius continued:

"But now the great way no longer prevails, the world is divided up into private families. People regard only their own parents as parents and only their own children as children. They acquire goods and labor for their own interest. A hereditary aristocracy is established, and the different states build city walls and moats for defense. The principles of propriety and righteousness serve as principles of social discipline, in accordance with which people maintain the official status of rulers and subjects; parents and children, elder brothers and younger brothers, husbands and wives, learn to live in harmony; social institutions are established; and land and dwellings are distributed. The physically strong and the mentally clever are raised to prominence and each one carves his own career. In this way, selfish plots and enterprises thrive, and war inevitably follows. . . . This is the age of the minor peace."

The fact that Confucius labored for the establishment of the minor peace while he envisaged the ideal of the great commonwealth shows that he was not a pure utopian and dreamer. Realizing that the great commonwealth was too high an ideal in this far from perfect world, Confucius devoted his life to the art of practical government, to the principles of propriety and righteousness, to the ideal of goodness in interpersonal relations, with the hope that the minor peace might be a reality.

The Art of Government

The epidemic of regicides and patricides that was inflicted upon the feudal body politic was unquestionably the primary concern of

Confucius, the moral therapeutist. A regicide or a patricide, Confucius thinks, is not an accident that occurs suddenly in a day or night, but is a consequence of a long process of social and political malady. One has to study the past in order to understand the present and to judge the future.

The root cause of all social and political ills, Confucius discovers, is semantic in nature. A disciple, by the name of Tzulu, once asked what Confucius would consider the first thing to be done if he were to administer a state. The master answered: "What is necessary is to rectify names!" "You are wide of the mark!" retorted the disciple. "Why must there be such rectification?" The master said:

"If names be not correct, language is not in accordance with the truth of things. If language be not in accordance with the truth of things, affairs cannot be carried on to success. When affairs cannot be carried on to success, ritual and music will not flourish. When ritual and music do not flourish, law and justice will not be proper. When law and justice are not proper, the people will be at a loss even as to the movement of hands and feet."

What to the realist appears to be "wide of the mark" is the very first principle of government to the idealist. A good government should begin by rectifying the names (defining the terms) of all things so as to distinguish between the true and the false, the right and the wrong, the just and proper and the unjust and improper, in other words, to set up a standard of moral values.* The absence of such a standard, Confucius argues, spells social discord

---

* Thomas Hobbes begins his *Leviathan* with a long series of definitions. He accuses philosophers of enjoying the "privilege of absurdity." "For it is most true that Cicero saith of them somewhere, that there can be nothing so absurd but may be found in the books of philosophers. And the reason is manifest. For there is not one of them that begins his ratiocination from the definitions, or explications of the names they are to use; which is a method that hath been used only in geometry, whose conclusions have thereby been made indisputable." *Leviathan,* i, 5.

Because the ruler can't be a ruler, the minister can't be a good minister.

and political turmoil. To create order out of chaos, it is necessary first to set up a definite standard of moral values.

Of all the names that have to be rectified, those denoting social and political positions and relations are the most important. A duke asked about government. Confucius replied: "Let the ruler be ruler, let the minister be minister; let the father be father, let the son be son." The first "ruler" refers to the ruler as a real person, while the second "ruler" is the name or concept of the ideal ruler. Likewise for the other terms. If the actual ruler is the ideal ruler, the actual minister the ideal minister, the actual father the ideal father, and the actual son the ideal son, then there will be no regicides and patricides and there will be peace and order throughout the world.

who will decide

In order to define the ideal ruler, minister, father, and son and to censor the actual ruler, minister, father, and son, Confucius wrote the *Spring and Autumn (Ch'unch'iu)*, a chronological record of the major events from 722 to 481 B.C. He registered therein editorially, with approval or with condemnation, many instances of regicides and patricides and of feudal states that were vanquished. The *Spring and Autumn* may be considered as an application of the doctrine of the rectification of names to the decaying conditions of the feudal body politic. Through the *Spring and Autumn* Confucius attempted to set up a standard of moral values, which was a matter of prime importance to the restoration of the feudal regime. It may be added that in all his works Confucius aims at teaching proper human relations. Such phrases as the following recur frequently in his works: The prince must be princely, the minister ministerly, the father fatherly, the son sonly, the husband husbandly, the wife wifely, the brother brotherly, the friend friendly. He defines carefully and with examples what qualities constitute princeliness, fatherliness, brotherhood, and friendship. He sets up all the proper -nesses, -hoods, and -ships in all inter-personal relations.

If to govern means to rectify, it may be asked, who is to rectify,

The ruler by personal example

no incentive.

and how? The answer of Confucius is, the ruler is to rectify. If the
ruler is good, the people will naturally be good. "The character of
the gentleman is like the wind, and the character of the commoner
is like the grass. The grass bends, when the wind blows across it."
The ruler then must be a wise and virtuous person himself before
he can rectify the people.

Government is not merely a framework of conventions and institutions, but is primarily a human organization. When there are
good rulers, the government is good; when there are bad rulers,
the government cannot be good, even though the constitution may
be perfect. "The principles of the government of Wen and Wu
[founders of the feudal system]," says *Central Harmony,* "are well
preserved in the records—the tablets of wood and bamboo. With
the right rulers, such a government flourishes; without them, it
decays and ceases to be. Therefore, the administration of government depends upon men." The dissolution of the feudal system, or
of any other system, is seldom due to any flaw in the system itself,
but rather to the lack of right rulers to administer it.

There are two kinds of government, Confucius thinks. One is
government by virtue, the other government by law. Confucius
believes in the government by virtue, by moral influence, by personal example. "A sovereign who governs a state by virtue may be
compared to the north polar star, which remains in its place while
the other stars revolve around it." Moral influence is greater and
more profound than legal coercion, for virtue can win the hearts
of the people while law can only control their external behavior.
"If the people are governed by law and regimented by punishment,
they will try to keep out of jail and have no sense of shame. If
the people are led by virtue and regulated by the rules of propriety, they will have a sense of honor and moreover will become
good."

A government has to perform three important functions, says
Confucius. "There must be sufficient food for the people; there
must be an adequate army; and there must be confidence of the

people in the ruler." If necessary, a government should go without the army first and without sufficient food next, but no state can exist without the confidence of the people in the ruler. The most important single factor in any state is a wise and virtuous ruler, whose moral influence can command the willing support of the people.

The idea of government by man was evolved from the personal character of the feudal relations between the superior and the inferior. In the simple feudal society, the superior had direct contacts with the inferior, and the inferior were personally bound to the superior to observe certain obligations and duties. The feudal government was a personal government, radically different from the modern, impersonal, legal government. Wishing to restore the feudal regime, Confucius naturally attached paramount importance to the personality of the ruler.

Practically the entire body of Confucian ethics is devoted to the problem of cultivating the mind and character of the ruler. Confucius divides men into the gentleman and the commoner class. The gentleman cultivates virtue and character, while the commoner seeks profits and goods. The gentleman understands what is right, while the commoner understands what will sell. The gentleman develops upward, while the commoner develops downward. The gentleman must learn the art of government, while the commoner is to obey but not to know.

Like Plato and Aristotle, Confucius is aristocratic by nature. In the Platonic Republic, there must be three classes, producers, warriors, and counselors and magistrates, in addition to slaves, who are excluded from citizenship. If Plato declared that, until philosophers are kings, there will be no cessation of ills for states, Confucius might have said that, until men of virtue and knowledge are rulers, there will be no peace throughout the world. According to Aristotle, men differ in capacity, and some are by nature masters who can command and direct and some are by nature slaves who can only carry out orders. Similarly, Confucius divides men into the superior class that is naturally endowed and intellectually trained to govern and the inferior class that can only follow and obey.

Confucius began to rationalize the feudal system as it was in the process of disintegration, just as Plato and Aristotle began to analyze and classify the principles of a political life that was fast waning. Confucius was a great admirer of the Duke of Chou, the real organizer of the feudal system, just as Plato, and to a less extent Aristotle, fell under the influence of Lycurgus and Solon, lawgivers of Sparta and Athens respectively. As a result, both the Confucian and the Platonic and Aristotelean political philosophies were explications of the past rather than anticipations of the future.

Yet it would be difficult to overestimate the influence of these pioneer thinkers upon later centuries. Throughout the middle ages and even in modern times, Plato and Aristotle have exercised a philosophic influence than which there is none greater. Confucianism is still a predominant pattern of political thought in China today, two millennia after the extinction of the feudal regime. So retrospective is the philosophic gaze of man and so leisurely in fact is the movement of society that these ancient philosophers loom large on the horizon of modern consciousness.

3. THE IDEALISTIC SCHOOL: MENCIUS AND HSÜNTZU

The Lives and Works of Mencius and Hsüntzu

MENCIUS and Hsüntzu were the most distinguished orthodox disciples of Confucius. Both purported to interpret the true meaning of Confucianism, but they differed widely in methods and in postulates, though not so much in conclusions. Throughout the ages the Confucians have inclined either to Mencius or to Hsüntzu, and the Confucian school has virtually divided itself into the Mencius and Hsüntzu branches.

If an historical analogy is warranted, the trio of Confucius, Mencius, and Hsüntzu may be likened to that of Socrates, Plato, and Aristotle. Confucius and Socrates are the first original philosophers. Mencius and Hsüntzu are the greatest systematizers and molders of Confucianism, just as Plato and Aristotle are the most eminent interpreters and elaborators of the Socratic doctrine. The analects of Confucius and the maxims and aphorisms of Socrates are both handed down to history by their immediate followers. The works of Mencius, in seven books, are a collection of conversations and interviews, just as the writings of Plato are in the dialectic form. The works of Hsüntzu, in thirty-two books, are in excellent though difficult prose, just as the tomes of Aristotle are mainly in the form of exposition. The intellectual peculiarities and temperamental inclinations of Mencius and Hsüntzu are very similar to those of Plato and Aristotle respectively. Mencius and Plato are imaginative and poetic, while Hsüntzu and Aristotle are factual and critical. The styles of Mencius and Plato are incomparably beautiful, brilliant, and graceful, while those of Hsüntzu and Aristotle are rather ponderous and humorless. Ideas present themselves to Mencius and Plato more through metaphor and analogy, to Hsüntzu and Aristotle more through the process of logical analysis. For Mencius and Plato the ethical ideas of goodness and justice are the main subjects of discourse, while for Hsüntzu and Aristotle institutions and conventions constitute the chief objects of observation. Mencius and Plato are tender-minded philosophers who add grace and dignity to human history, while Hsüntzu and Aristotle are tough-minded philosophers who subject man and society to close scrutiny and examination.

Mencius (*circa* 372-289 B.C.) and Hsüntzu (*circa* 320-235 B.C.) lived about two centuries after Confucius. Though they were contemporaries for some years, they never met each other. Like Confucius, they were politically minded and were anxious to revive the dying feudal regime. Like Confucius again, they were both disappointed and never had a real opportunity to carry out their political ideals.

Mencius was of noble descent, though without a fief or a title. Having early lost his father, he was brought up by an able and ambitious mother, who intended that he should become a great scholar-statesman and who did everything she could to mold the character of the child. It is said that she moved her residence thrice in order to find a proper place for the child. While living near a graveyard, Mencius played the "coroner" with other children. She said to herself: "This is no place for my son!" She moved to a house near a market place, where he played the "merchant." Again she said: "This is no place for my son!" Finally she moved to a school neighborhood, where he learned to play "the ritual of sacrifice." She was then happy, saying, "This is the real place for my son!"

A fatherless son, nurtured by a purposeful mother, Mencius set up an unusually high level of aspiration for himself. Being poor and obscure, he worked hard toward political distinction. "When heaven is about to confer a great office upon a man," said Mencius, "it first exercises his mind with suffering, and his sinews and bones with toil. It exposes his body to hunger and subjects his person to poverty. It confounds his undertakings. By all these methods, it stimulates his mind, tests his temper, and increases his ability to perform the otherwise impossible."

Mencius was no philosopher of the ivory tower, no shy or solitary soul, but decidedly a man of the world. He spoke of his own vast and expansive nature which filled up all between heaven and earth. The following definition of the great man is characteristically Mencian:

"To dwell in the wide house of the world, to stand in the correct position in the world, and to walk along the great path of the world; when in office, to practice one's principles for the good of the people; when in retirement, to practice them independently; when riches and honors cannot make one dissipated, poverty and obscurity cannot make one swerve, and power and force cannot make one bend oneself: these are the characteristics of the great man."

Mencius spent many of his mature years in wandering among the contending states. He interviewed the rulers of Liang, Ch'i, Tsou, Sung, and Teng, who were anxious to make their states powerful and wealthy. But instead of teaching them the arts of military or economic expansion, he preached the moral principles of Confucius. Consequently, though he was politely received, he was never appointed to a high office. Toward the end of his life, after many instances of frustration, Mencius retired, not without "murmur against heaven and grudge against men." Asked why he was unhappy, when he left the state of Ch'i, Mencius made a statement which disclosed how greatly disappointed this great man of destiny really was. "It is heaven that does not wish that the empire be tranquil and in good order. If it wish this, who is there in the world besides me to bring it about! How should I be otherwise than unhappy?"

The early life of Hsüntzu is not known at all. Born in the state of Chao, Hsüntzu at fifty went to the state of Ch'i, where he distinguished himself as an able polemist against many sophists, logicians, and philosophers, and became the most eminent scholar in the state academy. Possibly someone slandered him to the king, so Hsüntzu left the state of Ch'i. For several years he traveled in Ch'in and Chao, where he had audiences with the rulers and attempted to dissuade them from military activity. When he was about sixty-five he was appointed magistrate of the Lanling district in the state of Ch'u, a small post, which he held for some fifteen years until shortly before his death.

During the magistracy, Hsüntzu wrote his philosophy. Unlike Confucius and Mencius, who had many disciples, Hsüntzu had few students (one of whom, Hantzu, became the greatest Legalist). It is tempting to conjecture that Hsüntzu was probably a perfectionist, a rigid disciplinarian, cold, distant, austere, and severe. More of a pure intellect than any of the other early philosophers, Hsüntzu lacked that sense of humor which was characteristic of Confucius, and that expansive feeling of warmth and friendliness which Mencius happily possessed. He wrote a book in which he assailed and vituperated twelve famous philosophers, including Tzuszu (Confucius' grandson) and Mencius. Self-righteous and self-willed, Hsüntzu was a difficult person socially.

Undoubtedly, Hsüntzu felt the call to take up the mantle of Confucius, the uncrowned prince of the world. He was to fulfill the historic mission which Confucius left undone, the mission of restoring the feudal order. Unfortunately, like Mencius, Hsüntzu was destined to fail. While the feudal states were busily engaged in the "vertical alliance" and the "horizontal coalition," in the interbalancing of power, while the social and economic structure of feudalism was rapidly being destroyed, Mencius and Hsüntzu preached the moral gospel according to Confucius, that a wise and virtuous ruler, even of a small state and without an army, would be able to triumph over force and to create order out of chaos—a gospel honored at a distance but never taken seriously by any practical homo politicus. So in the end, both Mencius and Hsüntzu failed to secure any high offices, and devoted the last years of their lives to writing and teaching.

Although they never realized their ambitions in political life, Mencius and Hsüntzu, the most learned scholars in the period of the Contending States, were not without their compensations. They found satisfaction in their own moral and intellectual developments and in having bequeathed upon posterity immortal spoken and written words. Mencius was eminently justified in saying:

> Let the rulers have their riches;
> I have my goodness.
> Let the rulers have their titles;
> I have my righteousness.
> Wherein should I be dissatisfied
> as inferior to them?

Equally justified was Hsüntzu in saying:

> Having developed a strong will,
> One may defy the rich and high;
> Having prized truth and virtue,
> One may despise kings and dukes;
> Having examined the inner mind,
> One may slight external things.

Thus, it seems that the political frustrations of Mencius and Hsüntzu were compensated, albeit partially, by their moral and intellectual achievements. Neither Mencius nor Hsüntzu was inclined to involutional melancholia; both lived to be healthy octogenarians.

Human Nature

That man is a social and political being is a common assumption of all the Confucians. Mencius and Hsüntzu both think that the state and society come into existence because human beings are by nature not isolated individuals. "Every man," says Mencius, "has a mind which cannot bear to see the sufferings of others. Having a commiserating mind, the ancient king established a commiserating government." Hsüntzu approaches the problem from a different angle: "Man is not as strong as the bull, nor can he run as fast as the horse. How is it that the bull and the horse are used by man? The answer is that man is sociable, while the bull and the horse are not."

If human nature is the stuff of which the state and society are made, it is a logical starting point of political speculation. Regarding the original nature of man, Mencius and Hsüntzu are as nearly in diametric opposition as Rousseau and Hobbes. Mencius assumes that human nature is good, that man tends to be good as water tends to flow downward, much as Rousseau argues that man is naturally good. On the other hand, Hsüntzu asserts that the nature of man is evil, just as Hobbes contends that man is by nature violent and intrepid and is intent only upon attacking and fighting. It seems that Mencius and Rousseau are as charming and innocent as Hsüntzu and Hobbes are grouchy!

During a discourse when a disciple brings up three current views that human nature is neither good nor evil, that it may be either good or evil, and that some men are by nature good and some evil, Mencius makes the following celebrated statement:

"If men follow their original feelings, they will all be good. This is why I say that human nature is good. If men become evil, that is not the fault of their original endowment.

"The sense of mercy is found in all men; the sense of shame is found in all men; the sense of respect is found in all men; the sense of right and wrong is found in all men. The sense of mercy is what we call charity; the sense of shame, righteousness; the sense of respect, propriety; the sense of right and wrong, moral consciousness. Charity, righteousness, propriety, and moral consciousness are not drilled into us; we have got them originally with us."

In direct opposition to Mencius, Hsüntzu declares that human nature is evil.

"Man is by nature rapacious; therefore strife arises and courtesy disappears. Man is by nature sadistic; therefore murder occurs and faith disappears. By nature man is sensual and libidinous; therefore there is adultery and disorder, and civilization thereby passes away. If men follow their natural desires and impulses, society will start with struggle, lose all distinctions and principles, and end in tyranny."

This is a very dark picture of the original man. Inclined by temperament to observe the seamy side of man, and impressed by the evil conditions of the times, Hsüntzu probably could not help but entertain the none too cheerful thought that "man's passions are far from beautiful."

The conceptions of human nature largely determine the methods of education, social organization, and government. To Mencius the method is simple; it consists in following the natural feelings of man, in realizing the full humanity in man. But to Hsüntzu the method consists in overcoming the natural desires and impulses of man through moral discipline. Mencius emphasizes the free development of the individual, whereas Hsüntzu lays stress upon the necessity of moral authority and sanction. In consequence, to Mencius morality is an inner state of mind, having to do with the motives and attitudes of man; but to Hsüntzu it is an outward conformity with socially recognized rules and standards of behavior. The good man, to Mencius, is the natural blossom of the original bud in him, but to Hsüntzu, an artificial figure that is carved and chiseled out of the raw stuff constituting his nature. These views are best stated by Mencius and Hsüntzu themselves. In the most charming manner Mencius says: "The great man is he who has not lost the heart of a child." In an incomparably pithy remark Hsüntzu declares: "The nature of man is evil; his goodness is only acquired training."

Although they differ widely in the conceptions of human nature and in the methods of education, Mencius and Hsüntzu both assume the moral equality of men.* To Mencius all men are originally good; all men have the same sense of mercy, shame, respect, and of right and wrong. To Hsüntzu all men are by nature equally bad and the original capacities of all men are alike. That some men become superior and some inferior is not due to any innate inequality but due to difference in training and development. Mencius and Hsüntzu both believe in the infinite potentialities and improvabilities of all men. Hsüntzu does not believe, as does Calvin, that man is a totally depraved and sinful being and can be saved only by the grace of divine power, although both think that human nature is evil. The Chinese are singularly free from the idea of divine salvation. Mencius says that "every man may be a Yao or Shun," model kings of legendary antiquity; and Hsüntzu says that "the man in the street can be as perfect as the great Yü," founder of the Hsia dynasty. Thus, Mencius and Hsüntzu, who start with opposite conceptions of human nature, end in the same optimistically idealistic view that all men, being essentially equal, are capable of infinite moral perfection.

* It is interesting to compare Mencius and Hsüntzu with Rousseau and Hobbes again. In *A Discourse on the Origin of Inequality*, Rousseau says: "It is easy to conceive how much less the difference between man and man must be in the state of nature than in the state of society." In the *Leviathan*, pt. i, ch. xiii, Hobbes says that the difference beween man and man is not considerable. "That which may perhaps make such equality incredible is but a vain conceit of one's own wisdom, which almost all men think they have in a greater degree than the vulgar."

The Nature of the State

Apologists of the feudal regime, Mencius and Hsüntzu conceive of the state as a hierarchical organization of society. Although they believe in the essential equality of men, they argue the necessity of divisions and distinctions between the superior and inferior classes, the ruling and ruled classes. The state must needs be a hierarchical structure.

In the beginning before the state came into being, Mencius contends, people lived in ignorance of proper human relations and in constant fear of natural calamities and wild beasts. Ancient sages arose, who invented the arts of farming, housing, and weaving, and who taught the people how to defend themselves against floods and animals and how to live together peacefully. The sages naturally became sovereigns, whose duty it was to govern the people. In this way the historic state came into existence.

The business of government naturally belongs to those who are morally and intellectually superior. Not all people are able to conduct the affairs of the state. Arguing against the anarchistic school of Hsü Hsing, who advocates that the wise and virtuous should cultivate the ground, equally and along with the common people, and eat the fruit of their own labor, Mencius says: "Some labor with their minds and some labor with their strength. Those who labor with their minds govern others; those who labor with their strength are governed by others. Those who are governed by others support them; those who govern others are supported by them. This is a universal principle." The administration of public affairs must be vested in the intellectual class, just as farming, manufacturing, and trading must be in the hands of those who are by training and experience skillful in these pursuits. The division of labor is a fundamental principle underlying the organization of the state.

That society is divided into the ruling and the ruled is, according to Hsüntzu, a necessity arising from the evil nature of man.

The desires of men are many but things are few; therefore, strife is inevitable. "If there is no prince to rule the subject, if there is no superior to rule the inferior," the country will be in disorder and chaos. Government is instituted in order that the people may not give rein to their desires and may restrict properly their elemental impulses.

The ruling class, Hsüntzu thinks, should be composed of those who are superior in wisdom. "Originally all men are alike in intelligence and stupidity, but developmentally they are differentiated into the wise and the ignorant." Those who have become wise should govern those who remain in ignorance. The differentiation of wisdom and ignorance with Hsüntzu, as the division of mental and physical labor with Mencius, is a fundamental principle in the structure of the state.

Although they are apologists of the feudal system, Mencius and Hsüntzu do not defend the heredity principle of feudalism. They wish to transform the hereditary nobility into a form of moral and intellectual aristocracy within the general scheme of the feudal constitution. They are democratic in their belief in the essential equality of all men and in the fact that they themselves are of the title-less and fief-less intellectual class, but they are aristocratic in the theory that the ruling class should be composed of moral and intellectual gentlemen. Thus, they are successful in harmonizing the democratic principle of human nature and the aristocratic ideal of government.

Commoners can't rule unless they tranform to gentlemen with wisdom & virtue.

Royalty and Tyranny

The Confucian school generally classifies governments according to the qualities of rulers or sovereigns. This is a logical principle of classification for the Confucians to whom the theory of government by man is fundamental. According as rulers are wise and virtuous or stupid and evil, governments fall under the categories of royalty and tyranny. Roughly, the royal government is distinguished by moral and educational influence, while the tyrannical government is characterized by military force and legal coercion.

The writer has searched the thesaurus for the English equivalents of the characters, *wang* and *pa,* and has chosen the words, royalty and tyranny, as nearest to the original conceptions. These terms are employed by Plato and Aristotle to denote two types of government. The bases of the Confucian and the Platonic and Aristotelean classifications are different. Plato adopts the number of persons exercising supreme authority and the relation of the government to law as the bases of classification. The following table shows the Platonic classification:

Number	*Subject to Law*	*Unrestrained by Law*
The rule of the one	Royalty	Tyranny
The rule of the few	Aristocracy	Oligarchy
The rule of the many	Democracy	Democracy

Aristotle classifies governments first according to the number of persons who exercise sovereign authority, and second according to the end to which the government is directed. If the government aims at the perfection of all citizens, the government is pure; if it aims at the interest of the governing body alone, it is corrupt. The Aristotelean classification may be shown as follows:

Sovereignty of	*Pure Form*	*Corrupt Form*
The one	Royalty	Tyranny
The few	Aristocracy	Oligarchy
The many	Polity	Democracy

Following the Confucian tradition, both Mencius and Hsüntzu make the distinction between the royal and the tyrannical government. Mencius very clearly defines the royal and the tyrannical sovereign: "The ruler who, using force, makes a pretense to benevolence is a tyrant. . . . The ruler who, using virtue, practices benevolence is a royal sovereign. . . . When the ruler subdues the people by force, they submit, not in heart, but because of inadequate power to resist. When the ruler wins the people by virtue, they are pleased in their hearts and sincerely submit." The royal sovereign, in Mencius' mind, is an extremely idealistic conception of moral perfection. No less idealistic is Hsüntzu's conception of the royal sovereign, who must be "the most discriminating and enlightened of men, in order to administer the empire, the mightiest and largest and the most populous of human organizations"; and who must be the most perfect man in conduct to whom the people may look up as a model. Hsüntzu's conception of the tyrant is one who may conquer a nation or an army but cannot win the hearts of the people, who is egotistic and rapacious, and who knows how to punish the criminal but not how to reform the people.

The conceptions of royalty according to Mencius and Hsüntzu are somewhat different. The royal government is to Mencius a benevolent government, to Hsüntzu a ritual government. Believing in the original goodness of man, Mencius would establish a government that fosters the spontaneous flow of kindness and sympathy among the people; whereas Hsüntzu, who thinks that human nature is evil, would have a government that restricts the blind impulses and desires of the people by rites, ceremonies, and rules of proper conduct. The benevolent government is guided by the natural feelings of commiseration or compassion, while the ritual government is maintained by the principle of authority. The former approaches the ideal of maternalism, the latter the ideal of paternalism.

In actual administration the benevolent government would first attend to the physical needs of the people. Mencius says: Let mulberry trees be planted, so that people of fifty years may be clothed with silk; let chickens and swine be reared, so that people of seventy years may be fed with flesh; and let none suffer from cold and hunger. These are the first steps of the benevolent government. Then, let the young be educated and let all the people learn the filial and fraternal duties. If the ruler loves music, let all his subjects enjoy the same; if the ruler loves beauty, let none of his subjects be unmarried men or women; if the ruler loves wealth, let none of his subjects endure poverty and want. "When the ruler rejoices in the joy of the people, they will rejoice in his joy; when he grieves at the sorrow of the people, they will grieve at his sorrow. A sympathy of joy and a sympathy of sorrow will pervade the empire. In such a state of things it cannot be but that the ruler will attain to the royal dignity."

If the benevolent government aims at satisfying the material and spiritual needs of the people, the ritual government proposes to regulate the evil impulses and desires of men by rites and rules of proper conduct. There are, according to Hsüntzu, mourning rites, sacrificial rites, court ceremonies, and social courtesies which people must observe. These rites are the basis of social distinctions between the noble and the base, the superior and the inferior, without which distinctions social peace is impossible. "Of the things that are in heaven there are none brighter than the sun and moon. . . . Of the things that are human there are none brighter than the rules of proper conduct. . . . The destiny of a country depends upon the observance of the rules of proper conduct." If the ruler observe the rules, then "from the west, from the east, from the south, from the north, none think but of obedience." Such a ruler, according to Hsüntzu, is a truly royal sovereign.

Evolution and Revolution

That society evolves from simplicity to complexity, from primitive natural existence to civilized moral life, is one of the fundamental conceptions of Confucius. The feudal system, it seemed to him, represented the highest stage of social evolution. So Confucius spent his entire life preaching the restoration of the feudal system, as though social evolution had come to a halt. So limited is the sphere of human thought by the horizon of experience that even the greatest of thinkers cannot transcend current sentiments and prejudices.

Following Confucius, Mencius spoke of the "earlier kings" and Hsüntzu of the "later kings" as models for the rulers of the world. While both looked backward to history to find authorities and sources of inspiration, they differed from each other regarding the nature of social evolution. Mencius seems to hold a deterministic view, and Hsüntzu a voluntaristic view, concerning the movement of history.

The progress of history, Mencius thinks, is inherently cyclical, and the duration of every cycle seems to be about five centuries. "The world has existed a long time, during the course of which there has been now a period of order and now a period of chaos and confusion." Yao, Shun, and the great Yü initiated a period of order, and Chieh (last tyrant of the Hsia dynasty) concluded the first cycle. T'ang Wang began another period of order, and Chow (last tyrant of the Shang dynasty) ended the second cycle. Wu Wang and the Duke of Chou inaugurated the third cycle, which terminated in chaos in the period of Spring and Autumn. By the period of the Contending States, Mencius felt, a new cycle was overdue. So he was looking forward to the emergence of the heaven-promised sage-king who would create order out of chaos.

Against such a deterministic view, Hsüntzu formulates a voluntaristic theory of history. Whether an age is orderly or chaotic, he argues, is not dependent upon heaven, for the same sun and moon shine upon the royal sovereign and the tyrant alike; nor is it dependent upon time, for every year has the same spring, summer, autumn, and winter, nor yet dependent upon place, for the good earth is always the same. The law of nature is constant; it does not alter itself in order to preserve the royal sovereign or to destroy the tyrant. Human nature being constant, the ancient age and the modern age, the golden age and the dark age, are the same. When the king rules wisely and virtuously, the world will be orderly; if he is stupid and wicked, the world will be in chaos.

It is the will of man, not the will of heaven, that changes the course of history.

Neither Mencius nor Hsüntzu, however, grasped the real nature of social evolution. Like Confucius they looked retrospectively and thought that the period of the Contending States would evolve into a new era similar to that established by the "earlier" and "later" kings. As to how the new era was to be brought about, Mencius and Hsüntzu developed a democratic theory of revolution.

The maintenance of the sovereignty of the king, Mencius thinks, depends upon the will of the people. When the king wins the hearts of the people, he wins the empire; when he loses them, he loses the empire. Yao gave the throne to Shun and Shun gave it to Yü, not because Yao and Shun had the power to give the throne away, but because the people supported the selections. Chieh and Chow, the last tyrants of the Hsia and Shang dynasties, were put to death, because they outraged the feeling of humanity and the sense of righteousness. They were not true sovereigns, but mere individuals, mere robbers and ruffians, who should be deposed.

No less eloquent is Hsüntzu in defending the sovereign right of the people. The tyrants, Chieh and Chow, did not lose the empire; they simply did not have it, for by their beastly deeds they had forfeited their sovereignty long before they were deposed. The model kings, Yao and Shun, did not give the empire away, for upon their deaths the empire naturally passed into the hands of those whom the people supported. "The prince is the boat; the common people are the water. The water can support the boat or capsize it."

Mencius and Hsüntzu anticipated a peaceful and gradual revolution which would depose the tyrants of the times and put on the throne a truly royal sovereign. They did not anticipate a revolution of the discontented classes, the rising middle classes or the serf and slave classes, against the traditional nobility. Being idealists, they failed to diagnose the feudal body politic realistically and to visualize the shape of things to come. Unaware of the new social and economic forces which doomed the revival of the ancient regime, they indulged in the wishful thought that a wise and virtuous prince would be able to win the people and to unify the empire. Brilliant disciples of Confucius, Mencius and Hsüntzu remained the last of the moral apologists of a regime that was in the stage of final disintegration.

4. THE NATURALISTIC SCHOOL: LAOTZU

The Life and Work of Laotzu

THE identity of Laotzu, the supposed author of the *Tao Teh Ching* and founder of the Taoist school, is a virtual Gordian knot which no academic Alexander has yet been able to untie. Traditionally Laotzu is thought to be a contemporary and a teacher of Confucius. He is believed to have been a native of the southern primitive state of Ch'u and later an historian in the archives of the Chou capital. Interested in the study of the feudal institutions and conventions, rites and ceremonies, Confucius journeyed to Chou, where he became acquainted with Laotzu. On his departure, Laotzu proffered the following advice: "A man who is brilliant and thoughtful is often in danger of his life because he likes to criticize people. A man who is learned and clever often endangers his life because he likes to reveal people's foibles. Do not think of yourself only as a son or a minister at court!" To Confucius, who considered that the relations between father and son and between prince and minister constituted the central axis of human society, this advice of Laotzu, the individualist and anarchist, was as disconcerting as it was incomprehensible.

Confucius and Laotzu, the greatest original thinkers of China, may be said to represent two polar patterns of life, two opposite ways of thought and action. In the Middle Kingdom, Confucius typifies the northern pattern, and Laotzu the southern. Confucius is practical, interested in social and political reform, while Laotzu is speculative and theoretical, and tries to escape from the world. Confucius is concerned with the conservation of the moral values that are embodied in institutions and conventions, while Laotzu wishes to return to nature where human artificialities and hypoc-

risies are unknown. The early Confucians were generally northerners who inherited the great traditions of the Hsia, Shang, and
Chou dynasties, while the Taoists were mostly from the state of
Ch'u, which was then in a very primitive stage of human evolution.

Had Laotzu remained in the state of Ch'u, he might not have
created the great Taoist system of philosophy. Fortunately or unfortunately, he was destined to settle in the center of the northern
culture and to achieve distinction as an historian in the royal
archives. It is conceivable that he never felt at home in the north
and was always longing for the south, the state of mother nature,
where he could find peace and happiness. The following verse is
an illuminating description of his mental state:

> All men are seething and beaming,
> As though feasting upon a sacrificial ox,
> As though mounting the spring terrace;
> I alone am placid and give no sign of stirring,
> Look like a babe which has not yet smiled,
> I alone look miserable as one who has no home to return to.
>
> All men have enough and to spare:
> I alone appear to possess nothing.
> What a simpleton I am!
> What a muddled mind I have!
> All men are brilliant:
> I alone am dumb:
> I alone am dull.
> All men are sharp, sharp:
> I alone am mum, mum!
> Bland like the ocean,
> Aimless like the wafting gale.
>
> All men settle down in their grooves:
> I alone am stubborn and remain outside.

But wherein I am most different from the others is
That I know how to suck the breasts of my mother!

Laotzu had a delicate sense of self-esteem or self-regard, which prevented him from associating freely with people and which was not infrequently offended and outraged. He maintained a consciousness of self-importance as well as a feeling of self-disparagement, thereby suffering from an inner tension between ego-maximization and ego-minimization, which tension was in fact the mainspring of his creative vitality.

Totally unprepared for strife and competition, Laotzu forever longed for the security he had enjoyed during childhood in the primitive community. His constant wish was to return home, to return to the state of nature, to recapture the simple paradise of the childhood of the human race. This regressive and retrospective orientation was coupled with an intense introversion. His solitary mode of life is revealed in the following famous verse:

Without passing out of the gate,
The world's course I prognosticate;
Without peeping through the window,
The heavenly reason I contemplate.
The further one goes,
The less one knows.

"Block all passages and shut all entrances!" Laotzu said, "Then you will be inaccessible to intimacy, inaccessible to estrangement, inaccessible to profit, inaccessible to injury, inaccessible to honor, inaccessible to disgrace!" Between the subjective and the objective world, Laotzu built a thick wall so that nothing could invade or disturb him. Within that wall, in splendid isolation, he found his ego, not only unimpaired, but also in supreme sublimity.

It is said that after having lived in Chou for some time, he resigned his post and left the world behind. It is not known where he ended his life. Prior to his final escape, at the urging of a friend, he produced the *Tao Teh Ching,* which, although a mere 5,000-word document and no formal treatise on philosophy, contains a systematic body of principles. The style is aphoristic—terse and rhythmic. From beginning to end, the book runs on in a series of dialectic paradoxes and contradictions, beautifully couched in parallel lines, occasionally interspersed with short paragraphs of prose.* This is unquestionably the work of a concentrated genius whose inner tension expresses itself vibrantly in dithyrambic measures. It is probably the most compact, pregnant, and trenchant piece of literature in Chinese history.

The General Character of the Taoist System

The keynote of the Confucian school is the character *jen,* which denotes goodness in interpersonal relations, while the central theme of the Taoist school is tao which signifies the first principle of, or the ultimate reason in, the universe. The former school is concerned with the relations between man and man, the latter with the relations between man and nature.

There is an ultimate reason in the universe, Laotzu thinks, which lies behind all phenomena and appearances and which is well-nigh beyond human comprehension.

> Look at it but you cannot see it!
> Its name is formless.
>
> Listen to it but you cannot hear it!
> Its name is soundless.

with Heraclitus

* Laotzu's mode of expression is very similar to that of the Greek philosopher Heraclitus. Both thinkers love to express their ideas in dialectical paradoxes and contradictions. For instance, Laotzu says: "All things under heaven are born of existence; existence is born of non-existence." "The tao gives birth to one; one gives birth to two; two gives birth to three; three gives birth to all the myriad things." Heraclitus says: "All is one, the divided and the undivided, the begotten and the unbegotten, the mortal and the immortal, reason and eternity, father and son, God and justice." "The beginning and the end are one." "Life and death, sleeping and waking, youth and age are identical."

Grasp it but you cannot get it!
Its name is bodiless.

These three are unfathomable;
Therefore they blend into one.

Laotzu is not entirely satisfied with this agnostic description of the first principle and, prompted by a strong metaphysical craving, he proceeds to characterize that thing-in-itself, that form of the formless and image of the imageless.

Now what is the tao?
It is something elusive and evasive.
Evasive and elusive!
And yet it contains within itself a form.
Elusive and evasive!
And yet it contains within itself a substance.
Shadowy and dim!
And yet it contains within itself a core of vitality.
The core of vitality is very real,
It contains within itself an unfailing sincerity.

If this verse is less agnostic than the preceding, it is still a very obscure picture of that elusive and evasive thing-in-itself. Though Laotzu finds it extremely difficult to express the idea he has in mind, he tries again.

There is something undefined and yet complete in itself,
Born before the heaven and earth.

Silent and boundless,
Independent and changeless,
Moving through immensity tirelessly,
It may be regarded as the mother of the world.
I do not know its name;
I style it "tao";
And, in the absence of a better word, call it "the great."

The word tao literally means the way. As Laotzu uses it, the tao is the ultimate reason, which is eternal and immutable, inherent in the entire existence and manifest in all phenomena and appearances.

The ultimate reason as such, according to Laotzu, is neither moral nor theistic; it is a naturalistic concept, devoid of human volition and emotion. "The heaven and earth are not human," declares Laotzu, "for they treat all creatures alike as straw dogs." "The great tao is universal like an ocean, which cannot be turned to the right or to the left. All creatures live upon it, and it denies nothing to anyone." In other words, the tao is a neutral and impartial principle that governs all things—plants, animals, and human beings alike. Laotzu seems to deplore the fact that man is notoriously anthropomorphic. The Confucian, for instance, assumes that the universe is benevolent and righteous in its very constitution, and the Mocian believes that the universe is governed by a god that wills the good. The Taoist, on the other hand, is not at all impressed by the humanity of the universe. This is neither an ethical nor a theistic universe, the Taoist thinks, but a natural universe, pure and simple, in which man, which is but one creature among many, breathes, moves, and has its being. This naturalistic world-outlook is a distinctive contribution of Taoism to Chinese philosophic thought.

If the universe is natural, man should not be contrariwise. Laotzu thinks that all institutions and conventions are man-made, are artificial, that all moral norms and standards are contrary to natural ways, and that the much ado of the busybody (such as Confucius!) is responsible for the miseries and misfortunes of the human race. Let there be no goodness, there will be no badness; let there be no beauty, there will be no ugliness. "When all the world recognizes beauty as beauty, this in itself is ugliness. When all the world recognizes goodness as goodness, this in itself is evil." Let all the "musts" and "shoulds" and "oughts" be done

away with, the people will return to natural simplicity and innocence. According to the Taoist scheme of universal life,

> Man follows the ways of the earth,
> The earth follows the ways of the heaven,
> The heaven follows the ways of the tao,
> The tao follows its own ways.

Taoism is thus a clarion call to return to nature and to escape
from culture. Laotzu's *Tao Teh Ching* is an indictment not merely
against the historic state but against the entire body of the cultural heritage of the human race, much as Rousseau's *Discourse
on the Arts and Sciences* and *Discourse on the Origin of Inequality*
are, according to Voltaire, the first and second books against the
human race.

Until philosophers are no longer kings, the Taoist thinks, there
will be no cessation of human ills in the world!

The Negation of the Historic State

If the Confucian mind is positive, tending to affirm the historic
state and the traditional morality, the Taoist mind is critical, inclined to question and to deny the authority of venerable moral
imperatives. Inasmuch as politics and ethics are as completely
blended in Taoism as in Confucianism, it is inevitable that Laotzu
should simultaneously attack the historic state and the traditional
morality.

If Confucius was profoundly disturbed by the epidemic of regicides and patricides of his time, Laotzu was equally distressed by
the fact that the people were prevented from pursuing their peaceful lives by the much ado of the ruling class.

> Why are the people starving?
> Because those above them are taxing them too heavily.
> That is why they are starving.

Why are the people hard to manage?
Because those above them are too meddlesome.
That is why they are hard to manage.

Why do the people make light of death?
Because those above them make too much of life.
That is why they make light of death.

The people have simply nothing to live upon!
They know better than to value such a life!

These lines were an accurate expression of the sentiment and
thought of the people living under the yoke of tyrannical and corrupt government. A then popular ballad describes vividly and in
simple words how the normal life of the people was interrupted
and interfered with by the state.

> We used to have our farms,
>   But you have robbed us of them;
> We used to have our kinfolk,
>   But you have taken them from us.
>
> Here is one who is innocent,
>   But you want to condemn him;
> There is one who is guilty,
>   But you want to pardon him.

Laotzu held the feudal governments directly responsible for the
widespread miseries and misfortunes of the people, who were simple and innocent and, if let alone, would live peacefully and
happily.

To Laotzu, the state appears to be the greatest destroyer of
human society—the greatest cause of social turmoil and paroxysm.
The rulers of the world use the instruments of law and war
presumably to maintain order and peace, but actually to disrupt
the normal pursuit of happiness. Laotzu warns that these instruments are of no avail and are contrary to the law of nature. The

administration of law assumes the obedience of the people. But if the people are not obedient, how can the court function? "If the people are not afraid to die, how can they be scared by the specter of death?" Therefore, law as an instrument of justice is utterly futile. As to war as an instrument of national policy, Laotzu warns that it augurs evil. "He who knows how to guide a ruler in the right path does not try to override the world with force of arms. Arms invite retaliation. Where great armies are quartered, briers and thorns grow. After a great war, famines invariably follow." Furthermore, war is absolutely contrary to the nature of man. "Even a victory is no cause for rejoicing. To rejoice over a victory is to rejoice over the slaughter of men!" It is inconceivable to Laotzu that any human being can delight in the slaughter of his fellow men.

Laotzu may be considered as a forerunner of the Physiocratic and Classical economists and the philosophical radicals, when he declares: "The more restrictions and prohibitions there are in the world, the poorer the people become. . . . The more laws and orders are issued, the more robbers and thieves arise." Let the people alone; let them enjoy their homes and farms; let them carry on their ordinary pursuits; let them follow their natural ways of life. The human world, just as the physical universe, will then of itself be in a state of permanent peace and harmony. It would be easy to criticize the naïveté of this laissez-faire theory but it is unnecessary to do so. What appears paradoxical is that Laotzu, who, like many another great man, is a keenest and most sophisticated thinker, remains a naïve and innocent child at heart. He is the prime example of the Mencian ideal of the great man who "has not lost the heart of a child."

More revolutionary than the eighteenth-century economic theorists and more radical than the philosophical radicals, Laotzu is opposed not only to state interference and regimentation, but also to the entire moral and intellectual superstructure of society. The Confucian lays the cause of social and political ills to the absence of a standard of moral values, but the Taoist regards the very presence of virtue and intelligence as a symptom of human illness. In the state of nature, man knows not what constitutes goodness or badness, beauty or ugliness, truth or falsehood. Only after the rise of the philosopher-king does the world begin to suffer from moral confusion and mental disorder.

> When the great tao is abandoned,
> There appear charity and duty.
> When intelligence and wit arise,
> There appear great hypocrites.
> When human relations are not harmonious,
> There appear filial piety and paternal kindness.
> When darkness and disorder reigns,
> There appear loyalists.

Laotzu would destroy all moral imperatives and intellectual sophistries as the first step towards restoring mankind to the state of natural simplicity and innocence.

> Drop wisdom and abandon cleverness,
> Then the people will be benefited a hundredfold.
>
> Drop charities and abandon duties,
> Then the people will return to natural affections.
>
> Drop shrewdness and abandon sharpness,
> Then robbers and thieves will cease to be.

Much as the Greek Cynic would abolish the whole system of logic and natural philosophy and give up literature, science, and art, the Taoist would do away with all rules and standards of conduct and all criteria of reason.

Laotzu is not only a political anarchist, but a moral and intellectual anarchist as well. As a political creed Taoism is born of despair and resignation. It constitutes a desperate attempt to escape—to escape from political storm and stress, from the world that is too much for man. In a broader sense, Taoism stands as the sternest protest against Chinese culture and civilization. One of the most learned of men, Laotzu, vigorously condemns the damage that culture and civilization inflicts upon mankind.

The Taoistic way of thinking is very similar to the Sophistic. Both the Taoist and the Sophist split the intricate mass of the universe into sharply divided sections by the use of the "either . . . or." With them both, nature and culture are in complete antithesis. The Confucian and the Socratic thinkers make no such antithetical bifurcation of the universe, and seem to possess a keener appreciation of the shades and nuances inherent in the nature of things. The Taoist and the Sophist by temperament or training reach a stage of abstract thinking, wherein the world seems either white or black and has no intermediate colors. Hobbes, Rousseau, and Locke are modern representatives of this Taoistic-Sophistic stage as they, too, make a sharp distinction between natural society and civil society.

In denouncing the historic state and in denying the blessings of culture, Laotzu quite logically proposes a return to the state of nature. The negation of the historic state and the affirmation of primeval society are inherently two phases of the Taoistic pattern of abstract thought.

The Affirmation of Primeval Society

From the point of view of mental orientation, human beings seem to fall under three general categories: those who look backward, those who look forward, and the army of world-as-it-is worshipers. There are political philosophers who tend to idealize the present and who regard the world as it is the best possible world. To them, the present represents the consummate synthesis of historical contradictions or the highest stage in human evolution. There are, however, other political philosophers who are discontented or dissatisfied with the present. They look either backward to a paradise lost or forward to a paradise to be gained; they gaze either retrospectively into some imaginary golden age of the remotest antiquity or far into some perfect utopia of the most distant future. The modern communists and anarchists (such as Marx, Engels, Proudhon, and Bakunin) are men who look forward to the coming stateless society. Laotzu the Taoist, Zeno the Cynic-Stoic, and Rousseau the child of nature are examples of those who look backward to the primeval age of human existence.

Laotzu was never at home in the center of northern culture and forever pined to return to nature, to the simple paradise of the childhood of the human race. The feudal governments, with their armies and courts, it appeared to him, had plagued the people with moral imperatives, with restrictions and prohibitions, laws and orders, and destroyed the very foundation of normal life. Gone were the days when people lived in simple innocence and blissful ignorance. Not strong enough to weather the political storm and stress, having neither a will to lead a revolution nor a desire to reform the world, Laotzu could see only one path open to him—the path leading directly back to the bosom of mother nature. He quietly chose that turn of the road and bid farewell to the world.

Posterity would have guessed correctly Laotzu's destination even if he had not left the following description of his utopia.

"Ah, for a small country with few inhabitants! Though there are highly efficient mechanical contrivances, the people have no use for them. Let them mind death and refrain from migrating to distant places. Boats and carriages, weapons and armor, there may still be, but there are no occasions for using or displaying them. Let the people revert to the use of rope-knotting [as an aid to memory]. See to it that they are contented with their food, pleased with their clothing, satisfied with their houses, and inured to their simple ways of living. Though there may be another country in the neighborhood of this, so that they are within sight of each other and the crowing of cocks and barking of dogs in one place can be heard in the other, yet there is no traffic between them, and throughout their lives the two peoples have nothing to do with each other."

This is no mean, intolerable, barbaric society, but a highly refined, self-sufficient, and self-contented community, in which, to borrow a phrase from Rousseau, man lives a "simple, regular, and solitary" life.

It is rather regrettable that, unlike Rousseau, Laotzu is sparing in words and does not give an elaborate and eloquent description of primeval society. The picture of natural society as Rousseau paints it is so fascinating and stirring that it makes Voltaire itch to go on all fours, but the Taoist conception of primeval society leaves the reader rather in a state of quietude and stillness. Rousseau wishes man to be a noble savage or, as Shelley put it, to live "like the beasts of the forest and the birds of the air," but Laotzu wishes man to be like an infant sleeping in its cradle, ignorant, innocent, and happy.

Laotzu and Rousseau, however, are really birds of a feather. Both denounce culture and civilization; both wish to return to nature. They assume that in the beginning man is a solitary and happy being. He is not the timid, miserable creature that Montesquieu describes, nor is he the energetic, aggressive monster of Hobbes. The primitive man does not injure others and is not afraid of being injured. He attends to his own well-being, in his individual way, while the world goes on of itself.

In the Taoistic-Sophistic way of thinking, nature and culture stand as two opposing symbols. If nature is the original thesis, culture is the antithesis. Laotzu seems to think that the world moves perpetually in a strange dialectical cycle, beginning with the thesis, going through the antithesis, and returning to the original thesis.

> To be great is to go on,
> To go on is to be far,
> To be far is to return.

There is no going without returning. Laotzu centers his interest in the returning phase of the dialectical movement. Says he: "While all things are moving, I contemplate only the return." In fact, "the movement of the tao consists in returning." The world has gone too far, Laotzu thinks, and it is time to return—to return to nature.

The political theory of Laotzu consists of two aspects, the negation of the historic state and the affirmation of primeval society. It is highly significant that Laotzu does not envisage a possible state that leaves man as free as he ever is in nature but preserves all the cultural heritage of history—a synthesis of the original thesis and the antithesis. To Laotzu, the world seems a great reversible machine, alternating between periods now of nature and then of culture. It remains for the modern political philosophers, Hegel and Marx, to bring the dialectic conception of history to maturity.

5. THE NATURALISTIC SCHOOL: YANGTZU AND CHUANGTZU

Yangtzu the Egoist and Chuangtzu the Mystic

LAOTZU, Yangtzu, and Chuangtzu are the most renowned obscure trio in Chinese history. While their ideas have struck the sympathetic nerves of many retiring thinkers throughout the ages, their lives have remained shrouded in complete mystery. Some scholars have gone so far as to deny the historicity of Laotzu the man, and some have even suggested that Yangtzu and Chuangtzu are the names of one and the same individual. So obscure are the early Taoists that in attempting to analyze their character one treads dangerously near the realm of pure speculation.

It is easily understandable why the Taoists remained incognito, as it were, behind the curtain of history. Unlike the illustrious trio of Confucius, Mencius, and Hsüntzu, who were Messianic world reformers, the obscure trio were esoteric fugitives from the prison of humanity. They could not plow the waves and ride the storms of life, so they slipped stealthily from the sea of teeming millions into the void of the unknown—over the lost horizon.

Yangtzu (*circa* 400-330 B.C.) and Chuangtzu (*circa* 360-290 B.C.) are among those who seek an entire escape from the world. These two thinkers, however, choose different exits, walk along different forks of the road, and consequently arrive at different terminals, for temperamentally and intellectually they are not of the same category. Yangtzu, it seems, is a free but tragic spirit, while Chuangtzu is a poetic and mystic soul. Yangtzu is utterly naked and stripped, with no moral inhibitions, while Chuangtzu is paradoxical, enigmatic, and often unfathomable. The former is completely worldly

74

—sensual and carnal; while the latter is transcendental—out of space and out of time.

Yangtzu is an egoist pure and simple, while Chuangtzu is a great mystic. The former exalts the position of the ego, while the latter transforms the ego into divine ether that dissolves itself in the great flux of the cosmos. To the former, every man is an individual atom having a free and independent existence; to the latter, all creatures—insects, butterflies, men—are one in the great uni-verse.

As a person, Yangtzu seems to have been deeply, if not mortally, wounded. What fatal hands administered the blow remains unknown. At any rate, it appears that he was a seriously crippled or amputated personality, bitterly resentful against the world, yet too weak and timid to encounter it; he was haughty and scornful, yet melancholy and resigned. As a reaction to a hostile world and as a defense against the tempest of life, Yangtzu plunged deep into the abyss of self-absorption and busied himself in ceaseless ego-assertion—to the total disregard of the external world. He himself was the only reality, and his own pleasure was the only pleasure conceivable.

Yangtzu feels life is a great burden and death is no relief therefrom. His keen sense of the fleetness and futility of life is thus expressed: "As our life is ours, we must bear it, yet scorn it; get what pleasures we can out of it and wait till we die. When death draws near, we must bear it, yet scorn it; look where it is leading and go on till the end. Scorn everything, bear everything. A little sooner, or a little later, does it matter?"

Man is "chained and ironed, in a dungeon cell," Yangtzu declares. The longest span of man's life is but a hundred years. Close to half of the time, he is a mere babe in arms or else is dim with years. And perhaps half of the years between are wasted in sleep or frittered away during the day. Half again may be lost in pain, illness, sorrow, bitterness, deaths, losses, troubles, and fears. There is hardly one hour free from anxiety. Life comes anon, and goes anon in death. While living, man must follow his natural instincts and get what pleasures he can. For death ends all. By birth human beings are not the same, but in death there is no differentiation. They are born wise or simple, high or low; when death claims them, they all stink, rot, melt, and disappear. Alive, they may be saints or sinners; dead, they are all a valley of rotten bones! "And rotten bones are all alike; who can tell them apart? Then let us make haste to live, and let after-death wait!" As "it is hard to get born and death is ever at hand," man in his transitory years should drain from life all of its pleasures.

In terms of western philosophy Yangtzu is a perfect Cyrenaic-Epicurean. Had he lived in Greece, he might have been the author of the famous line in Lucretius: "Where we are, death is not yet; and where death comes, there we are not." And instead of Aristippus, Yangtzu might have said to Socrates, "I beg to be enrolled amongst those who wish to spend their days as easily and pleasantly as possible."

Chuangtzu was probably as weary of the human world as was Yangtzu. But whereas Yangtzu escaped from the world into his own ego, Chuangtzu withdrew from society into nature, allowing his ego to fall into a state of mystic union with the entire universe. This beautiful allegory illustrates the mysticism of Chuangtzu.

"Once upon a time, I, Chuangtzu, dreamed that I was a butterfly, flitting hither and thither, to all intents and purposes a butterfly. I was conscious only of following my fancies as a butterfly, and was unconscious of my individuality as a man. Suddenly, I awakened, and there I lay, myself again. Now I do not know whether I was then a man dreaming I was a butterfly, or whether I am now a butterfly dreaming I am a man."

Chuangtzu was not a man of this world; he was as completely out of tune as any mortal could be. He longed to be a free being in the great universe—free from all temporal, spatial, and physical limitations. The lake might scorch up, he would not feel hot; the river might freeze, he would not feel cold. Were the mountain riven by thunder and the sea tossed up by storm, he would not tremble. In such a case, he would mount upon the clouds of heaven, cycle the orbits of the sun and moon, and pass beyond the confines of the finite world, beyond the pale of life and death.

It would be inconceivable that such a mystic should have been interested in social and political life. Once the state of Ch'u, as the legend goes, asked Chuangtzu to serve as prime minister. Whereupon the philosopher answered: "I would rather disport myself to my own enjoyment in the mire than be slave to the ruler of a state. I will never take office. Thus I shall remain free to follow my own inclinations." Mencius and Hsüntzu, the Confucian reformers, could never have resisted such an offer, but Chuangtzu declined it with a cynical smile. He would far rather remain poor, obscure, and unknown than govern the affairs of a state and submit himself to the powers that be.

This story reminds one of Diogenes the Cynic. Once when he was enjoying his bathtub, Alexander the Great came and said: "I am Alexander the Great King." "And I," replied Diogenes, "am Diogenes the dog." On another occasion when he was basking in the sun, Alexander, who was standing by, said, "Ask any favor you choose of me." Diogenes answered: "Cease to shade me from the sun!"

A sensitive and aesthetic nature, Chuangtzu must have been profoundly weary of the world in which he lived. Prone to melancholia and inclined to be retiring, he almost automatically found his haven of peace and rest in a return to the state of nature. He could not bridge the deep chasm between the universe of his artistic creation and the world of coarse and brutal realities. He was never at ease in this world of men and could see no ray of hope in the dark age. Fortunately, he had a keen sense of humor and a rare gift of imagination which saved him from becoming bitter and resentful. The storm and stress of life drove him to find shelter in the bosom of nature, where he at once was in a transport of delight. The following rhapsodical allegory is an eloquent expression of the nature-returning motif of his life. When Chuangtzu was near death, his disciples promised him a splendid funeral. His retort was: "With heaven and earth as my coffin and shell; with the sun, moon, and stars as my burial regalia; and with all creation to escort me to the grave—are not my funeral paraphernalia ready at hand?"

Like many other mystics, Chuangtzu found his raptures and ecstasies, not in the intimacies of human relations, but in complete union with the universe.

Naturalistic Philosophy

It will be remembered that Confucius the idealist thinks that the first duty of a government is to rectify the names (define the terms) of all things so as to distinguish between the true and the false and between the right and the wrong—in other words, to set up a standard of moral values. Yangtzu and Chuangtzu, the naturalists, think quite otherwise; even though they reason differently, they are equally opposed to any artificial standard of truth and goodness.

Looking skeptically at history, Yangtzu observes that all names, good and bad, are humbug. For instance, Yao and Shun, the sage-kings, have good names, but they are really the most miserable creatures that ever crawl upon the earth. Chieh and Chow, the famous tyrants, have bad names, but they get the most fun out of life. "From the oldest times until now is far more years than we can count. . . . Wisdom and folly, virtue and vice, success and failure, right and wrong, all crumble and disappear; a little sooner or a little later! To scorch and wear out soul and body to win the praise or blame of an hour, to conquer a name for a few hundred years after death, will that put fat on dry bones?" What is in a name? It is the reality that counts.

More significantly, Yangtzu thinks that all names as concepts or as species and generic terms have no real existence. Only individual things exist. "Names have no realities; realities have no names. Names are merely man-made." Yangtzu denies the realities of such ideal concepts as prince, minister, father, and son, and by implication denies the functions of any standard of moral values.

Live a natural life, Yangtzu would say, and forget all artificial distinctions between truth and falsehood and between goodness and badness. A nominalist, he counts only the individual ego; * a hedonist, he stresses the importance of the pleasures attainable during one's all too fleeting years on earth.

To Chuangtzu, the standard of human virtue is so obscure that it is impossible actually to know it as such. "Granting that you and I argue," says Chuangtzu, "if you beat me and not I you, are you necessarily right and I wrong? Or if I beat you and not you me, am I necessarily right and you wrong? Or are we both partly right and partly wrong? Or are we both wholly right and wholly wrong? You and I cannot know this, and consequently the world will be in ignorance of the truth."

The distinctions between yes and no, this and that, the positive and the negative, the subject and the object, are purely artificial, says Chuangtzu. The Confucian and the Mocian, for instance, are opposite schools, each denying what the other affirms and affirming what the other denies. They fail to see that there is nothing which is not this and nothing which is not that; that the positive and the negative may be reconciled; and that the subject and the object are really one. Everything is an infinity: this is an infinity and that

---

* Max Stirner, the egoist anarchist, assumes the same position. He says: "The species is nothing, and if the individual lifts himself above the limits of his individuality, this is rather his very self as an individual. . . . Man with a great M is only an ideal, the species only something thought of. To be *a* man is not to realize the ideal of *Man,* but to present oneself, the individual. . . . *I* am my species, am without norm, without law, without model, and the like." "They say of God, 'Names name thee not.' That holds good of me: no concept expresses me, nothing that is designed as my essence exhausts me; they are only names." *The Ego and His Own,* tr. by Steven T. Byington (New York: Benjamin R. Tucker, 1907), pp. 238 and 490.

is an infinity. In the central axis where all infinities converge, the positive and the negative, the subject and the object, blend into one infinite. Therefore, rather than judge whether the Confucian is right and the Mocian wrong or vice versa, Chuangtzu would transcend them both; rather than praise Yao and Shun as good kings and condemn Chieh and Chow as tyrants, Chuangtzu would forget them both. For from the vantage post of the infinite, all contraries and opposites are identical.

In this light, Yangtzu and Chuangtzu are true followers of Laotzu, who declares: "When all the world recognizes beauty to be beauty, this in itself is ugliness. When all the world recognizes goodness as goodness, this in itself is evil." All standards of virtue and knowledge are relative and artificial.

Yangtzu the Egoist Anarchist

It was Mencius who stigmatized Yangtzu as being an egoist anarchist. In his crusade against the forces and doctrines undermining the feudal order, Mencius attacked Yangtzu in these unsparing terms. "Yangtzu is an egoist, who does not acknowledge the sovereign" and who therefore "is a beast." The self-appointed defender of *status quo* warned that, if the "perverse theory" and "subversive practice" of the egoist anarchist were not suppressed, society would revert to the stage of barbaric existence and men would devour men.

The anarchism of Yangtzu, however, is not really the acme of disorder or the abyss of chaos. It is a utopia of free and independent introverts who follow their own natural instincts and do not interfere with one another. Addressing the chancellor of a state, Yangtzu says: "A man skilled in external business may not succeed in keeping order, but is sure to have a wretched life. A man skilled in internal cultivation may not create disorder, and is sure to have a good time himself. Take your way of bossing others: it may work for a time in a state, but it does not fit in with the human heart. Take my way of private life: if it could be extended to the whole world, the principle governing the ruler-subject relationship would naturally die out." The symptom of world illness, according to Yangtzu, is manifested in the abnormal phenomenon that there are people who rule and people who are ruled; and the cause lies in the extraverted and compulsive character of those who do not mind their own business and let others alone. Many are the people who feel called upon to reform the world in the name of justice or charity; they are really egomaniacs who unwarrantably filibuster and frustrate the normal pursuit of human pleasures.

Yangtzu is an egoist, not in the sense of seeking private ends at the expense of others, but in the sense of pursuing individual pleasures without interfering with others. He puts the egoist theory in a nutshell as follows:

"If the men of old could benefit the entire world by pulling out one hair, they would not do it. If they were offered the entire world for life, they would not take it.

"When no man hurts one hair and no man benefits, the world will be at peace."

There are two aspects of the egoist theory. On the one hand, the individual should not hurt his ego, not even by pulling out a single hair, for the ego is the only reality that counts. On the other hand, no one should take anything away from others, not even the tender of an empire. Critics of Yangtzu who, following Mencius, single out the first aspect and condemn the entire theory, do not estimate justly the egoist position.

Yangtzu may seem to exaggerate the importance of a single hair, but logically he is irrefutable. Granting the premise that no one can save the world by any effort, the conclusion is inevitable that no one should, under the grand delusion of saving the world, pull out a hair which, being part of the body, is as important as a limb or a pound of flesh.

As an intellectual, Yangtzu prizes wisdom and depreciates strength. Man is a small heaven and a small earth—a microcosm—and relies upon wisdom, not upon strength, for preservation. "Wisdom is noble, for it helps preserve the ego; strength is base, for it tends to grab things." If every man preserves his ego and if no man grabs things, the utopia of the egoist anarchist will be realized.

Like Laotzu, Yangtzu looks backward upon the state of nature and idealizes the prepolitical stage of society.

"The earliest men knew that life comes anon, and goes anon in death. So they followed their own hearts. They did not turn their backs on natural impulses, they did not forego any of life's pleasures. They did nothing with an eye to fame. They roamed as their nature listed, and did not fight against universal instincts. As they did not care for a name after death, they were above the law. Name and praise, sooner or later, the few or many of the allotted years, were not things they thought about."

But now men are corrupted by culture and civilization and are in perpetual warfare with one another. "There are four things that rob living beings of rest. The first is long life, the second fame, the third place, and the fourth riches. The man that holds by these four things fears ghosts, fears men, fears power, and fears the law. He is a runaway. He may be killed, or he may live: his fate is not in his own hands."

In order to restore the state of nature, every individual must live a simple life himself and let others alone. Then there will be no fears, no anxieties, no wars. There will be no kings and subjects, no rulers and ruled. No government is the best government; no law is the best law; no organization is the best organization. Such is the final anarchism of Yangtzu.

Chuangtzu the Mystic Anarchist

If the anarchism of the egoist is based upon the supremacy of the individual as against the state, the anarchism of the mystic is posited upon the universal oneness of all men, animals, and things. "The universe and I came into being together," says Chuangtzu, "and I and everything therein are one." Man is an integral part of the natural order which has its own law and reason. "There is the universe, its regularity is constant; there are the sun and the moon, their brightness is unceasing; there are the stars, their constellations never change; there are birds and beasts, they flock together without varying; there are trees and shrubs, they grow upwards without exception." Man should follow the law of nature and should not formulate rules and conventions against nature.

Chuangtzu believes that men have certain natural instincts: to weave and clothe themselves, to till and feed themselves. These are common to all humanity.

"So in the days when natural instincts prevailed, men moved quietly and gazed steadily. At that time, there were no roads over mountains, nor boats, nor bridges over water. All things were produced, each for its own proper sphere. Birds and beasts multiplied; trees and shrubs grew up. The former might be led by the hand; you could climb up and peep into a raven's nest. For then man dwelt with birds and beasts, and all creation was one. There were no distinctions of good and bad men. Being all equally without knowledge, their virtue could not go astray. Being all equally without evil desires, they were in a state of natural integrity, the perfection of human existence.

"But when sages appeared, tripping over charity and fettering with duty to one's neighbor, doubt found its way into the world. And then with their gushing over music and fussing over ceremony, the empire divided against itself."

This celebrated passage contains the essence of mystic anarchism.

Chuangtzu would return humanity to the state of nature in which all men and things are merged into an infinite whole.

Chuangtzu is absolutely opposed to all rules and laws which philosophers and sages impose upon mankind. "Away with wisdom and knowledge, and great robbers will disappear. Discard jade and destroy pearls, and petty thieves will cease to exist. Burn tallies and break signets, and the people will revert to their natural integrity. Split measures and smash scales, and the people will not fight over quantities." Utterly abolish all the rules of philosophers and sages, then the world will be a happy place in which to live.

It is tempting to compare Chuangtzu with Rousseau again. The following paragraph in the *Discourse on the Arts and Sciences* might have flowed from Chuangtzu's pen. "There is in Asia a vast empire, where learning is held in high honor, and leads to the dignities in the state. If the sciences improved our morals . . . the Chinese should be wise, free, and invincible. But, if there be no vice they do not practice, no crime with which they are not familiar . . . of what use were their men of science and literature? What advantage has that country reaped from the honors bestowed on its learned men?"

Man is born free and should not be bound in chains, according to Chuangtzu. "There has been such a thing as letting mankind alone; there has never been such a thing as governing mankind! Letting alone springs from fear lest men's natural dispositions be not perverted nor their virtue laid aside, what room is there left for government?" There is no government that really can govern, i.e., create peace and order. If let alone, people will live peacefully by themselves. The government is not only a highly unnecessary evil, but the very harbinger of war and chaos and the greatest destroyer of humanity.

The Place of Yangtzu and Chuangtzu in History

The illustrious trio of Confucius, Mencius, and Hsüntzu are the best representatives of the northern pattern of life, the northern way of thought and action; while the obscure trio of Laotzu, Yangtzu, and Chuangtzu are models of the southern pattern. The former are practical and conservative, while the latter are speculative and destructive. The former are interested in the maintenance of social and political hierarchy, of folkways and stateways, and of moral values that are inherent in civilized society; while the latter are engaged in denouncing all man-made conventions and institutions and in advocating the return to the state of nature.

In the fourth century B.C., one of the most troublous centuries in Chinese history, China produced four of her greatest thinkers: Yangtzu and Chuangtzu, the Taoists, and Mencius and Hsüntzu, the Confucians. It was a century when China was undergoing a great social revolution which struck down the traditional nobles as well as created havoc among the serfs and slaves hitherto under their protective, albeit none too benevolent, wings. When the new entrepreneur and landlord classes began to seize powers in the various warring states, the death-knell of the feudal body politic was sounded, and was echoed far and wide throughout the length and breadth of the Middle Kingdom. Wars were the order of the age, interstate wars and interclass wars, which engendered a high level of social tension and a high plane of universal insecurity. It fell to the intelligentsia, a floating class none too firmly attached to any stratum in the changing social hierarchy, to interpret the spirit of the times and to voice the thoughts and sentiments of the several classes of people. The galaxy of those brilliant minds in the fourth century was all the more luminous and dazzling in the darkness prevailing under heaven. Probably the heights of philosophic enlightenment are always attained only as the depths of social suffering and agony are reached.

Against the background of the total social milieu, Yangtzu appears to have been a degenerate noble turned a decadent intellectual, and Chuangtzu a disinherited noble turned an escapist mystic. Both lacked the aggressive and enterprising spirit of the bourgeois and landlord classes and both had little to do with the toiling masses. Yangtzu lived an easy, pleasant, leisurely life in the garden of pleasure where wines were served at all hours and women were constant companions. This garden of pleasure, however, never quite approached the paradise of happiness; it was merely a refuge from the ennui and boredom of life itself. Chuangtzu was a nonpolitical being who, disdaining the human world, fled into a transcendental realm where he "roamed with the creator and consorted with those who were beyond the pale of life and death and beyond the alpha and omega of the universe." This transcendental realm, though beautiful and noble in conception, was after all little more than a wild extravaganza of poetic frenzy.

The roles of Yangtzu and Chuangtzu in Chinese philosophy are very similar to those of the Cyrenaic-Epicurean and the Cynic-Stoic in Greek philosophy. The Epicurean and the Stoic constitute "a rebellion against the central Socratic philosophy," just as Yangtzu and Chuangtzu represent a revolutionary trend against the dominant Confucian school. The Socratic philosophy is a purely Hellenic product, while the Cyrenaic-Epicurean and the Cynic-Stoic philosophies are more or less non-Hellenic as they fall under the influence of the Semitic east and the Roman west. Similarly, the Confucian philosophy is a purely Chinese product, while the Taoist philosophy is the revolt of the more primitive southerners against the more civilized northerners.

Over two millennia passed before the philosophies of Yangtzu and Chuangtzu found distant echoes in the persons of Max Stirner and Rousseau. In some respects, Yangtzu may be called the "Max Stirner of antiquity" and Chuangtzu the "Rousseau of antiquity." Yangtzu and Stirner are both egoist anarchists, but they differ in certain significant aspects. While assuming the supreme importance of his own ego, Yangtzu concedes the existence and value of other egos. But Stirner thinks that he is not an ego along with other egos, but the sole ego, that he is unique. Yangtzu condemns force that grabs things or hurts men, but Stirner believes that might is right and that "he who has might has right." Chuangtzu and Rousseau are somewhat akin to each other in temperament and intellect. Both are extremely artistic and imaginative and full of easy-flowing, effervescent, intellectual life. Both idealize the state of nature and condemn the arts and sciences that make man a depraved animal. However there is at least one important difference: in his mature years Rousseau was able to create a revolutionary theory for the liberal movement in the eighteenth century, while Chuangtzu remained to the end of his life a complete escapist from the world. With Proudhon, Bakunin, and Kropotkin, leaders of the modern anarchist movement, Yangtzu and Chuangtzu have little in common, save their general opposition to the state. The modern anarchists are communistic and collectivistic and have a revolutionary program for the future, while the Taoists are individualistic and merely look backward to the paradise of the childhood of humanity.

6. THE UTILITARIAN SCHOOL: MOCIUS

Mocius the Man

IN THE history of Chinese political thought, Mocius stands as a
unique and strange character. He had neither any worthy predecessor nor any great successor. He did not come under the Confucian influence nor did he fall within the Taoist pattern. He was
equally opposed to the aristocratic culture of the Confucian and
the anarchistic spirit of the Taoist; he was inclined to accept
neither the rationalization of the feudal regime nor the idealiza-
tion of the primitive utopia. A man of independence and originality, Mocius created a new style of thought and action that was
as anti-Confucian as it was anti-Taoist.

Against the total social milieu, the Mocian school appears to
represent the lower middle classes, independent artisans and free
farmers, who were emancipated from the traditional feudal bonds
between the noble and the serf and slave classes. Neither wealthy
nor powerful, the lower middle classes were a common lot of
hard-working, self-supporting people. They could neither afford
to enjoy the Confucian luxuries of music and poetry, nor could
they comprehend the critical and skeptical attitude of the Taoist.
They were plain and practical people, busily engaged in manual
work and interested only in what was useful.

Of the lower middle classes Mocius was the first able spokesman. He lived in the fifth century (*circa* 470-390), B.C., after Laotzu and Confucius, who were in the sixth century, and before
Yangtzu, Chuangtzu, Mencius, and Hsüntzu, who were in the
fourth. Unlike Confucius, who was of noble descent, Mocius was
of common origin. A native of Lu or of Sung, he had a thorough
knowledge of traditional culture and was widely read. Even

though a student of Confucianism, he thought that the Confucian liberal and humanistic education was not useful or productive and was therefore unwholesome, that music and poetry, or rites and ceremonies, as taught by Confucius, served no practical purposes in society. So he rebelled against Confucianism.

Mocius was a skilled artisan and was more than once contemptuously dismissed by nobles as a mere commoner, a base or mean person. The aristocratic way of life was completely alien to him. He led a humble, assiduous, ascetic life, permitting himself no moments of leisure and no extravagant expressions of joy or anger. He was ultra-puritanic in self-discipline.

He was no philosophic genius. He lacked that power of human understanding which made Confucius what he was, and that metaphysic intuition which Laotzu happily possessed. Mocius was quite blind as to human nature and never touched upon deep metaphysical problems.

Nor was he a literary genius. Unlike Mencius, who had an effervescent and graceful style, and unlike Chuangtzu, who had the rare gift of imagination, Mocius was little more than an average literary man, who came upon ideas only through laborious processes and expressed them in a rather cumbersome and repetitious style.

Mocius was a Messianic world reformer of the puritanical and ascetic species. He was so extraverted that "he did not retain a single seat long enough to make it warm." He was so solicitous of the well-being of the world that he "would bear shame and humiliation to approach the rulers of the time." If he could benefit the world, he would "rub smooth his whole body from the crown to the heel." Once he walked ten days and ten nights and had to tear off strips of his garments to wrap his sore feet, all for the sake of preventing a vicious attack upon a weak state by a strong neighbor.

Living in an age in which war was the order, Mocius preached the doctrines of universal love and mutual aid, which he believed to be the only means of world salvation. "To refute my doctrines with any other doctrines," he said, "is like trying to destroy a boulder with an egg. All the eggs in the world would be exhausted before the boulder could in any way be damaged." He was as absolutely dogmatic in thought as he was completely self-denying and self-sacrificing in action.

Like Confucius, Mocius traveled from state to state preaching his doctrines to the rulers of the world. Obviously he was sailing against the current of the times and was naturally considered by the potentates of the world as an impractical and unrealistic pacificist. He is said to have been a minister in Sung and to have been put in prison for some reason. As a political man, he was quite as unsuccessful as Confucius before him.

After his failure in politics, Mocius established a school, to which young men from many states came to study. It was hardly a liberal school where different arts, sciences, and philosophies of the age were taught; it was rather exclusively a school teaching the Mocian dogmas. He had several hundred pupils who looked up to him with awe and admiration and who were willing to sacrifice their lives for his doctrines. They were a company of undubbed knights, brave and chivalrous, ready to defend any weak state against the attack of a strong neighbor. They labored day and night, and chose to wear shabby clothes and eat niggardly, holding their self-denial a virtue. In every respect, they were under the influence of the dominant personality of the master.

Fundamentally, Mocius was an authoritarian character, humorless and joyless, in dead seriousness all the time. The doctrines of universal love and mutual aid notwithstanding, Mocius was not a tender mind or a gentle nature, but decidedly a rigorous, severe, righteous personality. He wished to command all men to love one another; he hardly knew how to inspire human affection and kindliness.

There were two illuminating comments on Mocius, one by a Confucian and one by a Taoist. The Confucian Hsüntzu said that

"Mocius prescribed coarse clothing and poor food and brought anxiety undiluted by amusement" and that "Mocius was blinded by utility and did not know refinement." To the aristocratic Confucian, Mocius appeared vulgar and unbeseeming as well as heavily laden with anxiety and sorrow. The Taoist made an even more searching analysis of Mocius the man, an analysis very critical but extremely sympathetic.

"Mocius would have no singing in life and no mourning at death. He inculcated the doctrines of universal love and mutual aid. He condemned war and did not permit of anger. He was fond of learning. . . . He attacked ceremony and music. . . .

"That he taught such lessons cannot prove that he loved men; that he practiced them certainly shows that he did not love himself. . . .

"Notwithstanding men will sing, he condemns singing; men will wail, he condemns wailing; men will rejoice, he condemns rejoicing—is this truly in accord with human nature?

"Toil through life and niggardliness at death—this way is one of great unkindliness, making people uncomfortable and unhappy, and difficult to be carried out in practice. . . .

"Nevertheless, Mocius was one of the greatest souls in the world! . . . He was a superior man indeed!"

The Utilitarian Theory

Whereas the idealistic Confucian thinks that goodness or rightness is for its own sake and whereas the naturalistic Taoist denies the distinction between good and evil or between right and wrong, the utilitarian Mocian argues that what is useful is good and what is beneficial is right. Mocius is primarily concerned with the consequence of an idea in action and not at all interested in the abstract nature of goodness or rightness.

Once Mocius is asked, "The doctrine of universal love is a good

thing, but can it be of any use?" He answers: "If it were not useful, even I would disapprove of it. But how can there be anything
that is good but not useful?" In the Mocian canons, "the right"
is defined as "the beneficial." Instead of inquiring whether an idea
or institution is good, Mocius asks what it is good for; instead of
defining the right abstractly, he searches for the beneficial in a
concrete manner.

The following argument brings the difference between idealism
and utilitarianism into clear relief. Mocius asks a Confucian, "Why
do you pursue music?" He answers, "Music is pursued for its own
sake." Whereupon Mocius says: "You have not answered me.
Suppose I ask why you build houses. And you answer that it is
to keep off the cold in winter and the heat in summer and to
separate men from women. Then you will have told me the reason
for building houses. Now I am asking why you pursue music.
And you answer that music is pursued for its own sake. This is
like saying that houses are built for their own sake."

The famous doctrines of universal love and mutual aid, the central themes of Mocianism, are fundamentally utilitarian doctrines.
Says Mocius, "Whoever loves others is loved by others; whoever
aids others is aided by others; whoever hates others is hated by
others; whoever injures others is injured by others." Mocius
frankly admits that the doctrines of universal love and mutual aid
are based upon enlightened egoism. It is to the interest of the
self that universal love and mutual aid must be practiced.

However, although conscious of self-interest, the ideal Mocian
is a self-denying and self-sacrificing personality. Herein lies the
fundamental difference between the Mocian and the Benthamite.
The modern utilitarian regards pleasure and pain as two sovereign masters of human action, and tends to seek pleasure and
avoid pain. The Mocian, on the other hand, will forsake pleasure
and incur pain, if he can benefit others. The Benthamite theory
arises from the upper bourgeoisie in modern society, whereas the

Mocian theory originates from the lower middle classes, free artisans and farmers, in ancient China.

In politics, both types of utilitarianism have one common goal,
namely, the greatest happiness of the greatest number of people.
The famous Benthamite felicitous calculus, as is well known, runs
as follows: A maximum of men enjoying a maximum of pleasures minus a minimum of men afflicted with a minimum of pains
equals the greatest good of the greatest number. Mocius, though
less mathematical than Bentham, expresses the same utilitarian
principle in a pragmatic statement instead of a mathematical
formula. Says Mocius, whether an idea or act is good or evil is,
in the last analysis, to be determined by the test whether it is
beneficial or harmful "to the nation, the hundred families, and
the common people." Regardless of its abstract nature, an idea or
act is good if it is beneficial to the majority of the people and is
evil if it is harmful.

To explain this quantitative principle Mocius employs many
illustrations. For instance, war is evil, says Mocius, because "the
invader gets no profit, neither does the invaded. War does not
benefit anybody." Supposing a large country attacks a small
country. "In the country invaded, the farmers cannot till and their
wives cannot weave, all being engaged in defense. Nor in the
aggressor country can the farmers till and their wives weave, all
being engaged in the attack." Even a victory is not of advantage
to the victor. While the vanquished loses everything, the victorious
acquires only ruined cities and devastated fields. Because it is
harmful to all, war is evil.

It is interesting to compare this utilitarian anti-war argument
with the idealistic. Sung Keng was about to advise the kings of
Ch'in and Ch'u (who were then warring) how unprofitable war
was. Whereupon Mencius said:

"If you, starting from the point of profit, offer your persuasive
counsels to the kings of Ch'in and Ch'u, and if those kings are

pleased with the consideration of profit so as to stop the movements of their armies, then all belonging to those armies will rejoice in the cessation of the war and find their pleasures in the pursuit of profit. Ministers will serve their sovereigns for the profit of which they cherish the thought; sons will serve their fathers and younger brothers will serve their elder brothers from the same consideration. The result will be that, abandoning goodness and rightness, sovereign and minister, father and son, younger brother and elder will carry on all their intercourse with the thought of profit cherished in their breasts. But there has never been such a state which does not end in ruin!"

Mencius the idealist thinks that a nation should follow the good or the right without any consideration of profit, but Mocius the utilitarian argues that the good is the useful and the right is the beneficial.

The Origin of the State

To Confucius the state appears a final product in social evolution from the primitive stage of individual existence and through the intermediate stage of family life. To Laotzu the state comes into being when the philosopher-king imposes artificial and arbitrary laws and rules upon the people. But to Mocius the state seems to be the consequence of a deliberate and rational action, a social contract between the sovereign and the people. In this respect, Mocianism anticipates the social contract theories of Hobbes, Locke, and Rousseau.

In common with the later contract theorists, Mocius does not think that there is an actual contract between the sovereign and the people, which formally institutes the body politic. The contract is rather a logical deduction from an hypothetical state of nature, which is described in the following famous passage.

"In the beginning there is no ruler, and men have conflicting wills (ideas or purposes). Where there is one man, there is one will; where there are two men, there are two wills; where there are ten men, there are ten wills. The more the men, the more the wills. As all men affirm their own wills and oppose those of others, they are in the state of mutual antagonism. Therefore, fathers and sons as well as elder brothers and younger brothers become enemies and cannot live together in harmony. The deadly hand of each is against all. The strong do not help the weak; the rich do not feed the poor; the enlightened do not teach the ignorant. The human world is in the state of chaos, similar to the animal world."

This state of nature immediately recalls the Hobbesian. In fact, the Mocian conception of the state of nature cannot be better summarized than by the famous dictum of Hobbes, *bellum omnium contra omnes.*

Mocius is not so systematic a political philosopher as Hobbes. The former merely assumes the chaotic state of nature without entering into the psychological motives and material conditions of the early man, whereas the latter builds his conception of the state of nature upon a critical analysis of human nature and a careful description of the primitive environment. Unlike Hobbes, who is a closet philosopher, Mocius is an anxious reformer, having neither the leisure nor the inclination to work out any comprehensive system of political philosophy. Yet it is to the permanent credit of this extraverted man of action to have developed a body of political principles which, as will be seen, run closely parallel to those of the English speculative philosopher.

The state of nature being what it is, Mocius argues, the necessity of political association inevitably arises. In the course of time men begin to realize that the natural condition of chaos is due to the absence of a universal ruler. Therefore, one bright day, men gather together and decide to elect the most virtuous and capable among them to be emperor in whom the government of the world is entrusted. As the emperor alone cannot govern the world, the people elect "three ministers" to assist him. As the emperor and the ministers cannot administer the entire world, the people then elect governors of various territories, magistrates of districts, and heads of villages. The governor of a territory must be the most virtuous and capable in that territory; the magistrate of a district or the head of a village must be the most virtuous and capable in that district or village. Thus, by a series of popular elections, the entire political hierarchy is created.*

The body politic is essentially a contractual institution. Says Mocius, "The sovereign, the ministers, and the people are bound in alliance by contract." As to the nature of the contract, however, Mocius does not make any explicit statement. When men find the state of nature intolerable, they organize themselves into a state by electing a government. By this act, presumably, they covenant that they will give up their own particular wills and submit themselves to the will of the elect. In assuming the sovereign power the emperor, presumably, agrees to maintain peace and order in the world and to unify the conflicting wills, ideas, and purposes of the people.

This hypothesis of the origin of the state should be interpreted in the light of the social position of Mocius. As a representative of the lower middle classes, Mocius opposed the traditional feudal nobility and by implication rejected the principle of heredity. He projected the hypothesis that, in the beginning when the state was instituted, the people elected the entire governing and administrative body. Upon the basis of this hypothesis, he argued effectively that the virtuous and capable among the commoners should be elected to replace incompetent aristocrats.

* There is some controversy over the meaning of "election." According to some authorities, it is heaven that elects the emperor, and it is the emperor who appoints the ministers and other dignitaries. But according to others, it is the people who elect the emperor, the ministers, and other officials. The writer has adopted the latter view, believing that by "election" Mocius does not mean "appointment" or "self-appointment."

The Mocian Leviathan

Having outlined the process whereby the state is created, Mocius discusses the power and function of the ruling body. Here a great paradox appears. What is democratically created turns out to be a monstrous Leviathan that claims an absolute control over the soul and body of every citizen.

According to Mocius, the state is to unify the conflicting wills, ideas, or purposes of the people. It is to be a universal empire under one supreme will, which identifies itself with the will of heaven above and with which are identified the wills of all below.

The process of identification begins from the base to the apex of the political hierarchy, from villages to districts, then to territories, then to the empire, and finally to heaven. The head of the village, upon election, is to issue the following proclamation:

"All you people of the village are to identify yourselves with the magistrate of the district. What he thinks to be right all shall think to be right; what he thinks to be wrong all shall think to be wrong. Put away your evil speech and learn his good speech. Put away your evil conduct and learn his good conduct. Then there will be peace in the district."

The magistrate of the district will command the people to identify themselves with the governor of the territory, and the governor of the territory will command the people to identify themselves with the emperor. Then, behold, a universal empire emerges. "What the emperor thinks to be right all shall think to be right; what he thinks to be wrong all shall think to be wrong."

Mocius and Hobbes see eye to eye the necessity of a universal standard of conduct, set up by the sovereign and followed by all citizens. Hobbes condemns the doctrine that "every private man is judge of good and evil actions" as seditious. Mocius does not permit any private citizen to judge for himself what is right or wrong. In neither Leviathan is there room for individual conscience.

There is, however, one limitation upon the will of the emperor. Upon election, the emperor becomes the representative of heaven and is obliged to execute the will of heaven. Now what is the will of heaven? The answer, according to Mocius, is that men love and aid one another. The principles of universal love and mutual aid constitute the will of heaven. It is the duty of the emperor, therefore, to issue the following proclamation to the world:

"All you people must report those who love and aid others and those who hate and hurt others. I will reward those who report the good behavior of others and punish those who do not report the evil behavior of others. I will reward those of good behavior and punish those of evil behavior. Then peace will reign in the empire."

Thus, the will of the emperor represents the will of heaven on the one hand and unifies the wills of all the people on the other.

The will of heaven is supreme. If the emperor does not carry out the will of heaven, he will be punished; if he does, he will be rewarded. If the people do not obey the will of heaven, heaven "will send down cold and heat without moderation, and snow, frost, rain, and dew untimely. As a result, the five grains cannot ripen and the six animals cannot mature; and there will be disease, epidemics, and pestilence." The Mocian Leviathan thus becomes an absolute theocratic monarchy.

It may be stated as a general principle that those thinkers who wish to have an authoritarian regime frequently project the hypothesis that the state of nature is chaotic and brutal, and those who are anarchists or individualists tend to imagine a beautiful paradise of nature. Mocius and Hobbes fall under the first category, while Laotzu and Rousseau are of the second. If the state of nature is intolerable, the necessity of authoritarian government is easily defended. On the other hand, if the state of nature is blissful, the *raison d'état* falls of itself.

Public Administration

Mocius is perhaps less a theorist of the state than a student of public administration. With a practical turn of mind, he is more interested in how public affairs are to be administered than in the origin and nature of the state.

The aim of public administration, Mocius repeatedly declares, is threefold: the wealth of the nation, the increase of the population, and the orderliness of legislation and adjudication. To achieve the threefold aim, Mocius argues, it is imperative that the ruler employ the virtuous and capable in the government. "All the rulers of the world desire their countries to be wealthy, their people to be many, and their jurisdiction to be orderly. But what they obtain is not wealth but poverty, not multitude but scarcity, not order but chaos. This is because the rulers have failed to promote the virtuous and employ the capable." "They have, indeed, missed the very foundation of public administration."

This personnel principle of public administration is first expressed by Confucius and is therefore not original with Mocius. But the latter presents a far more cogent and effective argument than the former. Supposing, says Mocius, the ruler wants a cow killed, he will certainly look for a skillful butcher. If he wants a garment made, he will look for a skillful tailor. If he has a sick horse that he cannot cure, he will look for an experienced veterinary doctor. Or, if he has a tight bow that he cannot draw, he will look for a deft archer. For these, he will not employ his relatives because he knows they are incapable. "But," Mocius continues, "when it comes to the affairs of the state, all is different. The relations of the ruler—the rich but unworthy and the handsome but stupid—are all promoted. Does it not seem that the ruler loves his country even less than a tight bow, a sick horse, a garment, or a cow?" If menial matters have to be attended to by specialists, how much more do public affairs have to be managed by experts?

There seems to be a fundamental difference between the Confucian conception of the public servant and the Mocian conception. Confucius thinks that the public servant should be a philosopher, a scholar, a poet, a musician, a ritualist, or an historian—in other words, a man trained in the general humanities. On the other hand, Mocius seems to argue that the public servant should be a man who can master and solve certain concrete problems. Mocius does not think that liberal arts and sciences can cure all political ills. "Upon entering a country," he says to a disciple, "one should locate the need and work on that." If the country is in chaos, one should prepare to be a statesman to establish an authoritarian regime. If the country is in poverty, one should be an economist to reduce public expenditures. If the country is indulging in melodies and wines, one should be an ascetic moralist to teach the anti-music and anti-fatalism principles. If the country is insolent and disgraceful, one should be a religious leader who can lead the people in the reverence of heaven and in the worship of the spirits. If the country is engaged in aggression and conquest, one should be a pacifist crusader, who can preach and practice the doctrines of universal love and mutual aid. As the ills of different countries are not the same, Mocius does not prescribe a universal panacea. The public servant of a country need not be a philosopher or a poet, but should be a practical man of affairs.

Further to illustrate how Mocius is concerned with practical problems of administration, let us quote his famous analysis of the "seven causes of anxiety" in a state. These are: (1) When the outer and inner city walls are not fortified while the palace is under construction. (2) When an enemy is approaching and yet neighbors do not come to the rescue. (3) When the resources of the people are exhausted without producing any profit and the national treasury is emptied in entertaining idle companies. (4) When the officials value only their salaries and the sophists only friendship, and when the inferior officers dare not remonstrate the superior. (5) When the ruler is over-confident and makes no preparation against external danger. (6) When the trusted are not loyal and the loyal are not trusted. (7) When the crops are not sufficient and the ministers are not responsible, and when rewards cannot make people happy and punishments cannot make people afraid. This analysis touches upon some of the central problems of public administration, such as personnel and finance, and places Mocius as a pioneer student of public administration.

The Place of Mocius in History

During the last three centuries of the feudal age, Mocianism, Confucianism, and Taoism were the three most powerful rival schools of philosophy, which were said to have trifurcated the Middle Kingdom. But in the last twenty centuries, Mocianism has for all practical purposes ceased to be a living school, while Confucianism and Taoism have remained the two most dominant currents of political thought. The rapid ascendancy and the total eclipse of the Mocian school constitute one of the unusual phenomena in the history of political thought.

In its heyday, the Mocian school was better organized than the other two rivals. Within the school, Mocius was the supreme and absolute leader and held a position similar in authority to that of the Pope in the Catholic Church. He could send any disciple on any mission to the rulers of the age and could recall any disciple from any office in any state. Confucius did not have such powers over his followers, and Laotzu would certainly have disdained exercising them.

Upon his death, Mocius appointed a successor, who in turn became the supreme and absolute leader of the school. The line of succession continued for some two centuries. Had the Mocian school succeeded in seizing political power, China might have undergone an age of absolute theocratic monarchy.

Mocianism was a product of the age when the central authority was declining and the local feudal states were in constant war with one another. Unlike Confucianism, which represented the aristocratic class, Mocianism voiced the sentiments and opinions of the new middle classes that were opposed to the hereditary nobility. Against the anarchistic tendency of the Taoist school, Mocianism advocated the establishment of a strong centralized monarchy. Confucius looked backward to the restoration of the feudal hierarchy and Laotzu to the revival of the state of nature, but Mocius rather anticipated the emergence of a centralized monarchy that would inaugurate a new era of peace and prosperity.

As a man, Mocius was an authoritarian character. In theory, he was the first Chinese to create a great Leviathan, which was quite foreign to the thinkers of his day and which was the most distinctive innovation of his system. But notwithstanding his exaltation of the state, Mocius fundamentally had the interest of the people at heart. He was antagonistic to the leisure, unproductive, aristocratic class that had usurped the power of the state and oppressed the toiling masses. For him, the state did not exist for its own sake, but for the sake of the people as a whole.

Even though Mocius anticipated a unified regime, he failed to realize that the coming empire was to be brought about, not by popular election, nor through the spread of the doctrines of universal love and mutual aid, but by wars and conquests which he eloquently though ineffectively attempted to prevent. He was the spokesman of the new middle classes which in the fifth century were neither powerful nor wealthy and did not constitute a threat to the declining nobility. It was not until the third century, when the upper middle classes arose to seize the powers of the feudal states, the classes represented by the Legalist school, that a new empire loomed as a distinct sign of the times.

7. THE REALISTIC SCHOOL: HANTZU

Hantzu The First Political Scientist

IF POLITICS and ethics are more or less blended together in the Confucian and Mocian systems, they are distinctly separated in the Legalist philosophy, of which the most outstanding exponent is Hantzu (*circa* 280-233 B.C.), the first political scientist of China.

Hantzu is the spirit that symbolizes the greatest political metamorphosis in China, the transformation from the feudal regime to the monarchical order. More than any other thinker, Hantzu intellectually marks the omega of the feudal age and the alpha of the monarchical era. He is the child of the disintegrating feudal society but the pontiff of the monarchical order. In the annals of history, there are few thinkers who surpass him in prophetic vision and historical acumen.

One of the princes of the Han state, a weak state between the powerful Ch'in and Chao, Hantzu devoted himself to the studies of penology, epistemology, law, and statecraft, wishing that he might someday chart the course of the ship of state through the troubled waters of the times. He studied with Li Ssu under the great Confucian Hsüntzu, who was then the supereminent scholar of the Middle Kingdom. Li Ssu was a strong man, a man of affairs, but Hantzu was a far greater scholar and thinker. Both were geniuses who, it is understandable, accorded with each other as harmoniously as dynamite and fire. It was during this school life that Hantzu sowed the seed which ripened into a final tragedy.

In his mature years Hantzu lived in his native state. He submitted memorials and presented counsels to the King of Han, but was completely ignored. He wanted to improve the laws and institutions of the land and proposed measures to enrich the country and strengthen the army, but he hardly won a hearing. Thereupon he became highly incensed at the ruler who elevated frivolous and dissolute men to high posts above men of real merit. He was resentful against unprincipled ministers and lawless cavaliers. It was under such circumstances that Hantzu wrote *Solitary Indignation, Five Vermin,* and other works.

When the King of Ch'in, who was later to become the first imperial monarch of all China, read *Solitary Indignation* and *Five Vermin,* he immediately recognized the genius in the author and exclaimed, "Lo! If only I, the King, could meet this author and become friendly with him, I would have no cause to regret my death thereafter!" "These are the works of Hantzu," remarked Li Ssu, Hantzu's schoolmate, who had become a minister of Ch'in.

Soon after, Ch'in launched an attack upon Han. The King of Han, who had not hitherto taken Hantzu into service, now sent him as a good-will envoy to Ch'in. When the King of Ch'in met Hantzu, he instantly entered into mental rapport with the scholar and saw in him a man after his own heart.

Li Ssu, the minister, who had always suffered feelings of inferiority and insecurity in the presence of Hantzu, began to slander the newcomer. He said to the King: "Hantzu is one of the princes of the Han state. As Your Majesty is now planning to conquer all the feudal states, Hantzu will in the long run work for the Han state and not the Ch'in. Such is the natural inclination of human nature. Now, if Your Majesty does not take him into service and, after keeping him thus long, sends him home, it is to leave a source of future trouble. It is best to kill him for an offense against the law."

Considering this admonition reasonable, the King instructed his officials to pass sentence on Hantzu. In the meantime, Li Ssu sent men to bring poisonous drugs to Hantzu and ordered him to commit suicide. Hantzu wanted to plead his own case before the throne but could not secure an audience. Later the King regretted

and instructed the officials to pardon him. But the scholar had
already passed into history.

Thus ended the tragic career of the most brilliant political
scientist of ancient China, a man who was a novice in real politics
but who composed the most realistic treatise on politics.

Hantzu visualized a universal state, under one sovereign, one
regime, one supreme law—a universal state which would put an
end to the age of war and confusion. It was probable that, when
he met the King of Ch'in, he recognized in him the man destined
to unify the world. The King, on his part, must have been delighted in meeting a mind that understood him. Hantzu saw in
the King of Ch'in what Aristotle had seen in Alexander and what
Goethe was to see in Napoleon—a political genius who was to
create unity and order out of a chaotic world. But as Aristotle and
Goethe were powerless in the marches of Alexander and Napoleon
respectively, Hantzu came to a tragic end before the curtain of
history unveiled a new scene.

It was not, therefore, in the march of events, but in the realm
of ideas, that Hantzu figured as a significant historic character.
In actual life he was socially inhibited and politically frustrated,
and was an habitual stutterer. In thought he was of the toughest-
minded of men in history, condemning sentiments of mercy or
sympathy and admiring qualities of physical strength and mental
coldness. He was a scholar of keen observation and a writer of
extraordinary force and elegance. Indignant as he was against the
shape of things then obtaining, Hantzu ever remained on a high
rational and intellectual plane. He studied men and institutions
as they were, with all their comedies and tragedies; he never
indulged in utopian dreams and wishful fantasies. Unlike other
philosophers who gazed retrospectively at the glories and gran-
deurs of the early Chou feudal regime, at the mythical sage-kings
such as Yao and Shun, or at the primeval paradise of the human
race, Hantzu broke completely with the past, faced the realities
of the present with unusual objectivity, and looked forward to

the immediate future with an insight that was prophetic. It was this realism—realism of a high rational and intellectual order—that enabled him not only to synthesize all the theoretical elements of the Legalist school, but also to absorb as well as to discard components of the Confucian, Taoist, and Mocian systems, thereby distinguishing himself as the last and most eminent political thinker of ancient China.

The Meaning of History

To Hantzu the realist, history is a continuous flow, a perpetual flux, of men, events, and ideas. Ages come and go; dynasties rise and fall. The past is neither to be repeated nor regretted; only the present and the future remain to challenge human intellect and power.

"Both Confucius and Mocius," says Hantzu, "followed Yao and Shun. Though they differed in matters of acceptance and rejection, yet both claimed to represent the true Yao and Shun. Now that Yao and Shun are not able to come to life again, who can determine whether Confucius or Mocius is right?" Hantzu thinks it impossible to know accurately the ways of Yao and Shun, who are supposed to have lived three millennia before the period of the Contending States. "To insist upon anything that has no corroborating evidence is stupid; to abide by anything that one cannot be sure of is self-deceptive. Therefore, those who freely quote the early kings and dogmatically speak on behalf of Yao and Shun must be deceitful, if not stupid." Hantzu deplored the fact that the Confucians and the Mocians had duped and misled the princes of the world by preaching the ways of Yao and Shun of which they themselves had but the vaguest notions. A courageous and radical thinker, Hantzu attempted to overthrow the authority of history, the weight of which had been deeply impressed upon the Chinese mind through the teachings of Confucius and Mocius.

Hantzu divides history into three periods: remote antiquity, middle antiquity, and recent antiquity. In remote antiquity human beings were few while beasts were many. A sage appeared who fastened trees to build nests (shelters), in order to protect men against savage beasts. He was made king and known as the Nest-Dweller. In those days, people ate raw vegetables and meats and contracted all alimentary diseases. Another sage appeared who used a drill to make fire for cooking. He was likewise made king and known as the Fire-Driller. In middle antiquity came a great deluge, wherefore the great Yü opened channels to drain off the water. In recent antiquity Chieh and Chow became tyrants, wherefore T'ang and Wu overthrew them. Now, says Hantzu, if anyone in middle antiquity fastened trees to build nests or used a drill to make fire, he would certainly be ridiculed, for the age had outgrown these primitive inventions. Again, if anyone in recent antiquity opened new water-courses, he would certainly be ridiculed, for there was no deluge. That being so, if anyone were to laud the ways of Yao and Shun to the present generation, he would certainly be ridiculed by the modern sage. "That is the reason," Hantzu concludes, "why the sage seeks neither to follow the ways of the ancients, nor to establish any fixed standard for all time, but examines the things of his age and then prepares to deal with them." Hantzu thus turns the retrospective gaze of philosophy at the dead past into a pragmatic look at the dynamic reality of the living present.

Not only does Hantzu understand more clearly than any other ancient thinker the dynamic nature of social evolution, but he formulates a theory of historical materialism, which destroys completely the Confucian and Mocian illusions of the remote golden age and of the moral superiority of the ancients to the moderns. In olden times, says Hantzu, men did not till, nor did women weave. People were few while supplies were ample. Neither large rewards were bestowed, nor were heavy punishments inflicted, but people governed themselves. At present, however, people have become numerous while supplies have become scanty. People therefore quarrel and fight so much that, although rewards are doubled and punishments repeated, disorder remains the order of the day. Human beings are more or less alike, the ancients and the moderns, but material conditions are different.

When Yao and Shun were Sons of Heaven, Hantzu continues, they ate unpolished grains and coarse greens, wore deerskin garments in winter and rough fibre cloth in summer; they enjoyed no more comforts than the gatekeeper. When the great Yü was Son of Heaven, he wielded the plow and the spade; he toiled as hard as the slave. In view of such hardships, anyone who abdicated the throne was simply leaving the lot of the gatekeeper or the slave. On the contrary, the prefect of today hands down luxurious chariots to his descendants. Therefore, in the days of yore the Son of Heaven found it easy to resign, while at present even the prefect does not wish to abandon his post. The difference in reality lies between meagerness and abundance.

Summarizing his materialistic theory, Hantzu concludes:

"In the spring of famine years men do not even feed their infant brothers, while in the autumn of abundant years even strange visitors are always fed. Not that they cut off their blood relations and love passers-by, but that their feelings are different in times of abundance and scarcity. For the same reason, men of olden times thought lightly of goods, not because they were benevolent but because goods were abundant; men of today quarrel and pillage, not because they are brutish but because goods are scarce. Again, in the days of yore men made light of resigning from the dignity of the Son of Heaven, not because they were noble but because the power of the Son of Heaven was limited; while at present men make much fighting for government posts, not because they are mean but because the powers of the posts are great. Therefore, the sage governs according to quantitative considerations, such as the abundance or scarcity of supply and the ample-

ness or meagerness of income. So it is not charity to inflict light
punishments, nor is it cruelty to enforce severe penalties: these
measures are carried out in accordance with the folkways of the
age. Circumstances change with time, and ways of dealing with
circumstances change accordingly. . . . Different situations need
different preparations. . . . The ancient and the modern have different folkways; the old and the new necessitate different measures."

This materialistic theory was truly revolutionary at the end of
the Contending States. The Confucian deplored the deviation of
the age from a fanciful conception of the feudal regime, with
little understanding of the new economic and social forces that
made a restoration of the golden age impossible; he did no
more than lament the moral decadence of the age. The Mocian,
though more realistic, conjured up a vision of the Leviathan instituted by popular election and maintained through universal love
and mutual benefit. The naturalistic Taoist remained comfortably
in the dream of paradise lost and more or less inadvertently excluded the reality of the present from his consciousness. The
Legalist almost alone was alive to the changing configuration of
the body politic and able to offer a dispassionate and rational
analysis of history.

The Nature of Man

Hantzu, as a student of Hsüntzu, is inclined to believe that
human nature is evil. Man is not born with any moral consciousness or any ethical standard; rather is he born with certain likes
and dislikes. He likes to be free and lazy and dislikes toil; he likes
to receive benefits from others and dislikes to give benefits to
others; he likes to be safe and dislikes to be exposed to danger.
Such is the nature of man.

Even in the parent-child relationship, Hantzu observes, the

thought of self-interest is predominant. The father and the mother always congratulate themselves when a male child is born, but they sometimes murder a female child at birth. For they think that the son will be of benefit to them in the long run, while the daughter is forever a burden. If the relationship between parents and children is governed by self-interest, how much the more are other human relationships guided by cold-blooded calculations.

Hantzu thinks that love is not the principal factor in the relationship between parent and son and is much less so in the relationship between ruler and ruled. As the mother cannot preserve a family by love alone, Hantzu asks, how can the ruler preserve a state by love? To govern a state, the ruler must understand human nature. Men by nature welcome rewards and fear punishments, therefore the ruler must bestow rewards upon those who render service to him and inflict punishments upon those who act against him. This is a first principle in government.

Hantzu believes as does Machiavelli that it is much safer for the prince to be feared than loved. He argues, the mother loves the son twice as much as the father does, but the father is obeyed by the son ten times more than is the mother. The prince may not love the people at all, but he is obeyed by the people ten thousand times more than the father is obeyed by the son. The more loving the prince, the less is he respected; the more strict and severe, the more is he feared and obeyed.

"In ruling the state," says Hantzu, "the sage does not count on people's doing him good, but utilizes their inability to do him wrong. If he counts on people's doing him good, within the boundary there will never be enough such persons to count by tens. But if he utilizes people's inability to do him wrong, the entire state can be regulated. . . . Reliance not on rewards and punishments, but on the naturally good among the people, is not highly considered by the intelligent ruler. The law of the state must be applied to all the millions of the ruled. Therefore, the artful prince does not follow the good that happens by accident, but practices the way that prevails by necessity."

It is a far cry from the Méncian innocent faith in human nature to this realistic analysis of man—an analysis unacceptable to many because it is disturbing and disillusioning, nevertheless an analysis that marks the beginning of a dispassionate understanding of the forces of destruction in man.

The Nature of the State

As history is a continuous flux, Hantzu thinks, the state is never a permanent condition of being, an unchanging status. As conditions alter, so changes the state. In common with other Chinese philosophers, Hantzu conceives of the state as a set or a phase of human relations. In analyzing this phase, Hantzu makes a significant distinction between the ancient and the modern state. The relations between prince and minister in the old age are personal or tribal, while the relations between ruler and ruled in the new age are impersonal or purely political relations. In Hantzu's thought, this is perhaps the most fundamental generalization of history, for it is the basis upon which he breaks with old traditions and formulates a new political philosophy.

Developing this generalization more fully, Hantzu advances a theory of the evolution of the state in the following form. In the ancient age, when things are simple and problems few, the state is under the government by virtue. In the middle age, when things multiply and problems complicate, the state comes under the government by intelligence. In the modern age, when people are in continual struggle for existence, the state naturally falls under the government by force or power. The ancient ideal ruler is a moralist, the medieval a philosopher, and the modern a strong man. Therefore, the ancients cultivate virtue, the medievals develop intelligence, and the moderns use force. It is unwise for the medievals to cultivate virtue alone, just as it is unrealistic for the moderns to use intelligence alone.

Lord Shang, an earlier Legalist, formulates a theory parallel to Hantzu's. Says Shang:

"In the highest antiquity, people loved their relatives and were fond of what was their own; in middle antiquity, they honored talent and delighted in virtue; and in later days, they prized noble rank and respected office. . . . When the guiding principles of the people become unsuited to the circumstances, their standards of value must change. As conditions in the world change, different principles are practiced."

The essential characteristic of the state, according to Hantzu, is power or force or sovereign authority. Excepting Shentzu, no other political thinkers before Hantzu had touched upon this fundamental subject in politics. Hantzu defines sovereignty as "the instrument for the control of the masses." If the ruler can hold all under heaven in submission, it is because he has the sovereign power. Without the sovereign power, Yao and Shun would have been mere individuals and could not have maintained peace and order throughout the world; with the sovereign power, Chieh and Chow, who otherwise would have been mere individuals, succeeded in throwing the world into chaos and confusion. Sovereignty, therefore, is the distinguishing mark of the ruler and is the very essence of the political association.

Between royalty and tyranny, Hantzu makes no distinction. Whether a ruler is a saint or a sinner, or whether he is supported by the people or not, does not in the least alter the fact that he is sovereign as long as he is in a position to exercise the supreme power of the state. In the opinion of Mencius, when a ruler is a tyrant, he ceases to be sovereign and becomes a mere individual. Hantzu does not accept such an idealistic view. To him, what distinguishes a sovereign as sovereign is the power he exercises over the people, not his moral excellence or intellectual superiority. Sovereignty is solely the possession of the ruler and cannot be delegated or divided, according to Hantzu. The ruler who knows how to exercise his sovereign power can maintain the safety of his state; he who shares his sovereign power with his ministers endangers his throne. Hantzu does not divide the sovereign power into the legislative, the executive, and the judicial, as does Montesquieu. Rather he thinks, with Bodin, that the ruler is the person in whom the entire sovereign power is vested. The ruler apparently is the supreme law-maker, the head executive, and the chief justice, all in one. He is the absolute monarch, governing the life and death of every private individual without exception. Although theoretically he is to act in accordance with the law, the ruler, being the holder of sovereignty and hence the source of all legislation, is logically above the law and not under it. In the history of western political thought, Jean Bodin is the first to develop a conception of sovereignty that is strikingly similar to Hantzu's. Says Bodin, "Sovereignty is supreme power over citizens and subjects, unrestrained by the law."

Having exalted the august position of the sovereign, Hantzu analyzes the tissues and cells of the body politic. He thinks that the state does not represent a community, but always a conflict, of interests between the ruler and the ruled, between the public and the private. Such being the case, it is of primary importance that the state suppress the interests of the ruled or the private. Those classes of men who act contrary to the interests of the ruler or the public are to be exterminated: the literary class (the Confucians) who preach subversive doctrines; the hermit and recluse class (the Taoists) who escape from political duties and obligations; the cavalier class (the Mocians) who render no service to the army; and all other classes of unproductive parasites and harmful vermin of society. The highest aim of the state is power and wealth, to achieve which the state must so regiment and educate the people that they all become soldiers and farmers, the only classes who

can increase the power and wealth of the nation, and that all shall
be public citizens and none private individuals. For Hantzu the
state exists for its own sake and the individual must live and die
for the sake of the state. As Chang T'aiyen, an eminent modern
writer put it, "Hantzu sees only the state, but does not see man;
he sees only the group, but does not see the individual."

The Supremacy of Law

The Confucian school, it will be remembered, believes in the
principle of government by gentlemen, a principle derived from
the personal nature of feudal relations. This principle assumes
that society is naturally divided into the gentleman class who rule
and the commoner class who are ruled. From the principle results
an unwritten maxim of government: "Courtesy should not be
extended to the commoner and punishment should not be administered to the gentleman."

In direct opposition to this principle, Hantzu proposes the
principle of government by law. He conceives of a law, written in
clear and concise language and proclaimed to all people, a law
before which the high and the low, the clever and the stupid, the
gentleman and the commoner, are equal. Even the sovereign,
Hantzu concedes, must obey the law, once it is promulgated. The
law shall be applied rigidly to all people: punishments shall not
fawn upon the mighty, nor shall rewards go over the heads of the
humble. No minister or citizen may violate the letter or the spirit
of the law. This idea of the supremacy of law is first expounded
by Aristotle in the West. According to the Greek philosopher,
above every form of personal sovereignty, whether of the one,
the few, or the many, must be placed the sovereignty of the law.

To govern a state, Hantzu maintains, means to govern the
average people. There are superior people who will do good without consideration of punishments or rewards, and inferior people
who will do wrong regardless of punishments or rewards; but the

great majority of the people will do good if induced by rewards and shun evil if threatened with punishments. Therefore, in order to govern a state well, the sovereign should administer the laws to all people alike, whether they are superior, inferior, or average. Again, the rulers in history are average rulers, Hantzu thinks. There is but one Yao or Shun in a thousand generations, and but one Chieh or Chow in a thousand generations. The majority of the rulers are neither as good as Yao or Shun, nor as bad as Chieh or Chow. Therefore, it is necessary to have a legal system in accordance with which the ruler may govern the state. With a legal system, there will be a thousand generations of peace and order until the appearance of a Chieh or Chow; but without a legal system, there will be a thousand generations of chaos and confusion until the rise of a Yao or Shun.

The ills in the body politic, Hantzu thinks, are not caused by the lack of wise and virtuous rulers who are rare in any case but are due to the absence of a legal system that works perfectly and smoothly by itself, a machinery that runs automatically. The enlightened monarch must establish a legal system, within which all public citizens shall move, breathe, and have their being, and beyond which no private individuals may transgress—a legal system that serves as the universal standard of conduct. The business of government is to be conducted uniformly and regularly in accordance with the laws. The monarch will then have to "do nothing," for once established the system works mechanically of itself.

There are no eternal or immutable principles governing the state, Hantzu thinks, hence there can be no legal system that is permanent. The laws must change as history progresses. Every age has a general spirit that is uniquely and peculiarly its own. "There is order, when the laws change as the times march on. . . . There is chaos, when the times change but the laws remain unaltered." Hantzu thus anticipates Montesquieu, the French political thinker, who formulates the doctrine that the laws must conform to the general spirit, the morals and the manners, of a nation.

Hantzu is an absolute monarchist. The monarch should make the laws the only literature, and the law officials the only teachers, for the people, so that they may understand and observe the spirit and the letter of the laws. He should prohibit all subversive and reactionary literature and suppress all divergent schools of thought, which tend to create mental chaos and to disintegrate the body politic. The absolute state permits no freedom of thought and expression.

The Art of Administration

"The affairs of the state may be scattered in the four directions, but the key of administration lies in the center," says Hantzu. In every state there are numerous problems that arise daily and hourly. It is the duty of the monarch as chief executive to see that all affairs of the state are properly managed and regulated. In the person of the monarch lies the center of all administration.

It is obvious that the monarch himself cannot attend to all state affairs and must employ men to perform different duties. The crux of administration is to put proper men in proper places. "When the cock is made to preside over the night and the cat is commanded to catch rats, each being used according to its ability, the superior is without concern."

In dealing with ministers and officials, says Hantzu, the monarch must be reposed and observant, always ready to listen, but never anxious to assert himself. He should be distant and dignified. Never is he to move his lips and teeth before the ministers and officials do. Never is he to discuss matters of right and wrong or to join issues with them. "At the height of political order, no ministers can surmise what is in the ruler's mind."

Hantzu observes a basic conflict of interest between the ruler and the ruled. "Superior and inferior wage a hundred battles a day!" The ruler must defend himself against the aggression of the ruled. He must never enter into intimate relations with the ministers and officials, and never reveal his innermost thoughts and feelings to them. Thus Hantzu advises the ruler: "Never ennoble anybody in such wise that he may molest you; and never trust anybody so exclusively that you lose the capital and the state to him." "Make the powerful wane and the powerless wax." The ruler must at all times be ready to use his sovereign power to reward or punish ministers and officials.

The ruler must not burden himself with any administrative matters. He must "do nothing." He must rest in quiescence so that he may watch the business of the ministers. He must grasp the fundamental in order to supervise the execution of the detail. He must appear passive and soft but in reality he must be active and tough. He must always be mysterious and inscrutable so that he may inspire awe and reverence in his ministers. He should exercise his sovereign powers "with the speed of lightning and with the dignity of thunder."

The ideal goal of administration is the agreement between names and realities, i.e. words and actions. All offices or duties should have legitimate names. The ruler is to see that names correspond to realities, that offices correspond to performances. "The ruler holds to the names, and the ministers bring about the realities. When the names and the realities are in agreement, superior and inferior are in harmony."

Hantzu insists upon the absolute identity of names and realities as the goal of administration. Says he: "Whenever a minister utters a word, the ruler should in accordance with his word assign him a task to accomplish, and in accordance with the task call the work to account. If the work corresponds with the task, and the task corresponds with the word, he should be rewarded. On the contrary, if the work is not equivalent to the task, and the task not equivalent to the word, he should be punished. Accordingly, any minister whose word is big but whose work is small should be punished. Not that the work is small, but that the work is not equivalent to the name. Again, any minister whose word is small but whose work is big should also be punished. Not that big work is not desirable but that the discrepancy between the work and the name is worse than the accomplishment of the big work. Hence the minister should be punished."

Confucius advocates the doctrine of the rectification of names in order to maintain a standard of moral values. Hantzu advocates it as a standard of administration, as a means whereby the ruler may measure the performances of his ministers. The quality of administration is good or poor according as the correlation between names and realities is high or low.

The Place of Hantzu in History

Hantzu lived in an age when the feudal body politic had already disintegrated and a new form of absolute monarchy was gradually taking definite shape. The main classes then in conflict were the feudal nobility on the one hand and the rising upper middle classes, entrepreneur and landlord, on the other. At the same time, there was the powerful but restive intelligentsia, who had offered many a panacea for the ills of the world. The nobles, a class generally degenerated or disinherited, remained the last feeble defenders of the feudal *status quo,* while the entrepreneur and landlord classes, who represented a new social and economic force and a novel type of bold and energetic leadership, were the natural supporters of the monarchs that were rising out of the feudal remnants. It was in the midst of the great historic transitional stage that the genius of Hantzu found its fullest expression in a systematic theory of the state that not only corresponded closely to the political reality of the times but also foreshadowed the shape of things to come in the ensuing twenty-one centuries.

Hantzu did not live to see the coming universal empire, which the King of Ch'in established. Under the empire the freedom of speech and thought that was so characteristic of the period of Spring and Autumn and the period of the Contending States was completely suppressed. Books and records were burned; scholars and thinkers were buried alive. The First Emperor began a new page of history, prohibiting the teachings of ancient kings and philosophers and breaking completely with the traditions and customs of the past. He controlled and exercised the absolute power of the state and proclaimed laws to be obeyed by all under heaven. The political theory of Hantzu was quite thoroughly embodied in the political reality of the empire. It is a strange irony of history that Hantzu, the prophet of absolute monarchy, should have died under the very hands that created the first empire.

The place of Hantzu in the history of political thought is as significant as that of Aristotle in the ancient times and that of Machiavelli in the modern. As a general treatise on political science, the *Works* of Hantzu is almost as broad and comprehensive as the *Politics* of Aristotle. As a practical manual of statecraft, the *Works* contains no less a keen insight into the nature of man than *The Prince* of Machiavelli. As completely unmoral as any mortal can be, Hantzu is even more objective in observing and diagnosing the biology and the pathology of the body politic than Aristotle who, under the influence of Plato, enters into a moral inquiry concerning the highest good of the state. Possessing a lively sense of wit and humor, Hantzu appears more mellowed and tempered and less of an "unholy necromancer" than Machiavelli.

Besides Aristotle and Machiavelli, the names of Bodin and Montesquieu suggest themselves in connection with Hantzu. In respect to method, the French philosophers are eminent representatives of the historical and inductive school, as is Hantzu. They all study objective phenomena and material conditions as bases of political philosophy. As to content, Bodin works out a definition of sovereignty that recalls the doctrine of Hantzu, while Montesquieu interprets the general spirit of the laws with the same historical insight that characterizes the Legalist philosophy. Bodin is as much an absolute monarchist as Hantzu, but Montesquieu tries to save and reform the institution of monarchy by the principle of check and balance, the necessity of which never occurs to the Chinese philosopher.

Throughout the ages the name of Hantzu has been much abused and execrated in China. Successful politicians and eminent scholars have denounced the unmoral teachings of Hantzu, although actually they have followed many of the maxims and adages of the great realist. Accepted in practice but rejected in theory, Hantzu goes down in history as a severe critic of humanity whom the world will not forgive. It is a sad paradox that Hantzu, though a realist, does not really know men, for he insists on treating them as they are, while they wish to appear as they ought to be!

Part Two

THE MONARCHICAL AGE

8. MONARCHICAL INSTITUTIONS AND CONVENTIONS

The Founding of the Monarchy

THE transformation of the feudal order into a monarchical regime, which took place in 221 B.C., is unquestionably the most significant political development in Chinese history. From 221 B.C. to A.D. 1911—a period of twenty-one centuries—the Chinese body politic, although undergoing a series of changes and modifications, remained essentially a monarchy. The feudal age constituted the first cycle of Chinese history, the monarchical age made up the second, third, and fourth cycles. The Ch'in and Han dynasties began the second cycle, the Sui and T'ang the third, and the Ming the fourth.

While the ideological prophet of the monarchical age was Hantzu, the real founder of the monarchical system was the First Emperor of the Ch'in dynasty, the greatest political genius in ancient China. Having "liquidated the six feudal states and unified the four seas," the First Emperor took upon himself the task of building an everlasting, universal, centralized, monarchical state. Instead of creating new feudal states, he divided the country into provinces and counties. Instead of preserving the ancient freedom of thought, he burned all philosophic and literary works and buried alive many independent scholars. He was the master engineer who completed the Great Wall—a supreme engineering feat and monument in China. An imperialist, he conquered and colonized all the land from the Yangtze River down to the South Sea, thereby laying the territorial foundation of the Chinese nation. He was brutal and brilliant. He was a combination of an Alexander and a Napoleon in military genius but greater by far in political acumen. He founded an empire, commensurate in size with the Roman Empire, but far more closely knit and far more enduring.

The most abiding institution which the First Emperor established was the provincial and county system. The originator of the system was Premier Li Ssu, Hantzu's schoolmate and murderer. To the proposal of a minister that new feudal states should be established, Li Ssu objected, arguing that the fall of the Chou regime was due to the weakness of the central authority and the independence of the feudal lords. Instead, he proposed that the country should be divided first into provinces (*chün*) and then into counties (*hsien*), so that the Emperor could directly control the provincial governors and county magistrates. In this proposal the First Emperor concurred, saying: "The world has long suffered from war because of the existence of rival feudal states. Now that the world is unified, if we establish feudal states, we shall be creating independent military centers and sowing the seed of future unrest and chaos. I think, therefore, that Li Ssu's proposal should be adopted." Thereupon the First Emperor divided the country into thirty-six (later forty-eight) provinces.

The provincial and county system, thus established by the First Emperor, has been more or less preserved to the present time, although it has naturally been modified in different dynasties. In the Han the country was divided first into territories (*chou*), then into provinces (*chün*), and finally into counties (*hsien*). In the T'ang and Sung it was divided into circuits (*tao* or *lu*), then into prefectures (*fu*), and finally into counties (*hsien*). In the Ming and Ch'ing, it was divided into provinces (*sheng*), then prefectures (*fu*), and then counties (*hsien*). Since the Republic the country has been divided into provinces (*sheng*) and then into counties (*hsein*). Although feudal states were created by some dynasties, they never lasted long. The provincial and county system has thus been a permanent institution in the Chinese body politic, while the institution of hereditary estates, whether royal or noble, has long become anachronistic.

The second political measure for which the First Emperor has justly won the title of a tyrant was the suppression of freedom of thought. Again this measure was proposed by Li Ssu. During the feudal age China enjoyed complete freedom of thought under which the ancient great philosophical systems developed. When the First Emperor unified the country he found that scholars and thinkers as a class were admirers of ancient institutions and conventions and were therefore critical of and inimical to the new state. Whereupon Li Ssu, the political strategist, made the following proposal:

"The ancient five kings did not imitate each other, nor did the three dynasties repeat themselves, because policies must change in accordance with times. . . . In the old days the feudal lords who were in constant struggle wished to secure the services of best talents and hence encouraged scholars. Now that the world is unified and all laws emanate from one source, common people should devote themselves to agriculture and industry and scholars to laws and regulations. Unfortunately, instead of learning the present laws, scholars are studying the ancient dynasties; they seek to criticize the present government and poison the minds of the people . . . I venture to propose that all historical records, save the Ch'in, be burned; that all libraries of literature and philosophy, except those under the custody of imperial doctors, be destroyed; that all people who recite poetry or discuss history be executed; that all those who raise their voices against the present government in the name of antiquity be beheaded together with their families; that only books on medicine, divination, and forestry be preserved; that students be required to study laws under officials."

In 213 B.C. the First Emperor burned all books that the government could discover, and in the following year he buried alive no less than 460 scholars who dared to criticize him.

No regime, however great, can suppress all the people all the time. While the First Emperor did succeed in regimenting the entire nation, there was a great deal of suppressed resentment and anger. No sooner had the First Emperor passed away than revolts spread throughout the country, resulting in the overthrow of the Ch'in dynasty and the establishment of the Han.

It must be pointed out that the greatness of the First Empire was to a large extent a result of the cross-fertilization of the Chou and Ch'in cultures. The Chou people represented the "purely sinitic" culture which prevailed in the lower basin of the Yellow River, while the Ch'in were an "alien" and "primitive" stock from the upper basin. The mixture of the two strains accounted for the vitality and ruthlessness on the one hand and the discernment and wisdom on the other of the First Empire.

The Stabilization of the Monarchy

The Ch'in initiated the monarchical system, the Han stabilized it, the T'ang perfected it. The short-lived Ch'in was succeeded by the Han, which lasted for more than four centuries (206 B.C.-A.D. 219), during which the monarchical system was improved, elaborated, and stabilized.

Following the Ch'in, the Han organized the central government as follows: Under the monarch there were three grand ministers: prime minister whose duty it was to assist the monarch in civil administration, commander-in-chief to assist in military administration, imperial censor to criticize governmental measures and officials. All great matters of state were deliberated and decided upon by these three grand ministers in council.

Below the grand council there were nine ministers: minister of ceremonies, minister of palaces, minister of finance, minister of justice, minister of royal families, minister of territorial colonies, minister of chariots and horses, minister of mountain and sea resources, and minister of police.

In reaction against the centralized despotism of the Ch'in, the founder of the Han created sixteen feudal states. This was an unhappy experiment, for some of the feudal princes incited armed rebellions against the central authority. After the suppression of the rebels the central government abolished the law of primo- geniture and divided the feudal estates equally among sons of deceased or banished feudal princes. By this process all the feudal estates were reduced to political nonentities in the course of a few generations.

In the administration of justice the Han adopted the Legalist philosophy—the philosophy of government by law, written in clear and unambiguous language. In economic policy the Han followed the Taoist philosophy—the philosophy of laissez-faire—which fos- tered the free development of industry and agriculture, resulting in the creation of a capitalist and landlord class. Most significantly, the Han was the dynasty in which Confucian philosophy tri- umphed. It was the Han that made Confucianism the official doc- trine of the state. By this act the Han set up a universal moral standard, although it did not in the least suppress freedom of thought and belief.

At the proposal of Tung Chungshu, the metaphysical monarchist, the Han established national universities and colleges where stu- dents studied the Confucian classics in preparation for govern- mental service, and instituted an examination and recommendation system whereby men who knew the classical literature and lan- guage were appointed to government posts either through examina- tions or through recommendations by local authorities. Thus began the civil service system—a system which was perfected by the T'ang dynasty.

After the fall of the Han, China went through a dark age, an age of civil war and foreign invasion, lasting for some four cen- turies (A.D. 220-588). This age produced many escapist poets and radical thinkers—among whom was the little-known but highly gifted sociological anarchist, Pao Chingyen—but no constructive political philosophers. The Sui unified the country and initiated many new political measures; but it was a short-lived regime which was succeeded by the T'ang.

Enlightened Monarchy

The political system of the T'ang was the most elaborate and complete in the long monarchical age. Like the Ch'in, the T'ang system was a product of the cross-fertilization of native and alien cultures and hence was characterized by the mixture of new vigor and ancient wisdom.

Generally speaking, the T'ang was probably the most liberal and enlightened of all dynasties in Chinese history. The political system as set up by the founders was such as would greatly limit the powers of the monarch when and if it worked well. Theoretically the T'ang monarchs were Taoists and as such they were perhaps more inclined to reign but not rule, although actually some of them were great rulers, not merely titular heads, of the nation.

Immediately under the throne was the highest office of the land, the privy council, which consisted of three imperial instructors (*sanshih*) and three imperial lords (*sankung*). The council had no administrative power. Its main duty was to advise the crown on matters of state policy.

The most essential organs in the national government were the central secretariat (*chungshu sheng*), the public chamber (*menghsia sheng*), and the cabinet (*shangshu sheng*). The director of the secretariat, the president of the chamber, and the prime minister of the cabinet were equal in rank and independent of one another. The central secretariat drafted imperial edicts and laws, and the public chamber received, examined, and disposed of memorials and proposals presented by officials or commoners to the throne. All edicts and laws drafted by the central secretariat, even if they were sanctioned by the throne, might be vetoed by the public chamber. These two organs really constituted the legislative arms of the national government. It was said that no imperial orders became the supreme laws of the land unless they were passed by both the phoenix hall (central secretariat) and the crane tower (public chamber). After being passed by these two organs imperial orders were promulgated and carried out by the cabinet.

The cabinet consisting of a premier, a left vice-premier, a right vice-premier, and six ministers was the real executive organ. The premier was the head of the national administration. The two vice-premiers each supervised three ministries. Under the left vice-premier were: the minister of civil service, who was in charge of the selection, appointment, promotion, demotion, pension, and punishment of civil servants; the minister of finance, in charge of vital statistics, government revenues and expenditures, money and exchange, and normal and charity granaries; and the minister of education and religion, in charge of public schools and colleges, temple services and ceremonies, and receptions of delegates from outlying territories. Under the right vice-premier were: the minister of war, who was in charge of armies, fortresses, topographical surveys, chariots and horses, and arsenals; the minister of justice, in charge of judicial administration and legal interpretation; and the minister of public works, in charge of city-planning and road-building, colonization and reclamation, mountain and sea resources.

Independent of the cabinet, independent of the central secretariat and the public chamber, was the unique office of the imperial censor, whose duty it was to supervise the political machinery, to interrogate and impeach government personnel, and even to censor the conduct of the monarch himself. This was not a novel institution in the T'ang dynasty, but it was during this dynasty that it became a powerful and independent organ.

The civil service examination system was perfected in the T'ang. Hitherto there had been no unified and systematic procedure for recruiting civil servants. Students of national universities and colleges—who constituted a privileged class—were appointed to government posts without examinations. Men of humble origin might be appointed through examinations or through recommendations by local officials. The Sui dynasty initiated, the T'ang perfected, a system of competitive examinations—open to all, students of national universities and colleges and of private schools alike, on the basis of complete equality—as a means of securing the services of the best talents of the country. Since the T'ang this system has been in operation, although the subject matter of examinations and the degrees or titles have changed from time to time.

In addition to dividing the country into circuits or provinces, the T'ang established six colonial districts and ten military areas in the outlying territories. Some of the colonial and military governors grew powerful and started revolts against the throne, which were in part responsible for the fall of the dynasty.

After the fall of the T'ang, which reigned three centuries (618-906), as after that of the Han, China entered upon an age of civil war and foreign invasion, which lasted four and a half centuries (906-1367). The Sung dynasty that came to power in 960 had ever a precarious existence. It was compelled by the Tartars to move south in 1127 and was eventually conquered by the Mongols in 1277.

The Sung regime was never as enlightened as the T'ang. The founder of the Sung concentrated all civil and military powers in himself. He reduced the premiership and the vice-premiership to nominal posts and abolished the colonial and military governorships. When the Mongols established the Yüan dynasty, they copied many Chinese institutions and conventions but actually instituted a reign of terror and oppression.

During the hazardous existence of the Sung dynasty, there arose a very great reformer-stateman, Wang Anshih, the new dealer, and a highly original thinker, Ch'en Liang, the political synthesist, in addition to an illustrious roster of pure philosophers and men of letters. Both Wang and Ch'en have been severely condemned by conservative Confucians, the former for his radicalism, the latter

for his unorthodoxy. Only in recent years have they been admitted
to the circle of respectability.

Absolute Monarchy

As a result of the Mongol reign of terror and oppression, the
first truly nationalistic movement in Chinese history was organized.
The reign lasted a whole century, during which many sporadic
nationalistic revolts broke out over the country but were all quelled.
It was not until Chu Yüanchang, a monk, organized a nation-wide
revolution that the Yüan dynasty was finally overthrown and the
Ming established (1368).

In staging this revolution, Chu issued a nationalist manifesto,
the first classic manifesto of the Chinese nation, which should rank
as one of the most significant documents in Chinese history. The
manifesto declared in substance:

"From time immemorial the Chinese have always lived in the
Middle Kingdom and governed the barbarians in the outlying
territories. It is against the law of history to let the barbarians live
in the Middle Kingdom and govern the Chinese people. . . . Now
the Mongols have invaded China and ruled the Chinese. They
have destroyed the fundamental principles governing the relations
between ruler and subject, father and son, husband and wife, and
brother and brother, and have created a state of moral confusion
and depravation. We Chinese have regarded the ruler as the
father of the people, the court as the center of the nation, and moral
principles as principles of government. The conduct of the Mongol
monarchs violates the Chinese sense of morality and cannot be
exemplary. The Mongol ministers are dictatorial, the Mongol
censors arbitrary, and the Mongol judges prejudiced. The Chinese
people have been murdered mercilessly, and those living cannot
protect their flesh and bones. . . . It is said that 'no barbarians
ever reign for a century.' This saying must come true, now that

we have started a nation-wide revolution to overthrow the Mongol regime."

It might be expected that the leader of this nationalist revolution would establish a benevolent regime in view of the fact that he was first of all a Chinese and secondly an opponent of the Mongol tyranny. However, the truth was just the reverse. The founder of the Ming dynasty, which means literally the enlightened dynasty, is one of the most unenlightened autocrats in Chinese history. Ignorant, suspicious, brutal, Chu Yüanchang instituted a regime that was no less terroristic and oppressive than the Mongol which he had overthrown. As soon as he became monarch, he began to fear that the warriors and men of letters who had assisted him in conquest might themselves covet the throne. On small pretenses he ordered the execution of general after general and minister after minister, until practically all those who had participated in the nationalist revolution were liquidated.

In order to concentrate all power in the throne this autocrat abolished the premiership and personally directed the national administration. He did away with the office of the commander-in-chief (*tatutu*) and established five military offices (*tutu*), so that no general would be so powerful as to be ambitious. Considering the nation as the private possession of the Chu family, he established twenty-three principalities, and appointed twenty-three of his twenty-six sons to govern them. He divided the country into fifteen provinces, to each of which he appointed two administrative governors in charge of civil and financial affairs respectively, one judicial governor in charge of justice and law, one military governor in charge of "horses and soldiers," and periodically a censorial official to supervise and investigate the conduct of the governors, in order that no province would be under a unified administration or would find it possible to revolt.

The Ming fell to the Manchus who established the Ch'ing dynasty in 1644. This alien regime went a step further in dictatorship and brutality. While the Ming treated the people cruelly but equally, the Ch'ing discriminated against the Chinese and favored the Manchus. Politically the Ming and the Ch'ing constituted the age of absolute monarchism in Chinese history—an age that extended from 1368 to 1911.

It is no accident that absolute monarchism and alien domination produced the most systematic philosophers of democracy and nationalism respectively in the persons of Huang Tsunghsi and Wang Fuchih, who lived contemporaneously at the end of the Ming and the beginning of the Ch'ing dynasty. And as the age of monarchy was drawing to a close, there appeared K'ang Yuwei, the last of the Confucians, who advanced the theory of the great commonwealth and proposed the creation of a constitutional monarchy. K'ang came too late to stay the rising revolutionary movement which finally overthrew the monarchy in 1912.

The scope of this chapter does not permit a thorough treatment of the evolution of monarchical institutions and conventions. This brief account is intended to give a bird's-eye view of the political realities in which the political philosophers discussed in the following chapters lived, breathed, and had their being and their doing. It may be noted that all those philosophers, except Tung Chungshu, lived not in the great ages of the Han, the T'ang, and the Ming, but in the ages of civil war and foreign domination, just as the ancient philosophers lived not during the rise and expansion, but during the decline and fall, of the feudal regime. Political animals, even the most sensitive and original, do not generally venture into new realms of thought unless they are shocked out of the ivory tower or swept away from the beaten path by great political tempests or cyclones.

9. TUNG CHUNGSHU: THE META-PHYSICAL MONARCHIST

Tung Chungshu the Man

DURING the Han dynasty—which constituted the first half of the second cycle in Chinese history—when monarchy took firm root and flourished in Chinese political soil, no philosopher so dominated the realm of thought as did Tung Chungshu (*circa* 179-104 B.C.). Tung most eminently symbolized the spirit of the age and formulated the most systematic philosophy of monarchism.

As a youth Tung interested himself in the study of the Confucian historical work, *Spring and Autumn*. He received the degree of doctor of classics—the highest academic honor conferred by the court—when he was about thirty and distinguished himself as a great tutor. He taught for some ten years and had many pupils from different parts of the country. Apparently he tutored only advanced students, who in turn taught the newly initiated. Some of the freshmen and sophomores never even had the privilege of seeing the master in person. He was a closet philosopher, aristocratic in temperament, dreading human intimacy, shunning the uninformed and ignorant, avoiding the crowd. It is said that once for a duration of three years he confined himself to his study and, engrossed in thought, never so much as visited his garden. Austere and severe in countenance, this philosopher led a rational, orderly, puritanic life. Conceivably, he was more esteemed and respected from a distance than loved in intimacy, and his admirers far outnumbered his friends.

Tung remained a mere doctor of classics until he was about forty, when Emperor Wu ascended the throne. Immediately after his coronation, the young and ambitious monarch gave audience to Tung and put three questions of national policy to the philosopher, whose answers were so comprehensive and far-reaching that they won for him a permanent place in history. He proposed to establish Confucianism as the official doctrine of the monarchy and to suppress all unorthodox ideologies that tended to confuse the minds of the people and to disunify officialdom.

Although he was instrumental in establishing Confucianism as the state doctrine, Tung himself never became a cabinet minister. He was sent by the monarch to serve as minister first in one principality and then in another. Both princes whom he served were brothers of the monarch and were arrogant, licentious, and brutish creatures upon whom, it is said, the philosopher succeeded in exercising a moderating influence.

In the imperial government Tung never became a powerful figure. Once he was sentenced to death, but was pardoned by a special imperial decree. Kungsun Heng, a lesser scholar but a shrewder politician, had become prime minister while Tung remained humble, though not obscure. Out of envy and resentment, the philosopher condemned the prime minister as a flatterer and sycophant.

Undoubtedly, Tung himself was scrupulous and straightforward, noble-minded and high-principled. He would not play the game of real politics and was therefore constantly at the mercy of the powers that were. When he finally realized that he was a failure in politics, he retired from public life and devoted his last years on earth to literary activities. Of himself he wrote:

"Woe is me! Time comes so slowly but, ah, how swiftly it passes! While waiting for the hour to arrive, I shall soon return to dust. Sad am I; no longer do I expect high office. Thus long have I hustled about anxiously but to incur disgrace and humiliation. Henceforth, I shall turn hermit, that I may be blameless. . . .

"Alas! I am destined, not to enjoy the golden era of antiquity, but to suffer this late day and age, when the cunning and specious are promoted but the honorable and conscientious must retire. . . .

"Though I examine my mind every day, I float in a sea of doubt, knowing not whether to advance or retreat; but those flatterers and sycophants at court do not for a moment hesitate to say black is white or white is black. . . .

"Ah! How the world has gone astray! Whom may I befriend? Rather than follow the winding path of the world, I shall return to simple and pure life."

These lines reveal Tung Chungshu as an ambitious but frustrated old man, who had decided, as had many another sensitive and aesthetic philosopher before him, to retire from the world and return to "simple and pure life."

Tung was a man of ideas rather than a man of achievement, obsessively systematic in thought, but nervous and diffident in action. Blundering and bungling many years through the game of real politics, thwarted on all sides, the philosopher in his old age came to look upon the world as an alien and hostile place, a forest haunted, as it were, by cunning foxes and howling wolves. There was but one exit for him—the exit that led via the literary highway to the metaphysical realm of peace and security.

The most significant of Tung's writings is the *Interpretations of the Spring and Autumn* (*Ch'unch'iu Fanglu*), in which he attempted to work out systematically the philosophy of Confucius. It is well known that commentators or critics frequently read their own ideas into original works. Tung is no exception. In the *Interpretations,* he develops a metaphysical theory of the monarchical state, a theory quite as remote from Confucianism as the scholastic doctrines of Augustine and Thomas are from Platonism and Aristoteleanism respectively. As Paul's idea of Peter tells more of Paul than of Peter, so Tung's interpretations of Confucianism constitute the philosophy of Tung rather than of Confucius.

Not only did Tung read his own ideas into Confucianism, but

he virtually legislated his own preferences into eternal and immutable laws of the universe. Perhaps it is the "normal madness"—to use a phrase of Santayana—of man to project his own nature into the cosmic order, to create a world after his own image. Tung certainly falls into the metaphysician's fallacy of identifying his own being with the nature of the cosmos.

Behind the external countenance of a humble scholar, there existed in Tung an ego that was cosmic in breadth and length. When at the height of the metaphysical realm, Tung must have fancied himself as the supreme law-giver of the universe, ruling over the entire creation. No other great Chinese philosopher had reached such a grandiose and schematic conception of the universe as he. Confucius the humanist was frankly agnostic about the nature of the universe, and Laotzu the poetical naturalist stood in awe and admiration under the mysterious and glorious firmament. But Tung the dogmatic absolutist ordained that the human world and the natural order should be identical and that the fabric of the state and society and the structure of the universe should be governed by the self-same eternal and immutable laws that he had decreed.

The Cosmic Order

Whereas Confucius delves deeply into the human situation and all but ignores the physical world, and whereas Laotzu wishes to return to nature and withdraw from society, Tung Chungshu formulates a theory of the unity of nature and man, of the cosmic and the human order—a theory that serves as a Jacob's ladder connecting the starry heavens above and the mortal beings below. The social and political philosophy of Tung is metaphysical in the sense that it constitutes an integral part of the philosophy of things. In Tung's system, human beings and things are treated in like manner, and the fabric of the state and society is considered analogous to the structure of the universe. Man is a microcosm, the shape and form of which corresponds to the frame of the macrocosm, and the human world is a replica of the physical universe.*

The universe, according to Tung, is a grand unity, which manifests itself through the duality of positive and negative ether, which in turn expresses itself through the quaternity of spring, summer, autumn, and winter. The positive ether begins to swell in spring and reaches its maximum quantum in summer; the negative ether begins to swell in autumn and reaches its maximum quantum in winter. When the positive swells, the negative shrinks; when the negative swells, the positive shrinks. As the positive and the negative thus wax and wane, the seasons of the year rotate accordingly.

The ether is the incorporeal substance that fills the boundless space between heaven and earth and ebbs and flows rhythmically according to natural law. Besides the ether, there are five elements in the universe, wood, fire, metal, water, and earth, the temporal and spatial configuration of which is as follows: Wood is located in the east and is the main element of spring; fire is located in the south and is the main element of summer; metal is located in the west and is the main element of autumn; water is located in the north and is the main element of winter; earth is located in the center and is the sustaining element throughout the year.

The positive ether is the herald of life. It saturates wood in spring and fire in summer. Therefore, in the sweet spring, trees begin to grow and birds to sing; during the warm summer, all creatures rejoice and multiply. The negative ether is the harbinger

* Cf. Benard Bosanquet, *The Principle of Individuality and Value* (London: Macmillan and Co., 1912), page 311. "The treatment of the state in this discussion is naturally analogous to the treatment of the universe." L. T. Hobhouse, *The Metaphysical Theory of the State* (London: George Allen & Unwin, 1918), page 18. "This, then, is the metaphysical theory of the state. It is the endeavor to exhibit the fabric of society in a light in which we shall see it, in or through its actual condition, as the incarnation of something very great and glorious indeed, as one expression of that supreme being which some of these thinkers call the Spirit and others the Absolute."

of death. It pervades metal in autumn and water in winter. Therefore, when the west wind howls in autumn, leaves begin to fall and
ants and bees to quiver; when snow blankets the earth in winter,
creatures cease to crawl and "lie cold and low, each like a corpse
within its grave."

The positive ether represents the grace (or virtue) of the universe, whereby all things live, breathe, and have their being; the
negative ether represents the wrath (or punishment) of the universe, whereby all things must come to an end. Even as man has
spells of happiness and sadness, the universe rejoices in creating
life, but becomes gloomy when it announces the approach of death.
Thus, in spring and summer, when the earth is fresh and green
and the sun shines bright, the universe is happy; but as autumn
comes and winter approaches, the heart of the universe grows melancholy and painful.

At the basis of this extravagant, though systematic, conception of
the cosmic order, there is, Tung assumes, the all-ruling idea that
the universe is inherently rational and intelligent and is constitu-
tionally righteous and benevolent. From this kernel idea, all creation springs; in accordance with this idea, the entire cosmic order
arranges and regulates itself.

It is not difficult to see how the cosmic order, as thus anthropo-
morphically conceived by Tung, may serve as the supreme pattern
for the human order. The cosmic order is literally the prototype
of the monarchical order, *modus operandi*. The government of the
human race is but a miniature government of the natural world.
The emperor represents the will of heaven and earth; he has but
to administer society in accordance with the law of nature. Tung
goes one step further. As the universe is at heart righteous and
benevolent, so is the monarchy. As the cosmic order is inherently
rational, so is the human order. In all Chinese political philosophy,
there is no more plausible apology or more systematic rationalization of monarchy than the metaphysics of Tung Chungshu.

The Human Order

In the natural order, says Tung, all things are paired or coupled. The positive and the negative are complementary; they reveal themselves in such polar entities and ideas as heaven and earth, the sun and the moon, day and night, heat and cold, the high and the low, the right and the left, the male and the female. So in the human order are sovereign and subject, father and son, husband and wife complementary to each other. The sovereign is positive, the subject negative; the father is positive, the son negative; the husband is positive, the wife negative. These three relationships constitute the tri-ordinate axes of the human order.

Even though sovereign and subject, father and son, husband and wife, are correlative and reciprocal, they are not on an equal basis. The sovereign is the overlord of the subject; the father is the master of the son; the husband is the owner of the wife.

Of the tri-ordinate axes, the sovereign-subject axis is the most fundamental in the human order. The sovereign-subject axis is the central axis, to which the father-son and husband-wife axes are subordinate. Without the central axis, the entire human order will crumble.

The cosmos, says Tung, is divided into three main parts: heaven, earth, and man. The sovereign is the person who spans heaven and earth and governs the human race. The Chinese character for sovereign is *wang*, which consists of three horizontal lines representing heaven, earth, and man, and one vertical line that goes through the horizontal lines in the center. It is the duty of the sovereign to follow the first principles or laws of the cosmos.

There are four seasons that complete the annual cycle. Spring gives birth to all, and summer furnishes the staff of life. Autumn imposes trials and tribulations upon everything that animates or vegetates, and winter seals the doom of life. As there are four seasons in the year, so are there four moods in the sovereign. As the seasons rotate, so the moods of the sovereign change. There is a time when the sovereign is as merciful as spring; there is a time when he is as severe as autumn; there is a time when he is as happy as summer; there is a time when he is as angry as winter. The sovereign, who holds the supreme power of life and death over all subjects, should rule through the proper manifestations of mercy, severity, happiness, and anger, even as nature tempers itself through the variations of the four seasons.

Not only is the sovereign the administrator of the will of the universe, but the entire governmental system is a mirror of the cosmic order. There are, for instance, four grades of bureaucracy paralleling the four seasons, and there are three members to each grade paralleling the three months in each season. In establishing the government, the monarch selects and appoints, first, three lords who are sages; next, three ministers who are superior men; then, three secretaries who are good men; and, finally, three scholars who are men of honor. The twelve officials, thus selected and appointed, co-operate with one another so as to bring about a peaceful and orderly reign, just as the twelve months, following one another rhythmically, complete the annual cycle.

Finally, Tung deems the universe benevolent and righteous in its very constitution. The sovereign, who spans the distance between heaven and earth, is the very moral incarnation of the will of the universe. Being pure and correct, the sovereign may rectify the court, purify the officialdom, and raise the moral level of the entire populace, so that the winds and rains may come in proper seasons, plants and animals may multiply, and the human race may rejoice in the bounty of nature.

The sovereign, according to Tung, is directly responsible to the universe and is far above and beyond the people. When a wise and virtuous monarch sits on the throne—a monarch who carries out the will of the universe—the rains will come regularly and the winds blow mildly. But when a tyrant rises, who acts contrary to the law of nature, there will come ill omens and abnormal phenomena bearing warnings from the universe. According to the metaphysical monarchist, the only check upon the absolute power of the sovereign seems to be the wrath of the universe.

To moderns this metaphysical doctrine of monarchism must appear anachronistic and unscientific, if not altogether preposterous, but during the Han dynasty it was almost universally accepted. The Han period was an age in which astrologers, magicians, diviners, and alchemists grew into great popularity. Tung's was the master mind that synthesized all the prevailing black arts and occult sciences into a systematic philosophy of the universe which, couched in Confucian terminology, was offered in all seriousness to those in power as a sanctification of the *status quo*. While this mystic and weird Confucianism had its day, the original humanistic Confucianism dimmed into the shadow of the night.

In certain aspects, the metaphysics of the Han period is comparable to the theology of the medieval age in Europe. In the first place, the Han period and the medieval age were both inordinately sensitive to dualism or polarism in the nature of things. In the Han period, the positive and the negative, heaven and earth, and the sun and the moon symbolized the mercy and wrath of the universe and, hence, of the sovereign. In the medieval age, the sun and the moon, soul and body, and the sword of the spirit and the sword of blood represented the two powers of the world, sacerdotal and royal. In the second place, both the Han scholars and the medieval schoolmen appealed to superhuman authority for the sanctioning of societal organization. To the Han scholars the monarch was the administrator of the will of the universe. To the ecclesiastical debaters the Pope was the messenger of God, while to the secular writers the king was the minister of God, the revengeful executor of God's wrath and the benevolent dispenser of God's mercy. Finally, the Han scholars incorporated black arts and occult sciences into Confucianism, much as the medieval schoolmen introduced theological dogmas into the systems of Plato and Aristotle. The former made the all-too-human Confucius a master metaphysician, sitting on a magic carpet, waving an enchanted wand, divining the secrets and mysteries of the universe, while the latter baptized the pagan Plato and Aristotle with the Christian spirit if they did not actually turn the philosophers into the right reverend archbishops of the church.

The Theory of Dynastic Evolution

Not only did Tung the metaphysician discover a cosmic sanction of the monarchical order, but he also found an historical justification of the reigning dynasty.

History, Tung believes, is a continuous evolution, which is essentially cyclical in nature. There are three stages, three reigns or dynasties, in a cycle. When one cycle is completed, another identical one begins. In other words, history is a triple-timed divine comedy that waltzes on continuously, perhaps with occasional intermezzos, to the end of time.

The first reign in the cycle is a black reign, the second a white reign, and the third a red reign, according to Tung. During the black reign, the year begins with the month of the tiger. The dynastic color being black, the crown and the scepter, the royal robe and throne, all ceremonies and sacrifices, all emblems and insignia, and all imperial regalia should be black. During the white reign, the year begins with the month of the ox. The dynastic color being white, the crown and the scepter, the royal robe and throne, all ceremonies and sacrifices, all emblems and insignia, and all imperial regalia should be white. During the red reign, the year begins with the month of the rat. The dynastic color being red, the crown and the scepter, the royal robe and throne, all ceremonies and sacrifices, all emblems and insignia, and all imperial regalia should be red.

Applying this theory to history, the Hsia dynasty was a black reign, the Shang a white reign, and the Chou a red reign. The new dynasty that rose after the fall of the Chou was once more a black reign, thus initiating a new cycle.*

The rise and fall of one dynasty after another, therefore, follows an inexorable and mechanistic course that is inherent in the nature of things, according to Tung. When a new dynasty rises, says the metaphysician, it must have a new color, a new calendar, a new capital, a new governmental system, because the universe so wills.

Such a conception of dynastic evolution recalls the dialectic theory of Hegel. The black, white, and red reigns in the dynastic evolution are comparable to the triadic movements, thesis, antithesis, and synthesis, in historical evolution. The will of the universe preordains and predetermines the course of the black, white, and red reigns, much as the universal spirit reveals and realizes itself in the thetic, antithetic, and synthetic phases of historical evolution. Although the former is statically cyclical and the latter dynamically progressive, both conceptions are metaphysically deterministic; they tend to view every reign as the very moral incarnation of some transcendental being and to justify every age as the best possible age in history. Tung, as well as Hegel, might have declared: "What is rational is real; what is real is rational." Small wonder that in actual politics Tung eulogized and exalted the supreme virtue and wisdom of the Han sovereign and Hegel proclaimed the Prussian autocracy as the highest synthesis of world evolution.

---

* There was another theory of dynastic evolution prevailing in the Han period. It is based upon the five elements, which form a cycle that constantly renews itself. Earth is vanquished by wood. which yields to metal, which succumbs to fire, which is quenched by water, which is overcome by earth, so renewing the cycle. Each element is controlled by a celestial ruler: earth by the yellow ruler; wood by the green ruler; metal by the white ruler; fire by the red ruler; and water by the black ruler. Every dynasty reigns by virtue of one element and falls when the element passes to the succeeding element. To every dynasty on earth there is a corresponding celestial ruler.

Tung himself formulates another theory of dynastic evolution, which is divided into four stages, representing spring, summer, autumn, and winter.

The Theory of Class Harmony

When the feudal age ended and the monarchical era began, the new bourgeois and landlord classes were in power, replacing the hereditary aristocracy. Enterprising industrialists, iron masters and salt boilers in particular, protected as they were by the government, exploited and enslaved multitudes of laborers, while landlords exacted exorbitant rents from peasants. By the time of Tung Chungshu, society was so sharply polarized into the rich and the poor as to threaten the outbreak of a serious social crisis. As he described the situation: "The wealthy own thousands of acres while the indigent have not a square foot to stand on. . . . In the cities, the bourgeois are as powerful as potentates and in the villages the landlords are as rich as nobles. . . . In contrast, the poor live like cows and horses and starve like dogs and pigs, and they are furthermore under the oppression of corrupt officials." Indeed, the situation resembled that of France on the eve of the Revolution as depicted by Rousseau: "There are a few rich and powerful men on the pinnacle of fortune and grandeur, while the crowd grovels in want and obscurity."

Unlike Rousseau, Tung was no revolutionary philosopher who could inspire the malcontent and destitute. Alarmed by the possibility of a social crisis, he sought to ameliorate the sufferings of the masses by social reform. Therefore, he proposed to limit the amount of landownership and the practice of monopoly, thinking that the ancient institution of public landownership could not be restored and that industry and commerce could not be wiped out. He further proposed to abolish slavery and to reduce the amount of taxes and the number of conscripts, thereby to avert a grave crisis. These proposals were not adopted. It was not until a century later that Wang Mang, a prime minister who made himself monarch, carried out a series of new deal reforms, following the general proposals of Tung.

Fundamentally, Tung did not believe in class equality. He

thought that the rich should not be too rich nor the poor too poor. Said he:

"When the rich are too opulent, they become arrogant. When the poor are too stricken, they become panicky. The arrogant tend to be tyrannical and the panicky are likely to be rebellious. This is human nature. Therefore, the sage, who knows the nature of man, will establish such a human system as will maintain an equilibrium between the high and the low. The rich may enjoy fortunes without being arrogant and the poor may have the necessities of life without becoming desperate. That state which can harmonize the rich and the poor and unite all people in a community of interests is peaceful and orderly. But at present such a system is nonexistent. Everybody wants to satisfy unlimited desires. The big men wish to be more and more opulent, while the small fellows become thinner and thinner. The rich grow more miserly and less benevolent, while the poor become increasingly violent and disobedient. For this reason, it is difficult to maintain peace and order."

This is one of the most eloquent passages in Chinese literature that express a typical Confucianistic theory of class harmony. Rich and poor there will always be, the Confucian believes. In order to have a peaceful and orderly reign, let the rich be not too rich and the poor not too poor. As in the cosmic order, there are high and low, heaven and earth, the sun and the moon, so in the human world, there will inevitably be rich and poor, strong and weak, brilliant and dull, powerful and defenseless.

Confucianism as State Doctrine

The new plutocratic classes, bourgeois and landlord, were in theory and practice supported by the realistic Legalist school, which had produced a number of able administrators, economists, lawyers, and political scientists in the early days of the monarchy, when the influence of the Confucian school was temporarily eclipsed. Now Tung, who wished to establish Confucianism, found it necessary to condemn the worldly desires and pecuniary interests of the plutocratic classes. Says he: "Those who are busily occupied in digging the mine of wealth and are ever afraid of empty pockets are mere commoners, but those who seek after benevolence and righteousness and are concerned about exercising moral influence over the people are really superior men indeed." "The good men are those who follow the right regardless of interests and who unfold the truth irrespective of consequences." Such men, according to Tung the Confucian, should be in the ruling hierarchy, instead of money-changers, shopkeepers, and estate-holders.

The philosopher envisaged a monarchical regime administrated by an intellectual and moral aristocracy, a bureaucracy versed in the Confucian classics. He proposed to Emperor Wu that Confucianism be established as the state doctrine and Confucian scholars be employed as ministers and officials.

"Your Majesty labors from early morning to late night for the good of the people, and seeks virtuous scholars to administer the Empire. . . . Now the best place to train scholars is a university. The university is a community of virtuous scholars and is the basis of culture and education. . . . Your humble servant proposes that Your Majesty establish a national university, where enlightened teachers are placed and promising scholars of the Empire may be trained and frequently tested and examined as to their abilities and achievements. Then Your Majesty will be able to secure brilliant talents. . . .

"Let every district magistrate of the Empire nominate two scholars each year. If they are virtuous and gifted, the magistrate shall be rewarded; if they are not, he shall be punished. Then every magistrate will seek the really virtuous and gifted among the people. . . .

"The principle of grand unity in the *Spring and Autumn* is an immutable law in heaven and earth and is a universal truth in ancient and modern times. But now teachers have different doctrines and people have conflicting opinions. There are a hundred schools advocating as many policies and entertaining as many ideas. Consequently, those on high have no unity of mind and proclaim contradictory laws and rules, and those below do not know what to observe.

"Your humble servant proposes that all doctrines that deviate from the arts and classics of Confucius be suppressed completely. Once subversive and pernicious doctrines are quelled, the unity of the Empire may be maintained and laws and rules may be so clearly stated that the people will know what to follow."

This is a momentous proposal in Chinese history. It made Confucianism, hitherto one doctrine among many, the orthodox creed of the state. It transformed Confucianism from a feudalistic theory to a monarchical dogma. It destroyed the freedom of thought that was characteristic of ancient China and, by making the Confucian arts and classics the only legitimate discipline of scholarship, was to some extent responsible for the tautology and the sterility of social and political speculation in the middle ages. Acting upon this proposal, the monarch began to dismiss politicians, economists, and lawyers of the Legalist school who had become influential members of the government, and to select and employ scholars of the Confucian arts and classics as ministers and officials. A national university was established where famous doctors of Confucian arts and classics held professorial chairs and young scholars were trained and indoctrinated in the orthodoxy. A selection and examination system was instituted as a means of recruiting civil servants. China became an empire of scholars. Thenceforth, for two thousand years, during which China witnessed the rise and fall of some twenty dynasties, Confucianism continued invariably to be the official doctrine of the state and Confucian scholars remained the ruling bureaucratic class, until the outbreak of the Republican Revolution in 1911.

While Tung made the bold proposal to create a moral and intellectual aristocracy, he did not want to overthrow the powerful plutocratic classes. For the new Confucian scholarly class, as he must have foreseen, sprang in the main from among landlord and bourgeois families and hardly from among peasants and slaves. Although in theory the selection and examination system was a democratic process of creating a scholarly bureaucracy, in practice it was a channel through which estate-holders, shopkeepers, and money-changers sent their sons into public service. The system, however, did guard against the revival of a hereditary noble class and insure a periodic circulation and rotation of intellectual elites in Chinese society. When it was modified by the T'ang dynasty, the civil service system was open to all citizens on the basis of complete equality and became a truly democratic institution in the monarchical body politic.

In making Confucianism the official doctrine of the state and in rendering a cosmic sanction upon the monarchical order, Tung Chungshu was undoubtedly the best representative thinker of the Han dynasty. He was the first philosopher of the bimillennial age of monarchy.

10. PAO CHINGYEN: THE SOCIOLOGICAL ANARCHIST

The Revival of Taoism

THE Han period of unity and peace having ended, China entered upon a period of division and war—the second half of the second cycle. The empire was first trifurcated into Three Kingdoms which waged war one upon the other intermittently for some fifty years. With the rise of the Chin dynasty came the unification of the empire. But, no sooner had the new dynasty been established than the empire suffered foreign invasions at the hands of the Hunnish and Turkistanish tribes and was rent asunder into Sixteen Kingdoms. As the nomadic races, wave after wave, poured into the Yellow River basin, the Chinese migrated into the valley of the Yangtze River. By the beginning of the fifth century, China was divided into the Northern Realm (along the Yellow River) and the Southern Realm (along the Yangtze River). The throne of the Northern Realm was occupied by two dynastic houses in turn, while the scepter in the Southern Realm fell into the hands of four royal families in rapid succession. Finally in 589 the Sui dynasty arose to control the empire, thus ushering in the third cycle.

The Han period of unity and peace witnessed the transformation of feudalistic Confucianism into the metaphysical doctrine of the monarchical state. The following period of division and war, a period of perennial insecurity and profound disillusionment, occasioned the revival of the escapist and utopian philosophy of Taoism, a metaphysical refuge where men of delicate sensitivity and keen intellect hibernated in order to eschew the coarse and brutal realities of life.

While scholars in the Han period of unity and peace wrote commentaries and interpretations of the Confucian classics, intellectuals in this period of division and war explored the hidden riddles and obscure paradoxes in the works of Laotzu and Chuangtzu. Wang Pi and Ho Yin were the most famous interpreters of Laotzu, and Kuo Hsiang and Hsiang Hsiu were the most brilliant commentators of Chuangtzu. Unsuccessful in politics, shattered by the tempest of life, these thinkers attempted to transcend Heraclitean change and Parmenidean permanence alike and to nullify themselves in the great void beyond the four-dimensional universe.

In the midst of acute crises and chronic disturbances, there appeared a literary and philosophic circle, dedicated to wine and women, defying conventional morals and manners, writing fantastic poems and satirical essays, deliberately committing indiscretions and misdemeanors to shock the hypocrite and the innocent alike. The Seven Sages of the Bamboo Grove, as the members of the circle were known, were—to use a Nietzschean expression—boundlessly extravagant and boundlessly indifferent. They were free thinkers and free spirits, veritable children of nature, incurably thirsty souls and erotic satyrs.

Of this circle of anarchistic poets and philosophers, Yüan Chi (210-263) was the leader. In the *Biography of the Great Man,* a satirical and fictitious essay, he advanced these anarchistic ideas:

"In the beginning, when heaven and earth were created, all things lived and let live. . . .

"At that time, the brilliant did not conquer and the dull did not capitulate. The strong did not use force and the weak were not frightened.

"With no sovereign all things were settled and with no minister all affairs were adjusted. . . .

"Once the sovereign is established, tyranny rises; once the minister is appointed, robbery follows. Rituals and laws are promulgated in order to enchain the people.

"The bright deceive the ignorant and the clever abuse the clumsy. The strong become masters and the weak become servants and slaves.

"Were there no nobles, the humble would not grumble. Were there no men of wealth, the poor would not quarrel. All would be satisfied and none would complain."

Here then is the germ of the sociological theory of anarchism that was developed some decades afterward by Pao Chingyen.

Of the life of Pao nothing is known. He must have written some works, which have suffered the fate of who knows how many valuable treatises. The secondary source now available is, ironically enough, *The Refutation of Pao* (*Chieh Pao*) written by Ke Hung, a conservative monarchist. In refuting the anarchist theory, Ke Hung the monarchist unwittingly immortalized Pao Chingyen the anarchist.

The anarchist must have been contemporary with—perhaps senior to—the monarchist, who lived in the last quarter of the third century and the first quarter of the fourth. This was the time when the Hunnish and Turkistanish tribes were pouring into the Yellow River valley and the Chinese were migrating into the rich basin of the Yangtze. The northern plain ran red as it became the theater of the barbarian invasions and agrarian revolts, while the southern domain, newly cultivated and settled, abundant in grain and rich with pearls, was the stage of the class struggle between powerful and wealthy pioneers on the one hand and poor migrants and natives on the other. During this great transitional period, there was no centralized political authority and no common moral standard.

Intellectually, Pao was born into an atmosphere that was saturated with the Taoist spirit. The brilliant interpreters of Laotzu and Chuangtzu had produced their works and the famous Seven Sages of the Bamboo Grove had created a new pattern of life, when Pao was but a youth. He "enjoyed the works of Laotzu and

Chuangtzu and studied the discipline of dialectics and sophistry."
Apparently he was no mere commentator, nor was he a romantic
poet. He was, above all, a political thinker, at once original and
systematic, a thinker of high caliber, even judged by the frag-
ments of his writings as quoted by his adversary. It is a permanent
loss to the history of political thought that the works of this great
sociological anarchist have not been preserved.

The Sociological Concept of the State

During the Han period the metaphysical theory of the state dominated the realm of political thought—the theory that sanctified
the monarchical regime as the replica of the cosmic order. During
the period of confusion following the Han, the sociological theory
of the state constituted the most significant undercurrent in the
minds of thinking men. Tung Chungshu, the metaphysical monarchist, was the representative political philosopher of the Han,
while Pao Chingyen, the sociological anarchist, was probably the
most outstanding and outspoken thinker of the age of confusion.

The political theory of Pao is sociological in the sense that the
state is regarded as an institution created and maintained by the
dominant classes in society and imposed upon the weak and ignorant masses.* Contrary to the Confucianist idea that the state
on earth reflects the order in heaven, Pao makes the following
categorical declaration:

"The Confucian asserts that it was heaven that created the in-

* Franz Oppenheimer, *The State* (New York: B. W. Huebsch, 1922), page 15.
"What, then, is the state as a sociological concept? The state, completely in its
genesis, essentially and almost completely during the first stages of its existence,
is a social institution, forced by a victorious group of men on a defeated group,
with the sole purpose of regulating the dominion of the victorious group over the
vanquished, and securing itself against revolt from within and attacks from abroad.
Teleologically, this dominion had no other purpose than the economic exploitation
of the vanquished by the victors." See also the writings of G. Ratzenhofer, L.
Gumplowicz, and A. Loria.

stitution of government for the sake of man, as though the supreme empyrean were solicitous of human welfare.

"The state originated really in this manner. When the strong conquered the weak, the weak were made slaves; when the intelligent deceived the ignorant, the ignorant were made servants. The state was created when the strong vanquished the weak 'and the intelligent dominated the ignorant. Slavery and servitude were born of the unequal struggle between the strong and intelligent and the weak and ignorant.

"The blue heaven was scarcely responsible!"

In this celebrated passage, not only does Pao ridicule the Confucian rationalization of the state, but he also advances a sociological concept of the historic state which antedates the modern communist and anarchist theories by some fifteen centuries.* The genesis of the state, according to Pao, lies in the class struggle between the strong and intelligent and the weak and ignorant. As an institution, the state is not created by heaven or ordained by nature; it is purely a man-made institution, a sociological phenomenon, in human history.

* Karl Marx defines the state as "the official form of class antagonism in civil society." See *The Poverty of Philosophy* (Chicago: C. H. Kerr, 1910), page 190. Elaborating this thesis, Friedrich Engels says that the state is "an organization of the particular class which is *pro tempore* the exploiting class." In ancient times, it is the "state of slave-owning citizens; in middle ages, the feudal lords; and in our own, the bourgeoisie." See *Socialism, Utopian and Scientific* (Chicago: C. H. Kerr, 1908), pages 127-28.

P. J. Proudhon, father of modern anarchism, believes that the historic state is always a class state; that it divides society into hostile camps, the strong versus the weak and the rich versus the poor. See *Idée Générale* (Bruxelles, 1868-76). Peter Kropotkin says that "the mission of all governments, monarchical, constitutional, or republican, is to protect and maintain by force the privileges of the classes in possession, the aristocracy, the clergy, and the traders." See *Law and Society* (1886), page 20.

The Historic State

The state having come into being, class distance tends to polarize and class antagonism to increase, Pao thinks. As the rulers become richer and stronger, the ruled become more miserable and rebellious. Instead of maintaining social peace, the state perpetuates and intensifies class war.

The will to power and the desire for wealth feed upon themselves, says Pao. Few indeed are the rulers who do not wish to build towers that soar up into the sky and palaces whose wings spread over miles of land. They seek treasures under the ground and pearls under the sea. They are not satisfied even if they possess "forests of jade" and "mountains of gold." They tax the people heavily and strip them of everything they produce or possess. They destroy homes and break up families; they saw off people's legs and collapse people's lungs; they "murder the world" to gratify themselves. All these evils they can perpetrate because they have sovereign powers. Were they commoners, asks Pao, how could they commit such crimes against humanity?

The rulers know that the people who suffer hunger and cold and who are under oppression do not always remain obedient and complaisant. "When public granaries are full, the people are certain to starve; when public offices are many, the people are bound to pay heavy taxes." Under such circumstances they tend to revolt. Then the rulers become fearful of the ruled. They will arm themselves to forestall any revolt. They will raise armies and build fortresses and castles. "They are afraid that their bows and arrows are not strong enough, their armor not heavy enough, their spears not sharp enough, and their shields not thick enough." They will issue laws and promote morals to threaten or pacify the people. "Thus the lords tremble in high places while the masses murmur and grumble in the midst of misery." Were there no sovereigns, says Pao, such a state of affairs could not exist.

Furthermore, the rulers of a state are seldom contented with the territory they possess. They will invade and conquer neighboring states. To this end, "they will drive innocent people to fight against guiltless countries. As a result, corpses will lie in the battlefields by the thousands and human blood will flow like rivers. In every generation there are tyrants who bring chaos and disorder to the world. Good citizens are murdered within and simple folks are killed abroad." Were there no sovereigns but common folks, Pao declares, there would not be such interstate warfare. Commoners may quarrel and fight, but they have no territorial ambitions, nor the will to empire; they have no cities to defend and no treasures to protect. All war is the natural consequence of the institution of the state.

It is interesting to see the argument of Ke Hung who wrote *The Refutation of Pao*. If the state is man-made, Ke Hung argues, so are social and political evils. War is created by man, not necessarily by the sovereign. The anarchist points out only the worst features of the institution of government but fails to see the real functions of good government. "If man and man fight over some small profit and family and family litigate over a piece of land, and if there are no judges and no laws, then private struggles will be more widespread than public wars and more people will be killed in private struggles than in public wars. Had there been no sovereigns, the human race would have been long extinguished!"

Primitive Stateless Society

In the beginning there was no state, declares Pao. As an institution the state is contrary to human nature and violates the principle that all men should live and let live. Thus says Pao: "All beings (creatures) like simple and natural joys. It is against the nature of the tree to have its bark peeled or its trunk carved; it is against the desire of the bird to be plucked or caged; it is against the nature of the horse to be shod or harnessed; it is against the will of the ox to be yoked or burdened. . . . All these are contrary to the principle that all beings should live and let live." In other words, it is against the nature of man to be governed, enslaved, or murdered.

Living in an age of war and confusion, Pao had reason to denounce the historic state and to long for the primeval society. Thus he describes the primitive stateless society: "In the beginning there was no sovereign and no subject. People dug wells to secure water and ploughed fields to obtain food. They began to work as the sun rose and to rest as the sun set. Free and unchained, they knew true enjoyment. They were not competitive or enterprising, nor did they know glories or humiliations."

One cannot resist the temptation to compare this passage with the famous description of the state of nature by Rousseau, where man is happy and free, "wandering up and down the forests, without industry, without speech, and without home, an equal stranger to war and to all lies, neither standing in need of his fellow creatures nor having any desire to hurt them, and perhaps not even distinguishing them from one another." All his wants are satisfied and his days flow in all tranquillity.

Pao the anarchist goes on to describe the state of nature in the following passage.

"There were no paths over the mountains, nor ships on the rivers. People did not conquer one another, there being no communications between valleys and plains. People did not fight one another, there being no armed forces.

"Desires for power and profit did not arise; disorder and chaos never occurred. Military weapons were never used; cities and moats were never built. All beings were equal (identical) and forgot themselves in the universal way (tao).

"There were no diseases or plagues, and people lived long. Pure and simple in heart, they were not cunning or unscrupulous. . . . Their speech was unadorned, their behavior unpolished.

"How could there be any ruler who would collect taxes from and impose heavy penalties upon the people?"

It is a far cry from this primitive utopia (imaginary though it must be) to the state of civil society. Man has traversed long and toiled hard on the road to civilization and has never seemed to reach the goal of peace and happiness. In every age we find people who gaze backward to the forest primeval and wish to escape thereto. Pao's hymn to the state of nature is, therefore, not merely a distant echo to the voice of Laotzu, but the very voice of many a delicate and artistic soul that finds the world too much with him.

11. WANG ANSHIH: THE NEW DEALER

Political and Literary Genius

NO HISTORICAL accident is it that the T'ang dynasty—a period of vigor and expansion, constituting the first half of the third cycle in Chinese history—was a golden age of poetry and art yet produced no worthy political thinkers, while the Sung dynasty—a period of political decadence and asthenia, constituting the second half of the third cycle—witnessed the rise of a brilliant galaxy of great philosophers. Periods of political upheaval and social unrest give impetus to intellectual efforts. Man is slack to exert his mental powers unless confronted with problems or crises.

Of the political philosophers and statesmen of the Sung age Wang Anshih (1021-1086) was unquestionably the most eminent. He was the one man who anticipated and feared the downfall of the Sung regime and the disintegration of the Sung society, and devised ways and means to strengthen the state and improve the welfare of the people. He served as the target for much literary slander and satire; bureaucrats obstructed and hampered him; each and every one of his social and economic theories and experiments was viciously attacked by the reactionary army of landlords and plutocrats. He was considered a cunning and dangerous enemy of the state and society, a sort of wizard who combined the gifts of a Solon and a Rasputin. His memory thus execrated and abused, the name of Wang Anshih has gone down in history as anathema. So much advanced of his time was he that only in recent years have we begun to understand and respect him.

In addition to being a genius of political caliber, Wang is one of the greatest literary figures in Chinese history. In a modern edition, his complete works, comprising poems, letters, essays, memorials, government orders and mandates, inscriptions, interpretations of classics, and introductions to books, consist of twenty-four volumes. He is generally classified as one of the eight famous writers of the T'ang and Sung times.* In contrast to the works of the other seven writers which are outstanding purely for their literary qualities, Wang's contributions are distinguished for their remarkable intellectual power, for their depth of thought and breadth of culture, for their masterly combination of forcefulness and elegance. "Wang is like Hantzu in the cogency and perspicacity of his reasoning, while in the forceful pertinacity of his composition he may be likened to Mocius," says Tseng Kuofan, famous literatus and statesman of the nineteenth century.

With advantage of a scholarly background and by personal industry and ambition, Wang at twenty-one passed the civil service examination for the degree of doctor of classics *summa cum laude*. He believed himself a man of destiny, for he wrote of "my stout heart of youth, my desire for a name, and the feeling that heaven has marked me for fame." In his twenties he embarked on the road to fame by serving as a minor provincial official. However, as he approached his thirties, he was a mere county magistrate and seemed to be in a state of mental restlessness.

It was the rule of that time for a provincial official to take a higher official examination and spend one year on unsalaried probation at the capital before he was appointed to a national post. Wang Anshih could ill afford this probationary period. In 1051 Wen Yenpo, then Prime Minister, recommended him for special promotion, saying that as he was of a "modest and retiring disposition he should be exempt from observance of the customary procedure." Despite his desire for promotion, Wang declined the offer, not wishing to violate the proper procedure. Again in 1053 Ouyang Hsiu, then a high official, submitted a memorial to the throne, recommending Wang for promotion. The memorial read

---

* Han Yü and Liu Tsungyüan of the T'ang; Ouyang Hsiu, Tseng Kung, Wang Anshih, Su Hsün, Su Tungp'o and Su Tzuyu of the Sung.

as follows: "Every one speaks most highly of Wang Anshih's character and learning. He is one who will adhere to his principles even if by so doing he remains in poverty. He is a man of very strong will, not easily swayed by extraneous influences. He has had a considerable variety of official experience, and has a real insight into the needs of the time. Though he has frequently been ordered to take the higher official examination, he has thus far refused to do so. My appeal is that he be given a post in the Board of Censors." Again Wang would not go to the capital. A year later, upon the recommendation of Ouyang, the Emperor appointed Wang assistant librarian at the capital, which appointment Wang Anshih likewise refused, declaring that he would not be the first to break the customary procedure of official promotion.

In 1058, when Wang was thirty-seven, he was appointed chief justice of the Chiangtung circuit. It was at this time that he came to the capital to submit to the Emperor the famous *Myriad-Word Memorial (Wanyen Shu)* which, in the estimation of Liang Ch'ich'ao, ranks as "the greatest document on government since the times of the Ch'in and Han."

From then on Wang rose rapidly in power and prestige. In the position of first vice-premier (1068) and then premier (1070), he introduced many radical social and economic policies. For some fifteen years, 1069-1085, the new deal reigned as the supreme law of the land. In order to carry out the new deal faithfully, Wang found it necessary to dismiss or demote many venerable high officials, including his patrons Wen Yenpo and Ouyang Hsiu, thereby arousing the antipathy of the entire literati and bureaucratic class. In 1085 the leader of the opposition party, Ssuma Kuang, a famous historian, who had been inimical toward the new deal from the beginning, was appointed premier. Immediately upon the assumption of his premiership, Ssuma repealed one by one all the measures which Wang had put into operation. Before his death in 1086, Wang, an old man in retirement, was compelled to witness a complete reversal to the old deal.

Upon Wang's death, the new premier wrote: "For literary genius and personal character, Wang Anshih had many exceptional points of excellence. He was, however, of an unpractical mind and was too fond of pursuing wrong ideas. This led him to treat with scant courtesy the loyal and upright and afforded an opening for the specious and cunning. . . . Now he has most unfortunately passed away. Unprincipled folk will inevitably take this opportunity to slander him on a hundred counts, but my own opinion is that the court ought to honor him with the highest respect." This from the pen of the leader of the opposition party is indeed high tribute to Wang the man, though not to Wang the new dealer.

Reformism versus Conservatism

During the lifetime of Wang Anshih the Sung regime was virtually under the suzerainty of the Tartars and the Tanguts in the north, having to pay heavy annual tributes as a means of purchasing temporary peace. Although it maintained an army of over a million troops, the regime was never able to resist the aggression of the Tartars and the Tanguts. It was further marked by a recurring annual deficit of some twenty million dollars and an inequitable system of taxation.

In the face of impending military danger and serious financial crisis, the government adopted the traditional laissez-faire policy, believing that all problems would of themselves be solved in the natural course of time. Wang Anshih was the one person in the entire empire who demanded a new deal, a positive policy, which would improve the administration, strengthen the army, and improve the welfare of the people.

In advocating the policy of laissez-faire, the conservative school pretended to follow the ancient rulers. Wang Anshih, therefore, had to expose the fallacy of such pretension. "If we moderns follow what the ancients thought to be proper, we may not really act in accordance with the ancient idea of propriety. If we moderns follow what the ancients thought to be righteous, we may not really act in accordance with the ancient idea of righteousness. Is the world permanently unchanging? Between the ancient and modern times there are similar forms but different realities. If we moderns seek to conform to the ancient forms but fail to adapt ourselves to the present realities, we are like the ancients only in name but not in fact."

Ancient methods of government, Wang contended, were good only in ancient times. "We cannot follow the ancient law to the letter. Law changes according as the spirit of the times changes. The law of the Hsia dynasty underwent a transformation in the Shang; the law of the Shang dynasty likewise underwent a transformation in the Chou. These historical facts illustrate how law must meet the demand of the age."

In his famous *Myriad-Word Memorial* Wang Anshih went a step further in arguing that the positive policy which he proposed was really in agreement with the practice of the ancient rulers, while the do-nothing policy of the conservative school violated the very spirit of the ancient law. Thus Wang said to the Emperor:

"The internal state of the country at this time calls for most anxious thought, while the pressure of the hostile forces on the border presents a constant menace to our existence. The resources of the nation are approaching exhaustion and the public morale is fast deteriorating. . . .

"All this is the result of the prevailing ignorance concerning proper government. . . . It is not that we have no laws and regulations, but that the present system of administration is contrary to the general principles of the ancient rulers. . . .

"I am not arguing that we should revive the ancient system of government in every detail. The most ill-informed can see that a great interval of time has elapsed since the ancient age. I suggest that we should follow the general principles, not the minute details, of the ancient system.

"If we only follow the spirit of the ancient law, then the reform that I have proposed need not alarm the ears and eyes, nor excite the tongues, of the world, for it will bring the government of our day in line with that of the golden age."

Wang was extremely anxious about the security of the nation and the livelihood of the people. He used strong words in condemning routinists and conventionalists in power, those time-servers and men-pleasers at court, those members of the conservative school who indulged in thinking wishfully that the national emergency would miraculously pass away in due course of time. In 1060, two years after the *Myriad-World Memorial,* Wang submitted to the Emperor the *Memorial on Current Affairs (Shih-cheng Shu)*, in which he again urged the necessity of a positive policy.

"In high circles there is no sound policy and among the people there is much poverty. . . . I am compelled to say that the national situation gives cause for grave anxiety.

"It is possible that a laissez-faire policy, or even idleness or neglect, may bring no disaster upon the country for some length of time, but it should on no account be persisted in. . . .

"As I view things, there is still a chance to save the empire from the danger and disorder that looms above it. If anything is to be done it must be done immediately."

It was not until 1069 that Wang Anshih was appointed vice-premier and thereby given opportunity to save the desperate financial and military situation of the country.

The New Deal

The new deal, which Wang Anshih introduced, aimed at an increase in the production of goods and services and an equitable distribution of the national wealth. The guiding theme of the new deal was "the repression of the monopolists and the alleviation of the peasant and laborer classes."

Ssuma Kuang, leader of the opposition party, which represented the landlords and plutocrats, attacked the new deal as impractical or utopian and contrary to the ancient law. But Wang argued that it was the only practical policy that would save the people from recurring economic crises and as such embodied the very spirit of the ancient law.

The most significant measures of the new deal were the agricultural adjustment act, the commercial exchange act, and the public works act. The first act was to relieve the poor farming class, the second to help the small trade class, and the third to effect an equitable and progressive taxation system.

The agricultural adjustment act was promulgated in 1069 when Wang Anshih became vice-premier. The act was not a utopian conception in the mind of a Messianic dreamer, but a realistic measure to meet an urgent need of the poor farming class. In the spring of 1069 a provincial official reported that peasants were unable to buy seeds and that landlords were lending money and exacting interest at the rate of 4 per cent per month. It was imperative for the government to render immediate assistance to those in distress. Thereupon Wang Anshih conceived and promulgated the agricultural adjustment act.

In the Sung period there were two kinds of public granaries, the normal granaries and the charity granaries. The stocks of the normal granaries came from the land tax and usually were sold to the people at market prices in times of dearth, while those of the charity granaries were harvests of government-owned farms and were distributed in times of famine for relief purposes. Wang devised a plan to convert the public granaries into a revolving capital fund from which loans would be advanced to needy peasants, and into a stabilization fund which would fix the prices of foodstuffs.

In the first place, the administration was to distribute loans, either of money or of grain, to peasants at the rate of 2 per cent per month. The loans were to be disbursed in spring at the beginning of the farming season and to be repaid in summer or autumn after the harvest. In case of a flood or drought the repayment of the loans might be deferred to the next harvest. In this way agricultural production could be carried on and peasants would no longer be at the mercy of landlords.

In the second place, the administration was to sell public granary stocks to the people below the current price level in times of dearth and to buy surplus stocks from the people above the prevailing price level in times of plenty. This would prevent landlords, who usually engaged in speculation and hoarding, from controlling the prices of daily necessities. By thus regulating the market Wang hoped to stabilize the prices of foodstuffs.

Under the agricultural adjustment act, therefore, peasants could secure loans from the government in the interval between the seedtime and the harvest, while landlords could not exact high rates of interest. The public as a whole would benefit immeasurably by a stable price level.

The commercial exchange act, promulgated in 1072, like the agricultural adjustment act, was not the theoretical scheme of a reformer, but a practical plan growing out of the necessity to help the small trader class. Under the laissez-faire system, monopolistic combines could buy up surplus stocks from small traders when the price level was low and sell when it was high. As a result, large combines became larger as small traders became smaller. Wang Anshih decided, therefore, to restrict the monopolistic class by the promulgation of the commercial exchange act.

The act provided for the establishment of a government trade bureau in every commercial center. When commodities were cheap, the bureau was to buy at prices higher than the current; when they were dear, it would sell at lower than the prevailing prices. The purpose was to adjust the supply and demand of commodities and to stabilize the price level.

The bureau was to be not only a trading corporation, but also a commercial bank. It would extend credits to small traders when the market was bear and require them to liquidate the loans when the market was bull. The bureau could thus expand or contract the volume of credit according as business conditions dictated.

By the commercial exchange act, therefore, Wang hoped to check the excess profits of the economic royalists and to protect the interests of the humble traders, and further to establish a permanently stable price system and prevent the danger of business cycles.

The public works act was promulgated in 1070. This, too, was a necessary measure to remedy a great evil in political and economic life. It was to replace the ancient corvée system, under which farming and laboring people were impressed to serve, without remuneration, as masons, postal messengers, road builders, canal diggers, dam constructors, or tax collectors. Those exempt were officials, scholars, priests, and only sons of families. Landlords and plutocrats, while theoretically liable to such services, were seldom drafted in actual practice. The system became a powerful instrument of intimidation and graft in the hands of local governors and magistrates.

Seeing that the corvée system did great injustice to farmers and laborers, Wang proposed the public works act, which was really a taxation measure. The act provided that the upper classes should pay a general property tax—the rates of which were to be progressively adjusted according to amounts of wealth—while the lower classes would be exempt from such taxation. The tax was to finance public works. Farmers and laborers who were drafted to do public works would receive adequate wages. This act naturally aroused a storm of opposition from the aristocratic and bourgeois classes who were required to pay the additional tax.

The new deal measures were enforced, despite the antagonism of the conservative party and the landlord and monopolist classes. In a letter to Ssuma Kuang, who had consistently attacked all the new deal measures, Wang Anshih said:

"I consider that I have adopted the government method of the ancient rulers, having the object only of relieving the people of economic distress and eradicating certain public evils. . . . My proposals for economic and financial reform are in the interests of the nation as a whole. . . . The governing class has been too long addicted to a policy of laissez-faire. The great scholars and officials generally do not give much thought to matters of state; they regard the *status quo* as the *summum bonum*. . . . I cannot admit the cogency of your contention that a policy of quiescence and conservatism is what the country needs today."

Fundamentally, Wang believed that the state should not be an instrument for the maintenance of the *status quo,* but a dynamic agency for controlling the anarchy of landlordism and capitalism.

We need not go into the operation of the new deal. Let it suffice to say that the reform measures were in general well conceived but not properly executed. The main difficulty lay in administration. There were not enough competent and efficient civil servants. The powers of granting loans and fixing prices were frequently abused and the powers of collecting taxes and managing public works led to all forms of corruption and intimidation. That the new deal as a whole was a sound policy was admitted even by some conservative leaders. In actual administration, however, it was not entirely successful.

Both in theory and in practice the new deal is neither communistic nor socialistic, for basically it holds no brief against the institution of private ownership. The author of the new deal intends to restrict large land estates and big business combines and wishes to see a nation of free farmers and small traders, a nation where the forgotten men will once more live in peace and security.

He opposes the system of unbridled competition, the system of anarchistic landlordism and capitalism, but he does not advocate a policy of complete state ownership. To him, the state is an intermediary agency whose duty it is to regulate the competition between landlords and capitalists on the one hand and peasants and laborers on the other.

The Military Service System

In 1070 Wang Anshih announced officially the militia act, the main objective of which was to mobilize the people so that they could defend the nation against the menace of the Tartars and the Tanguts.

If the new deal policy was dictated by an economic crisis, the militia act was necessitated by the impending danger of invasion from the north.

At the time when Wang Anshih came into power, the standing army of the nation numbered no less than 1,200,000 hired mercenaries, who were overbearing, corrupt, soft, and decadent. The maintenance of the army absorbed more than two-thirds of the national revenue. Even before Wang introduced the militia act, conservative statesmen voiced warnings against the weakness of the military force. Said the great essayist Ouyang Hsiu: "The standing army fails to win the respect of the enemy on the one hand and acts arrogantly at home on the other. So long as such conditions obtain, the safety of the state cannot be guaranteed." The great poet Su Tungp'o counseled: "The greatest defect in the national life today is that the people as a whole are not versed in arms. . . . I propose that all able-bodied males have a turn at soldiering for a certain period of time and afterward return to civilian life. In this way the nation as a whole will become a potential fighting force."

The militia act as originally promulgated contained the following features: Ten families were to form a platoon; fifty families a company; ten companies a regiment. Each regiment was to have a commander, elected locally. In every family where there were two able-bodied males, one should enroll in the militia. The government would provide bows and crossbows when the militia was in training. Each company should have five volunteers who would act as watchmen and policemen to maintain public order. From this outline it appears that the immediate objective was merely to raise a local police force. In the course of six years, however, the total force of the militia reached the number of 7,200,000, divided into three sections, cavalrymen, bowmen, and crossbowmen. These probably constituted the strongest potential army China had ever had in history.

As a corollary of the militia act, Wang proposed the reduction of the standing army. In the course of six years, the regular army was reduced from 1,200,000 to 600,000, thus cutting the government budget by one-third.

The militia act was not without opposition. There were many habitual moralists in the conservative party who argued that the way to govern the state was to inculcate ethical principles and not to strengthen the military force. To this Wang Anshih replied: "It is quite true that the use of military force to strengthen the state is not the ideal way. A wise ruler should alternate between mild measures and strong measures. Although force should never be the only consideration, it is at present absolutely necessary for the preservation of the state. The ancient rulers held armed forces in high esteem and at the same time taught moral principles to the people. These two policies—government by force and government by ethics—may be consistently combined."

Unfortunately for the Sung regime the militia act, together with the new deal measures, was rescinded upon the advent of Ssuma Kuang to power. Some four decades later the Sung regime fell an easy prey to the Tartars and was compelled to move from the Yellow River basin to the Yangtze valley. The main cause of the dis-

aster lay in the abolition of the people's army created by Wang
Anshih.

The Civil Service System

The examination system, conceived by Tung Chungshu of the
Han dynasty and perfected in the T'ang, was the chief method of
securing men for civil service during the Sung dynasty. The current tests at this time were mainly confined to the fine art of verse-
making and essay-writing and to the memorizing of the classics.
Wang Anshih was a severe critic of the system which, he contended, selected only men of inferior intellect and barred those of
real administrative ability.

Long before he came into power Wang had thought that the
greatest problem of the age was that of getting capable civil servants. In his *Myriad-Word Memorial,* submitted to the throne while
he was but a provincial official, Wang laid down a series of principles of public administration, which remain valid and useful
even to administrators of the modern state. These principles govern the methods of training, maintaining, selecting, and appointing
officials.

In the first place, Wang says, students who aspire to political
careers should specialize in public law and political economy, instead of learning how to compose poems and essays and memorizing the classics. A man's capacity for government is best educed by
specialization and best ruined by a great variety of literary studies.
The literary curriculum not only fails to train competent civil servants, but it positively unfits them for the task of administration.

As to the problem of maintenance, Wang observes that the officials in the country as a whole are but average human beings, who
can easily become corrupt when they are poor but who are likely
to be upright when they are financially secure. The scale of official
salaries must be adequate; otherwise, it is impossible for a mediocre
official to be honest and self-respecting and it is useless to expect

that he should. When officials are corrupt, public affairs cannot be administered on a sound basis.

The traditional method of choosing officials, Wang thinks, is faulty. If a man has a colossal memory, can repeat extensive portions of the classics, and has some skill in composition, he is considered worthy and brilliant and is given high office. It requires little insight to see that the knowledge and skill of such a man in no sense fits him for a position of authority and distinction. A candidate should be tested as to his views on current affairs and his ability to execute orders and initiate reforms; after being selected, he should be placed in some office for a probational period. In the last analysis, moral character is far more important than literary skill.

Finally, with regard to the method of appointment, Wang says that men, being by nature varied in temperament and in ability, are thereby suited for different tasks and cannot be expected to take up any and every kind of government work. A financial expert should be placed in the ministry of finance, an agricultural expert in the ministry of agriculture, an economist on the board of trade, an engineer in the department of public works. Once properly placed, a civil servant should be allowed to remain in office for some length of time so that he may make valuable contributions to the state. He should not be freely transferred or arbitrarily dismissed.

"The laws," says Wang, "do not administer themselves automatically. It is men who administer the laws. We should ensure that an increasing number of capable men are available for the civil service and that right men are put into right places. Granted that, it should not be difficult to reform the present system of public administration on the model of the ancient rulers."

As indicated above, it was precisely this lack of right men in right places that was largely responsible for the failure of the new deal. To paraphrase Wang himself, the new deal could not administer itself automatically. It took men to make it a success or a failure. This Wang knew too well, for before he formulated the new deal policy he had worked out some fundamental principles of public administration, which in reality constitute the very heart of the science and art of government. Unfortunately, despite the fact that he succeeded in reforming the civil service system while he was in power, Wang could not produce a generation of competent civil servants in the short space of a decade. As soon as he retired, the old system was restored, and poets, essayists, and classical reciters returned to administer public affairs in the succeeding eight centuries. Had Wang's reform taken deep roots and further developed in these centuries, China today might have had the most efficient civil service system in the world.

12. CH'EN LIANG: THE POLITICAL SYNTHESIST

Ch'en Liang the Man

THE political synthesist of this chapter was not a calm and halcyon philosopher, but a restless and explosive character, whose inner life was a veritable sea of turmoil and storm.

Ch'en Liang (1141-1194) was a most typical product of the Southern Sung age. Born in the year when Yüeh Fei, one of the greatest military geniuses in Chinese history, was executed by the traitorous Premier Ch'in Kuei in an effort to appease the invading Tartars, Ch'en grew up in the tense atmosphere of national emergency. The Tartars, who had captured the last two sovereigns of the Northern Sung, were overrunning the Yellow River valley and threatening to invade the Yangtze basin, while the Southern Sung ministers and high officials, who as a whole were either cowardly politicians or circumspect intellectuals, did little to strengthen the nation and resist the invader. In no other age had public affairs reached a more sorrowful and dismal state than in the era of the Southern Sung.

Early in life Ch'en considered the fact of national humiliation as a personal wound. He buried himself in the study of military strategy and tactics, hoping to discipline himself into a great general. At eighteen he wrote *An Inquiry into History (Choku Lun)*, a masterful geopolitical study of the famous battles in history. The magistrate of Yungk'ang, Chekiang, where Ch'en lived, on seeing the document enthusiastically exclaimed: "This youth is destined to be someday the leader of the world!"

Ten years later Ch'en recalled how irritable and excitable he was while writing the *Inquiry*.

"I was but a youth of eighteen, but I had the high ambition of directing military campaigns throughout the world. Many a time did I lose my soul in drunkenness, rant and rave of the great heroes of history, and shout and sing in high spirits. As I then reviewed the course of human events, I resented the fact that praises and blames in history were always exaggerated and often unjustified. My body was strained, my mind never restful. One day I came across this passage of the philosopher Yang Kueishan: 'A man must be able to repose before he can move the world. Brilliant though he may be, a man cannot repose unless he possesses knowledge.' Finding myself at a total loss on reading this statement, I decided to isolate myself in the solitude of my study. Now a decade having passed away, still can I scarcely find peace of mind!"

At the age of twenty-nine Ch'en submitted *An Essay on National Renaissance (Tsaihsing Lun)* to the Emperor. In this extremely eloquent and lucid essay he formulated certain general principles of government and concrete strategical and tactical plans for the recovery of the northern plain. As he received no word of commendation from the Emperor, Ch'en once more cloistered himself in his study for another decade.

After ten years of intensive study, Ch'en again grew restive and agitated. Now he was thirty-eight, more matured but no more mellowed. Within the space of one month he submitted to the throne a series of three lengthy memorials—stirring and inspiring documents—warning of the imminent danger of invasion and urging an immediate war against the Tartars. The Emperor was moved but took no action. The memorials won Ch'en national recognition but did not afford him any opportunity to serve the state.

Once more Ch'en went into seclusion. The next decade saw him engaged in philosophic polemics with the leading thinkers of the age. At that time, though the state of public affairs was sad, the pursuit of philosophy reached a new peak in Chinese history. The most eminent philosophers then were Chu Hsi and Lu Chiuyuan, both of whom professed to be pure Confucians. Chu is an "empiricist" who thinks that "the mind can be pure and the will sincere" only through experience, only through "the investigation of things and the acquisition of knowledge." Lu is a "rationalist" in the sense that he believes that only by developing the innate power of reason and not by depending upon external knowledge will man fully realize his moral nature. Ch'en was a personal friend but a philosophic foe of both Chu and Lu. To him, "such philosophers are morbid and paralyzed creatures who are insensitive to the pains and agonies" of the times. He admitted that he was "inferior" to the philosophers in the elucidation of obscure meanings of reason and nature, but he contended that he was "superior" in conceiving grand strategy and tactics and conducting great campaigns. Ch'en declared that they were mere interpreters while he was a maker of history.

When he reached the age of forty-eight, Ch'en again felt the compulsory urge to enter into politics. He submitted a final memorial to the throne, giving an illuminating analysis of the political and military conditions of the world then obtaining and advising the Emperor not to await, but to create, an opportunity to avenge the two lost sovereigns.

"I hear," Ch'en declared, "it takes extraordinary men to perform extraordinary deeds. If you wish to achieve extraordinary feats but employ ordinary talents that can think only of ordinary policies and solve only ordinary problems, you are bound to fail. . . . Unfortunately, during this period of national crisis, the scholars of the country are well-versed in the theories of ethics but know little of the realities of politics; they wish to preserve moral values but they know not how to employ military strategies. They cannot free themselves from eternal occupation in rhetorical gymnastics!"

Ch'en thought himself a creator of history and bid for the supreme command of the national armed forces. When the memorial was all but ignored, Ch'en became uncontrollably distracted and frenzied.

Thus thrice frustrated, he decided to spend the remaining years of his life in the retreat of his garden. But after six years of assiduous horticulture, he was once again fevered with the spirit of restlessness. At fifty-four he humbled himself by taking the civil service examination and, fortune smiling, he won the doctor of classics degree, ranking first in his class. By ill fate, before he could assume his post in a military court, the first government post to which he was ever appointed, Ch'en passed away.

In the life history of this man we note a definite rhythmic pattern. It is apparent that unconsciously Ch'en followed a master plan which was punctuated by decennial periods. After each decade of self-absorption, of solipsism and autism, during which he devoted himself exclusively to academic pursuits, he would invade society by publishing a fervid essay or submitting an astonishing memorial to the throne, and would thereby become the center of an intellectual or political storm. By nature, however, the storm could not have left a lasting impact upon society. With the ensuing calm, society relapsed into normal apathy and inertia. Ch'en, thoroughly dejected, would then enter into another decade of introversion. Obviously he did not realize that political careers were seldom built by leaps and bounds. His temperament would not permit him to sustain a long period of political probation and training in the low strata of the administrative hierarchy leading to the zenith. At the end of each decade, in an epochal essay or memorial, he demanded implicitly that he should be appointed no less than prime minister or commander-in-chief of the national armed forces! Small wonder that he met such abysmal failure in politics!

There is no doubt as to his inflated self-opinion. On his own portrait he subscribed this rhetorical question: "In the contemporary world, who is the colossus (tiger) among men and the monarch (dragon) of letters?"

Synthesis of Idealism and Realism

In China as in the West political philosophy has seen many a battle royal between idealism and realism. Confucius and Plato are the greatest representatives of the idealistic trend of political speculation, maintaining as they do that politics, being ethics, strives to bring about a state as it ought to be. Hantzu and Machiavelli are the outstanding exponents of real politics that is completely divorced from ethics and takes human society as it is. In diverse forms and terminologies, political philosophers of all ages incline either to the one or to the other of these two dominant currents.

In distinguishing idealism from realism in politics, Chinese philosophers have followed the classic formula of Mencius. Idealism is embodied in the conception of royalty, while realism is expressed in the idea of tyranny. The royal way, says Mencius, is that which wins the hearts of the people by virtue, whereas the tyrannical way is that which subdues the people by force. In addition to this formula, Mencius uses the symbols righteousness and profit to characterize idealism and realism respectively. To the King of Liang, who asks what may profit his country, Mencius replies: "Why must you use the word profit? I am come to advise only on benevolence and righteousness." Ever since Mencius the Chinese philosophers have in general advocated the royal way and denounced the tyrannical, have upheld the principle of righteousness and disdained the very thought of profit.

Ch'en Liang was the first political theorist to bring about a synthesis of idealism and realism. The great philosopher Chu Hsi summarizes the political theory of Ch'en in the following neat formula: "Righteousness and profit are both to be promoted; the royal and the tyrannical way are both to be followed." Chu the pure Confucian offers this formula as a criticism and advises Ch'en not to consider profit and not to follow the tyrannical way. For

Chu thinks that Ch'en deviates from the narrow path of Confucianism.

Ch'en himself protests against this formula as a misinterpreta-
tion of his theory. Probably he objects to the connotation of the
formula, for no political theorist wishes to be regarded as a pro-
moter of profit or as an open advocate of tyranny.

As a matter of fact, the formula is a rather apt summary of
his theory, if it is rephrased as follows: "Social justice and individual interest are both to be promoted; the civil and the military
way are both to be followed." Ch'en is neither a pure idealist as
are Confucius and Mencius, nor a pure realist as is Hantzu, but a
synthesist of political idealism and realism.

Living in an age when the northern plain was entirely occupied
by the Tartars, Ch'en was extremely anxious to increase the
military power of the nation. He had no use for Confucian
philosophers who were eternally babbling of moral principles and
values. To him those pharisaical and sadducean chatterboxes
were but simpletons unaware of imminent national danger and incapable of clear thinking.

"The civil and military ways," says Ch'en in the preface to the
Inquiry into History, "are really one and the same. They are but
lately divided into two. The so-called scholar specializes in using
the pen, while the so-called warrior makes a profession of handling
the sword. When peace reigns the influence of the scholar pre-
dominates. When war comes the power of the warrior meets no
challenge." In the eyes of Ch'en, this is a pitiable situation. "What
I mean by a scholar," he goes on to say, "is not one who knows
solely the use of the pen, but one who possesses the gift of public
administration. What I mean by a warrior is not one who is adept
only in handling the sword, but one who has the ability to defeat
an enemy. Such gift and such ability are really one and the same
quality. The so-called civil and military ways are different only
in name."

Historically the Chinese philosophers on the whole have idealized the semi-mythical golden age of antiquity. The Southern Sung philosophers are no exception. They hold the view that only the three ancient dynasties, Hsia, Shang, and Chou, are established on the idea of righteousness and hence are the true examples of royalty, while the Han and T'ang dynasties are founded upon the idea of profit and hence are followers of the tyrannical way. The Chinese philosophers are notorious in this process of historical rationalization.

Ch'en, however, is a rare exception. He is too original and too critical a thinker to attribute every virtue to antiquity and every vice to the later ages. In a series of letters to Chu Hsi the philosopher, Ch'en argues that, if the Han and the T'ang had followed only the tyrannical way, then "the mind of the universe must have been in suspense and the heart of man must have ceased beating for some fifteen centuries." The truth is, he declares, that the world is an ever-growing concern. The three ancient dynasties may be virtuous and righteous, but the Han and the T'ang cannot be entirely evil and selfish. The ancient ages may be golden, but the middle ages cannot be a fifteen-century-old cast of brass and iron.

In his polemics with Chu, Ch'en is willing to concede, for the sake of argument, that in the ancient ages moral influence reigned while in the middle ages physical force predominated. But, says Ch'en, in politics both moral influence and physical force are essential. No state can be secure without brave soldiers and intelligent commanders, or can be stable without ethical and legal codes. The art of government consists of both the civil and the military way. The state depends upon the power of moral persuasion in normal times, but in the last analysis it has to resort to the might of the military machine. Both the civil and the military way must be followed. Let not either be pursued to the exclusion of the other, Ch'en warns the rulers of the world.

To Chu, again, Ch'en is willing to concede that the idea of righteousness governed all in the ancient ages while the idea of profit prevailed in the middle ages. But he is of the opinion that no man is ever entirely pure in thought or absolutely free from the consideration of personal interest. The state has simultaneously to promote social justice and to protect individual interest. It is as unrealistic to ignore the idea of profit as it is unidealistic to ignore the idea of righteousness. According to Ch'en, these two ideas are not inherently contradictory.

Thus, with unusual common sense and with courage and independence of attitude, Ch'en Liang the political synthesist bridges the intellectual gap between idealism and realism in politics, between the Confucian and the Legalist school of thought. To him no political idealist can truthfully "follow the right regardless of interests" as Tung Chungshu, the metaphysical monarchist, pretends to do, no more than any political realist can advocate materialism pure and simple to the total abandonment of moral principles.

Nationalism and Democracy

Not only does Ch'en Liang bring about a synthesis of the traditional conflict between idealism and realism, but he also anticipates the rising sentiment of nationalism and the emergent trend of democracy in the metamorphosis of the body politic. As will be seen in the following chapters, Huang Tsunghsi and Wang Fuchih formulated the philosophies of democracy and nationalism respectively some seven centuries after Ch'en.

Nationalism and democracy were two significant undercurrents of thought during the Southern Sung dynasty. The former was a natural product of the Tartar invasion, while the latter was a reaction against the Sung regime itself which was fast becoming an absolute monarchy.

In his first memorial to the throne, Ch'en begins with an exaltation of the Chinese nation. "The Middle Kingdom," he declares, "is the very embodiment of the cosmic spirit of righteousness; it is in the Middle Kingdom that the destiny of the world rests, the heart of man reposes, the essence of civilization lies, and the glorious heritage of the ages forever endures."

"Is such a Middle Kingdom," Ch'en goes on, "to be violated by the evil spirit of the barbarians? Unfortunately, she has already been violated. We have now brought our civilization to this southeastern corner of the Middle Kingdom. Although the destiny of the world and the heart of man are resting here for the time being, we have no assurance that we will be permanently secure. If all officials and citizens choose the line of least resistance by remaining in this ivory tower and entertaining the illusion of security, if they do not take the entire Middle Kingdom into consideration, then the cosmic spirit of righteousness will express itself elsewhere and the destiny of the world and the heart of man will not forever lie in this little corner."

In order to bring about a national renaissance, Ch'en believes, it is imperative to establish a sound political system and to map out a master grand strategy. In his *Essay on National Renaissance,* he begins by saying: "To administer a nation there must be a sound political system, and to defeat a strong foe there must be a master grand strategy. When a sound system is set up, then the body politic will function properly. When a master strategy is decided upon, then tactical operations can be carried out." He proceeds to draft amendments to the then existing political system and to suggest a strategic plan for the counter-offensive against the Tartars.

The Sung regime was evolving into an absolute monarchy. All political and military powers were concentrated in the person of the monarch. Every government measure was issued and every official appointment made by the monarch himself. As one historian put it, "The recruit of every single soldier, the levy of every single tax, and the protection of every single county were all in the hands of the sovereign himself."

Seeing the weakness of this system, Ch'en argues that "the primary duty of the monarch is to maintain the political system as a whole and supervise the general administration of the state, but not to attend to all the trivial details." He proposed the restoration of the old three-power system. All state policies should be debated and agreed upon by the three highest ministers, the executive prime minister, the legislative minister, and the censorial minister, and then submitted to the monarch. After obtaining imperial sanction, the legislative department was to draw up proper measures, the censorial department to study and criticize them, and the executive department to put them into practice. In this way matters of state would be freely discussed and carefully planned by all the three responsible departments, and the function of the monarch himself would be to reign but not to rule.

Ch'en interprets the old Chinese system much as Montesquieu interprets the British constitution. Both are to be credited with the advancement of the theory of check and balance, an essentially democratic theory, as it tends to restrict the autocratic power of the monarch as well as to limit the authority of any one particular department of government.

To defeat the Tartars, Ch'en suggested the following strategic plan. The main objective being the recovery of Hopei and Honan (north China), Ch'en argued, the government should raise and train a strong army in Hupeh and Hunan (central China) and should make Wuchang the military headquarters. While the enemy in the north anticipated a frontal attack from the south, we should carry out surprise assaults on the flanks and capture Shantung in the east and Shensi in the west. Once these two provinces, the right and left arms of the enemy, were captured, we should attack the main body from three directions, east, west, and south. The Tartars would be unable to withstand such an enveloping movement and would have to flee northward to Mongolia or Manchuria.

When but a youth of eighteen, Ch'en had already conceived many strategical and tactical ideas in the *Inquiry into History*. No great victories in history, says he, are ever won without grand strategies. Military successes are seldom due to the preponderance of armed forces alone; rather they are achieved by brilliant and daring deeds, by taking tremendous risks, by surprising and deceptive movements, in accordance with preconceived strategical plans.

There are two kinds of soldiers, regular and mysterious, says Ch'en. Regular soldiers are steady, advance or retreat slowly but surely, fight in accordance with definite instructions. Mysterious soldiers are mobile soldiers, who "come like the storm and fade like the thunder." A great commander should never follow the letter of any war manual; he should train both regular and mysterious soldiers.

War is both defense and attack, Ch'en says. It is not won by pure defense or blind attack. To attack a place that is well defended is not a good attack. To defend a place that is attacked by an overwhelming force is not a good defense. A good attacker will storm "as if from the ninth heaven" a city that the enemy fails to defend. A good defender will lie in ambush "as if in the ninth hades" where the enemy expects no resistance. Surprise and deception are essential elements of military science.

Finally, says Ch'en, war is not a good instrument of national policy. It is the worst of all measures and the greatest of all calamities. But, he admonishes, when a country is invaded, let it not purchase a temporary peace at the price of eternal slavery!

Unfortunately, the Southern Sung regime could neither democratize the monarchical system nor resist the invader. Instead of achieving national renaissance as Ch'en hoped, the decadent regime headed straight towards an eventual downfall.

During the Southern Sung dynasty the Confucian philosophers as a whole were under the complacent influence of Buddhism and Taoism. They either turned inward, as did the Buddhist, to seek self-enlightenment and self-purification, or looked backward, as did the Taoist, to some semi-mythical golden age of antiquity—both failing miserably to face the political realities then obtaining. Ch'en was the lone voice in the wilderness calling for political reform and military preparation. Though his essays and memorials were widely read, his proposals were never acted upon and his ideas were generally refuted.

Ch'en is one of the most brilliant thinkers China has ever produced. Orthodox philosophers have regarded him as an iconoclastic heretic who injects the Legalist spirit into the Confucian body of doctrines. Barred from a political career, he has been well-nigh a forgotten man in history. Only recently have the Chinese come to realize and appreciate the vision and originality of this once obscure political theorist of the Southern Sung dynasty.

13. HUANG TSUNGHSI: THE PHILOSOPHER OF DEMOCRACY

The Life of Huang Tsunghsi

JUST as the early halves of the first, second, and third cycles of Chinese history produced no original or radical political philosophers, so the early half of the fourth cycle—the Ming dynasty—failed to stimulate man to rearrange old ideas or formulate new theories. In times of peace and order man tends to be complaisant and conformable, but in times of storm and stress man is likely to be restless or aberrant and to tread upon unbeaten paths. The Ming dynasty (1368-1644), an age of external expansion and internal stabilization, was an age of political conservatism and social prophylaxis. It was not until the Ming began to fall and the Manchus to invade China that a brilliant constellation appeared in the intellectual horizon. The most illuminating political writers of this time were Huang Tsunghsi, the philosopher of democracy, and Wang Fuchih, the philosopher of nationalism.

The Ming dynasty was an absolute monarchy. Its founder rose from the rank of a commoner. He organized a strong army and overthrew the Yüan dynasty. Soon after he enthroned himself, he killed many generals and ministers who had assisted him in the establishment of the dynasty. He abolished the premiership and personally directed the ministers of state in the execution of national affairs. The Ming code which he adopted goes down in Chinese history for its severity and rigor. The founding of the Ming dynasty heralded an epoch of absolute monarchy, of absolute autocracy and dictatorship, that characterized the fourth cycle (1368-1911) of Chinese history.

As though the Hegelian law—every thesis creates an antithesis—

were at work in China, the absolute monarchism of the Ming produced the most persuasive philosophy of democracy in Chinese
history. It was in 1662, shortly after the fall of the Ming and at
the beginning of the Ch'ing, that Huang Tsunghsi published *A
Treatise on Political Science (Mingi Taifang Lu)*, which is probably the most systematic political treatise in the Chinese language.
It contains discourses on the origin of rulership, the origin of ministership, the origin of law, premiership, education, civil service,
the national capital, the provinces and principalities, the land system, the military system, the financial system, clerks and courtiers.

Born in 1609, Huang Tsunghsi was nurtured in a scholarly family. His father, a doctor of classics and a high official, was a leader
of the Eastern Forest party that opposed the party of eunuchs and
courtiers then in power. As a mere boy Huang learned much of
the real politics in the country. When he was sixteen, his father
suffered death at the hands of Wei Chunghsien, leader of the government party. Huang swore vengeance for the death of his father.
In the following year, carrying an iron hammer, he journeyed to
the capital, intending to strike the fatal blow at Wei personally.
Fortunately, when he arrived at the capital, Wei had already committed suicide.

Between the ages of sixteen and thirty-five, while a student of
history and philosophy, Huang was extremely active in politics.
In 1644 the party in power planned to arrest all the sons and
nephews of the Eastern Forest party founders, among whom
Huang was a leading figure. Just at this time the Manchus invaded Peking and conquered the Ming, and Huang fled to his
home town in Chekiang.

For the next decade Huang was a revolutionary leader, assisting
the Prince of Lu in an attempt to overthrow the Manchu regime.
Several times he barely escaped capture at the hands of the Manchus. He hid himself between the island of Chusan and the Sze-
ming mountain, which location afforded him opportunity to observe astronomical phenomena and study geopolitics. Finally when

the Prince of Lu was defeated, Huang retired to live the private life of a scholar.

After a tempestuous but unsuccessful political career, Huang settled down and made his real contributions to the world. For in the next fifty years he not only wrote *The Treatise on Political Science,* but also produced *The Lives and Works of the Ming Scholars* (62 volumes), *The Lives and Works of the Sung and Yüan Scholars* (100 volumes, completed by his student Ch'uan Hsiehshan), *The History of the Ming Dynasty* (244 volumes), *The History of the Sung Dynasty* (incomplete), and edited *The Selected Works of the Ming Scholars* (482 volumes), not to mention his works on geography, astronomy, and mathematics.

There were three distinct periods in Huang's life. As he autographed his own portrait, "First persecuted as an opposition party leader, next outlawed as a fugitive rebel, finally respected as a scholar, I have lived three lives! Am I a child of the age, or am I a man of multiple incarnation?"

Huang was certainly both. Had not the party of eunuchs and courtiers been in power, he might not have become leader of the opposition. Had not the Manchus invaded China, he would not have been a rebel. Had the Prince of Lu succeeded in driving out the invader, Huang might have attained the stature of a great democratic statesman. Yet, despite the vicissitudes of time, Huang would never have become a great political philosopher and historian had he not set for himself an extremely high level of aspiration and a noble ideal of life. To a large degree external conditions determined the course of his life, but he was certainly no victim of circumstances.

Remaining loyal to the Chinese nation, Huang never accepted a post under the alien regime. During the last decade of his life, he declined first an order and later a request from the Manchu monarch to serve as government adviser and official historian. He died at the venerable age of eighty-five, leaving this epitaph: "Here lies a man who refused to serve the monarchs and lords. . . ."

Origin of Rulership

The leading idea of modern democracy is that the state is created for man, not man for the state. In Huang Tsunghsi's language, the same idea is expressed as follows: The people are the hosts and the ruler is the guest. The hosts always live in the house, but the guest may be invited to stay or asked to leave.

In the beginning, says Huang, there were no rulers. Every man lived a private life and looked after his own interests. What might have been public good was not promoted; what was public evil was not eradicated. Then there arose a man who ignored his own interests in order to benefit the world and who paid little heed to his own danger in order to safeguard the world. Such a man must have worked a thousand times harder than the people. Now, Huang asks, to work a thousand times harder than the people but not to gain therefrom any personal profit, is not this contrary to the nature of man? This is why, according to Huang, in ancient times Hsüyu and Wukuang (presumably early anarchists) refused to be rulers; Yao and Shun (legendary model kings) abdicated voluntarily; and the great Yü (alleged founder of the Hsia dynasty) wished to resign but could not leave office. For no man craved the office of king.

But in later ages the concept of rulership underwent a radical change. The ruler bethought himself: "I am the world! All under heaven is my own private property, which I will bequeath upon my children, my children's children, my children's children's children, unto infinity!" At first the ruler was a little ashamed of his egotism; eventually he convinced himself that he was the rightful owner of the entire world. He could legitimately murder any men, seize any women, enslave any children—all of whom were mere increments to his grand capital.

This is a far cry from the ancient concept of rulership, says Huang. "In ancient times the people were the hosts while the ruler was the guest. The ruler planned and worked for the good of the people. In modern times the ruler is the host while the people are

the guests. The people labor and slave at the mercy of the ruler.
. . . The ruler has become a public enemy. Were there no ruler, the
people could live private lives and look after themselves. The original concept of rulership has been completely submerged in political
evolution."

"In ancient times," Huang continues, "the people regarded the
ruler as father; they respected and loved him. In modern times the
people harbor only resentment and hate toward the ruler, considering him a profligate gangster, calling him a solitary individual. Unfortunately, the so-called Confucians still think that, rulership being
a fundamental institution of the universe, even a tyrant should not
be deposed. These Confucians have even argued that T'ang Wang
and Wu Wang should not have revolted against the tyrants, Chieh
and Chow; they have entirely lost sight of Mencius' insistence
upon the right to revolt. Alas! Is not the blood and flesh of a million people more valuable than that of a million mice? Is it not
utterly unreasonable that out of millions of people and families
one person and one family should be the owner of the world?"

The state is not the private property of the ruler, but the commonwealth of all citizens, says Huang. Because the ruler considers
the state as his personal fortune, he is in constant dread lest some
ambitious and enterprising citizens should usurp his office. No
ruler, however intelligent and powerful, can permanently suppress
all ambitious and enterprising citizens desirous of seizing the
crown. This is why, according to Huang, many emperors and kings
have been slaughtered and many dynasties have risen and fallen
in history.

The duty of the ruler is to administer the affairs of state on
behalf of the people, Huang declares. If this were understood, few
would wish to be rulers; since this is not understood, every man
in the street wishes he were king.

Origin of Ministership

Ministership, declares Huang, is not created by the ruler nor for the ruler. The world being too spacious, no ruler can govern alone. Hence the origin of ministership. When a man becomes a state minister, Huang says, he serves not the ruler but the people, not the royal house but millions of humble families. This is the fundamental concept of ministership in Huang's political philosophy.

Huang repudiates the popular notion of good ministership—that a good minister is one who is personally loyal and devoted to the ruler. Huang asks rhetorically: Is he a good minister who obeys before the ruler commands? Is he a good minister who sacrifices his life unconditionally for the sake of the ruler? No, these are not ministers at all in the true meaning of the term. The former is at best a good eunuch, the latter is but a devoted mistress! For a good minister will not obey the explicit, let alone the implicit, order of the ruler, unless he knows it is in the interest of the people. He will disdain to stand at the court, let alone to die for the throne, if he thinks that the ruler is corrupt and selfish.

Unfortunately, Huang says, the world thinks that ministers are made by the ruler and for the ruler. When men are appointed state ministers, they are grateful to the ruler and do their utmost to protect his private property. They are concerned with the safety and permanency of the dynasty, but have little interest in the affairs of the people. Such ministers fail to understand the true function and duty of ministership.

Whether the world is orderly or chaotic, Huang declares, is not conditional upon the rise or fall of one family, but is measured by the happiness or misery of the people. When the tyrants Chieh and Chow fell, the world became peaceful and the people were happy. When the despots of the Ch'in and Yüan dynasties rose, the world was in pandemonium and the people were heart-sore. Therefore, the duty of a minister is not to assist any and every ruler in power, nor to lay down his life for any and every ruler who is overthrown.

He is a minister of the people and for the people. He is not a eunuch or a mistress of the ruler!

Finally, Huang advances the novel view that rulership and ministership are different in name but equal in fact. Rulers are not creators of ministers, nor are ministers creatures of rulers. Rulers hold no absolute sway over ministers, nor must ministers kowtow to rulers. In name they are different, having as they do different titles; but in reality they stand shoulder to shoulder, both being servants of the people.

Origin of Law

In line with his general democratic philosophy, Huang Tsunghsi declares that the purpose of law is to improve the material and spiritual well-being of the people as a whole, not to stand guard over the private fortunes of one dynastic house.

Huang is a great admirer of antiquity. He interprets the spirit of the ancient law as follows: Knowing that the people must be fed and clothed, the ancient kings gave them land to grow grain and mulberry trees; knowing that the people must be educated, they established schools and sanctified the institution of marriage. These measures were for the sake of the well-being of the people.

But in the later ages, says Huang, rulers were concerned only with the impregnability and perpetuity of dynasties, so they promulgated laws to protect royal houses, instead of safeguarding the welfare of the people. For instance, the First Emperor (Ch'in dynasty) abolished the feudal system and inaugurated the provincial and county system, in the belief that if the world were divided into provinces and counties the royal house would be eternally secure. The founder of the Han dynasty instituted many principalities, each under a royal prince, thinking that these would safeguard the divine power of the emperor. The founder of the Sung dynasty abolished the offices of the territorial military governors, fearing that these might revolt and overthrow the throne. All these laws were proclaimed with the sole objective of preserving private fortunes of the dynastic families.

The ancient law, Huang thinks, assumes that the world belongs to all. The fruit of the earth is not the exclusive possession of the ruler. Those in the court are not inherently nobles, nor are those in the field commoners by nature. Under such a conception and scheme of society law is simple, and the simpler the law, the better the social order. This is what is known as government by natural law (that is, law without benefit of law).

The modern law, however, assumes that the entire world constitutes the very purse of the royal family, Huang says. No profits should go to the people; all blessings are to flow into the royal house. When a ruler employs a minister, he does not trust him and will employ a second minister to check up on him. When the ruler issues an order, he is afraid that it may be violated and will issue another order to punish the potential violator. Night and day the ruler is concerned with the security of his purse. Where the purse lies there lies also his heart. He will decree many rules and regulations. The more complicated the law, the greater the social disorder. This is what is known as government by illegal law.

Huang thinks that illegal law must be eradicated and natural law restored. He repudiates the opinion that the men who administer laws, not the laws themselves, must be reformed. There must be good laws, says he, before there will be good administrators of laws. Illegal laws bind the hands and feet of all administrators. Even the most capable of administrators are compelled to conduct affairs within the bounds of the illegal laws. If there are just laws, then capable administrators can perform good deeds for the people while corrupt officials can do little harm to the world. Therefore, Huang concludes, although it takes men to administer laws, it takes good laws to produce good administrators.

Education and Examination

For many centuries in China education has been a state function both in theory and in practice. Generally speaking, it aims at producing scholars and gentlemen who usually become officials and ministers of state through civil service examinations.

Huang Tsunghsi the democrat advances a somewhat unique view as to the aim of education. That aim is not merely to train scholars and gentlemen, but primarily to create a state of intellectual freedom in which all political and social issues and all moral problems may be openly discussed and rationally solved. He is as much averse to academic dictatorship as to political autocracy. Says he: "What the ruler declares to be right is not necessarily right; what he declares to be wrong is not necessarily wrong. The ruler should not insist upon his private judgment as to right and wrong, but should accept the public opinion of the colleges and schools." Education as an institution, accordingly, plays a distinctive role in the body politic—the role of public critic and censor.

Unfortunately, says Huang, since the end of the ancient age, education has been an instrument for the training of intellectual serfs and slaves in the hands of the powers that be. "Whatsoever the ruler favors all intellectuals regard as right; whatsoever he disapproves they all regard as wrong." As a result, colleges and schools become factories for the mass production of literary serfs and slaves.

Huang cites a few exceptional cases, however. During the Han dynasty the National University, where 3,000 scholars assembled, was free to publish papers and stage demonstrations against the then ruling party of eunuchs and courtiers. And in the Southern Sung dynasty the National Academy, where 3,800 scholars were in training, was the center of many a political upheaval. It was institutions such as these, Huang says, that had maintained the ancient freedom of speech and press and time and again had restrained the autocratic monarchs and corrupt ministers of state throughout the ages.

The rulers in history were not always willing to heed the sentiments of colleges and schools. Huang cites a few cases in which educational institutions were suppressed by rulers. The Neo-Confucian School of Chu Hsi, the greatest philosopher of the Southern Sung dynasty, was persecuted as heterodox and fifty-nine members of this school were proscribed or imprisoned. The Eastern Forest College of the Ming dynasty was destroyed and its leaders (among whom was Huang's father) were murdered in cold blood. Instead of training scholars, some rulers in history, Huang deplores, have distinguished themselves by liquidating independent minds and extraordinary talents.

So much for education. As to the selection of civil servants, Huang formulates a general principle, which is contrary to the customary practice of the Ming dynasty. Instead of being strict in selection but liberal in employment, he says, the government should be liberal in selection but strict in probation and promotion. When the method of selection is too rigid, great administrative talents and heroic characters may forever remain unknown; when the condition of employment is too liberal, mediocre persons will readily fill officialdom. But if the method of selection is liberal, every gifted man will have his opportunity; if the probational and promotional procedure is exacting, no ordinary man can ever reach the apex of political hierarchy.

The traditional method of examination—literary and classical in nature—is too stringent, Huang thinks. Men who have little gift in writing poetry or prose, or no inclination to philosophic speculation or historical research, are always failures in such an examination. Many a potential statesman has thus died unknown! Huang suggests that, in addition to rating men by literary and classical examinations, the government should choose civil servants by professional tests of administrative ability and technical skill, and that, instead of following an automatic procedure of promotion, the government should advance the status of civil servants according to merits and achievements. In other words, the methods of selection should be liberalized while the standards of promotion should be raised.

Equalization of Landownership

Ever since the abolition of the so-called well-farm system, a system of public landownership, which is alleged to have prevailed in ancient times, the problem of the distribution of landownership has challenged the master social and economic statesmen throughout the ages. Mencius was in favor of the restoration of the well-farm system. Tung Chungshu of the Han dynasty, the pontiff of metaphysical monarchism, suggested a restriction of private landownership with a view to curbing large landlords and alleviating farmers and peasants. Su Hsün, the realistic political commentator of the Sung dynasty, argued that it was absolutely impossible to restore the well-farm system of an age that had long passed, while Fang Hsiaoju, eminent scholar of the Ming dynasty, contended that it was necessary and practicable to revive the ancient system. Even today the land problem remains a great political issue between the Nationalists and the Communists.

Huang Tsunghsi supports the Mencian view and offers probably the most convincing argument for the restoration of the well-farm system. Now, to revive a system that passed away some two millennia ago would appear to be a most retrogressive measure, but as a matter of fact the carrying out of such a measure would most certainly revolutionize the entire structure of Chinese society. It is a highly interesting paradox in the dialectics of political thought that revolutionary doctrines are frequently based upon extremely vague notions of antique society. Rousseau, father of modern liberalism, Marx, father of modern communism, and Proudhon, father of modern anarchism—all great revolutionary philosophers—assume the primitive state to be a utopian existence. So does Huang. Probably it is the common lot of political philosophers to live in the memories of the past as well as in the hopes for the future.

In ancient China land was owned by the public. Every square li of land was allegedly divided into nine squares and was known as a well-farm unit. Whether or not such a system ever existed we do not know. It has been an issue over which many political philosophers have debated, pro and con, throughout the centuries.

Huang Tsunghsi proposed to nationalize the ownership of land in accordance with the ancient practice and to redistribute land to all citizens on the basis of equality. To those who thought it impossible to bring about such a radical social revolution, Huang cited the administration of colonial farms as an illustration. The colonial farms were owned by the public. Every colonial family was given fifty acres of arable land. In the outlying territories at that time there were 64,500,000 acres of land, which supported more than 1,200,000 families. In the country as a whole there were 701,-400,000 acres of land, of which the colonial farms constituted about one-tenth. Now, Huang argued, if the colonial farms were owned by the public, all private farms could likewise be nationalized. There were 10,600,000 families in the country. If all families were given fifty acres each, they would cultivate 530,000,000 acres, and the government would still have 170,000,000 acres left. Even if these were all retained by rich families, the people as a whole would have enough farms to support themselves.

The Ming dynasty was beginning to decay toward the close of the sixteenth century. One of the most distressing phenomena then was the rise of the so-called wandering bandits, who were really landless peasants and disbanded soldiers. These wandering bandits overran the length and breadth of the nation and staged many sporadic agrarian revolts. Huang thinks that unequal distribution of land, the most essential form of national wealth, is the main cause of the perennial disturbances in Chinese society. Therefore he proposes a radical social revolution to equalize the ownership of land. Not until the livelihood of the people is secure, Huang argues, will the nation ever be permanently stable and peaceful.

Huang's Place in History

In the history of Chinese political philosophy Huang occupies a cardinal position. He is the first systematic philosopher of democracy. Although some democratic ideas were expressed in various forms by the ancient philosophers, notably Mencius, and certain democratic institutions were embodied in the monarchical regime, it was not until Huang wrote the *Treatise on Political Science* that the Chinese philosophy of democracy was formulated in a comprehensive and methodical manner.

Huang is known not only as a political philosopher but also as a red-letter historian. He it is who first attempted a critical history of philosophy *(The Lives and Works of the Ming Scholars* and *The Lives and Works of the Sung and Yüan Scholars).* To this day no historical works in Chinese can surpass his in royalty of style or maturity of judgment.

Just as the ancient Chinese philosophers were contemporaries of the ancient Greek philosophers, Huang Tsunghsi lived simultaneously with the Independents, the Levellers, and the Commoners in England. It was at the time of the Puritan Revolution that Huang wrote the *Treatise on Political Science.* He opposed absolute monarchy much as the Independents, the Levellers, and the Commoners resisted the autocratic claims of the Crown, the Church, and the hereditary nobility. Had Huang lived in England, he might have been the author of the Leveller's pamphlet, which asserted that "we the people" derive "from Adam and right reason" certain "natural rights" of liberty, property, freedom of conscience, and equality in political privilege. Being a Chinese, however, Huang made use of symbols and illustrations from Chinese history.

In depth of thought and breadth of learning, Huang can be properly compared with John Locke and J. S. Mill. He is a pure philosopher like Locke, an economist like Mill, and a political philosopher like both. Locke is an "empiricist," while Huang is a "rationalist" of the Wang Yangming school. Mill is an economist of the modern industrial revolution, while Huang is an economist of the ancient agricultural civilization. All three are democrats, believing as they do that the state is created for man, not man for the state.

14. WANG FUCHIH: THE PHILOSOPHER OF NATIONALISM

The Life of Wang Fuchih

IN 1619, when Huang Tsunghsi, the philospher of democracy, was but ten years old, a child, destined to be a philosopher of nationalism, was born of a scholarly Wang family in Hunan and christened Fuchih. At that time the absolute monarchy of the Ming was on the verge of total collapse and the nomadic forces of the Manchus were threatening a large-scale invasion. In 1644, when Huang was thirty-five and Wang twenty-five, they witnessed the downfall of the Ming and the rise of the Ch'ing, the latter being an alien regime and more absolute than the former. ¹

It seems to be in the nature of the body politic that absolutism as a rule generates the sentiment of democracy, and that alien rule inevitably creates or intensifies the feeling of nationalism. The transitional period between the Ming and the Ch'ing, therefore, saw a widespread revolutionary movement that was at once nationalistic and democratic in nature. Huang Tsunghsi and Wang Fuchih were the philosophers who translated popular sentiments into systematic doctrines of democracy and nationalism, respectively, and as such they were the most representative products of the age.

Wang started his schooling at the early age of three. A restless and precocious child, he could not remain quiet and docile at school. He is said to have been free, wild, unconventional, unwilling to submit to the usual school discipline. Nevertheless, when he reached the age of six, he had already committed to memory all thirteen Confucian classics. From that time on he became an avaricious reader, devouring practically all philosophical and historical works in the Chinese language. At twenty-three when he had passed the provincial literary examination *summa cum laude,* he intended to go north with a view to paying tribute to the gentlemen at the national capital. Displeased, his father said:

"I dare not say whether or not the so-called gentlemen are really gentlemen. In conducting yourself, you ought to know what is of primary and what of secondary importance. If you consider those gentlemen as of primary importance and yourself secondary, you will sacrifice your life for what they represent. Would you not rather dedicate your life to your own principles? Beware, my son. Once you enter a party you cannot quit. You cannot devote your life to your own principles, even if you wish to."

Obviously the father was a man of strong will and independent mind, who must have exercised great influence upon the son. Owing to the fact that a rebellion broke out in Hunan while he was en route to Peking, Wang decided to turn back to care for his father; he never reached the national capital.

Within less than two years Peking fell to the Manchus. When the sad news reached Wang, he fasted a few days and composed the famous national dirge, *In Sorrow and Anger (Peifeng Shih).* So profoundly affected was he by the alien intrusion that whenever he recited the hundred rhymes in later years he invariably burst into tears.

Just as Huang Tsunghsi assisted the Prince of Lu in resisting the invader in Chekiang, Wang Fuchih joined the Prince of Kwei who was the main leader of the opposition in Kwangsi against the alien regime. For several years Wang was a rebel in the eyes of the law. When the Manchus captured the city of Kweilin in 1650, he made a hairbreadth escape and hid on a river bank where he went without food and was exposed to incessant rain for four nights and days. After many months of traveling through circuitous and unbeaten mountain paths he eventually reached his home in Hunan.

In the next forty years Wang lived the lonely life of a hermit.

He was a political fugitive, unwilling to subject himself to alien rule, refusing to wear a pigtail (as ordered by the Manchus), wandering in the mountains amidst the primitive aborigines in Hunan. During these years he built three small abodes—first the Eternal Dream Cottage on Mount Lotus, then the Fallen Leaves Cabin on Mount Golden Lily, finally the Grass Hut on Mount Stone Boat— where he lived in seclusion, remaining incognito and assuming different aliases, forsaking the world as completely as ever a mortal could.

If Wang was politically inactive, he by no means became rusty or stale mentally. He made his greatest contributions to the world during these forty years when he left the world completely. Probably he had to be outside the world in order to see the powers and virtues, the frailties and foibles and tragicomedies of humanity in proper perspective. Many were the hours and days he spent sitting alone on mountain summits, watching the sun, moon, and stars that eternally course the celestial orbit, and the rivers and streams that flow serenely into the mighty Yangtze. He must have studied carefully the customs and mores of the aborigines—who to him represented the childhood of humanity—thereby acquiring a scientific insight into the evolution of the homo sapiens. A less imaginative person would have found such a solitary life boring if not unbearable, but to Wang it was more than he expected.

This era of world abstinence proved to be extremely fruitful. In seclusion he flowered into one of the greatest writers in history. His most significant works in the realm of politics are *Yellow Paper (Huang Shu)* and *Strange Dream (E Meng)*. The former, written in 1656 soon after his retirement, is a nationalistic thesis exalting the culture of the descendants of the Yellow Emperor. The latter, written in 1682 toward the end of his life, is a reiteration of the nationalistic thesis, in which he expressed confidence that his dream of national revival, though seemingly strange, would eventually be fulfilled.

In addition to these political works Wang wrote extensively on history and philosophy. The most famous of his historical works are the *Essays on General History (Tu T'ungchien Lun)* and *Essays on the Sung Dynasty (Sung Lun)*, in both of which the idea of nationalism constitutes the central doctrine. Likewise, in his philosophical works, such as *Reflections (Szuwen Lu)* and *Problems (Szuchieh)*, as well as his commentaries on the Confucian works and interpretations of the Taoist works, the same nationalistic idea expresses itself in various recurring themes. For first and last Wang is a nationalist, using history and philosophy as media of national exaltation. This is far from saying that he is not a high-ranking philosopher or historian. According to Tan Szut'ung, one of the foremost modern thinkers, Wang is "the only philosopher in the last five hundred years who truly understands man and the universe." And in the opinion of Liang Ch'ich'ao, Wang is "the best historical critic of the old school" and is so original an historian that "he literally reverses at least half of the traditional judgments and conclusions on history."

Wang suffered the fate of many a now famous author—that of not being recognized in his lifetime. All of his works were published posthumously. His manuscripts were hidden in mountain caves and scattered among his relatives and friends. It was not until the middle of the nineteenth century that Tseng Kuofang, a distinguished scholar-statesman, collected and published the *Works of Wang Fuchih (Ch'uanshan Weishu)*, consisting of no less than seventy-seven books in 250 volumes.

In the Grass Hut on Mount Stone Boat Wang passed away in 1692 at the age of seventy-three. On his tombstone he personally inscribed this epitaph: "Here lies Wang Fuchih, the last loyal minister of the Ming dynasty."

Reason and Force

In the history of Chinese political philosophy we have noted a profound cleavage between the idealist (or scholar) and the realist (or warrior) point of view. The idealist believes in the final validity of reason while the realist thinks that force is the ultimate arbiter in politics. The idealist, usually a loquacious salesman of morals, is seldom capable of facing political realities, while the realist who knows only the language of force and high pressure is unaware of political ideals.

Ch'en Liang was the first outspoken thinker to attempt a synthesis of idealism and realism, insisting upon the parallelism of the civil and military ways. Wang Fuchih goes a long step further in bringing about a metaphysical synthesis of idealism and realism. Ch'en is a keen political thinker but not a philosopher, while Wang is eminently a philosopher. Ch'en can see but the political parallelism of the civil and military ways, while Wang reaches a higher plane—a metaphysical unity of idealism and realism.

The gist of this metaphysical unity may be stated as follows: In the nature of things, says Wang, reason and force are identical. What is reasonable, i.e., what is as it ought to be in the nature of things, is inevitable; what is inevitable, i.e., what is dictated by the force in the nature of things, is reasonable. This is almost exactly equivalent to the famous Hegelian formula: "What is rational is real; what is real is rational." Of all Chinese philosophers Wang Fuchih comes closest to Hegel.

Wang expounds this theory of the unity of reason and force most eloquently in a comment on the following well-known passage in the *Works of Mencius:* "When right government prevails in the world, princes of little virtue and little worth are submissive to those of great virtue and great worth. When bad government prevails, small and weak states are submissive to those that are large and strong. Both these cases are in accord with the rule of nature."

Commenting on this passage, Wang says in substance: It is reasonable that princes of little virtue and little worth should serve those of great virtue and great worth, for this is as it should be in the nature of things. It is inevitable that small and weak states should serve large and strong states, for this is dictated by the force in the nature of things. Conversely, it is reasonable that princes of great virtue and great worth should rule those of little virtue and little worth, and it is inevitable that large and strong states should govern those that are small and weak. What is reasonable is inevitable; what is inevitable is reasonable. In the very nature of things, reason is force, and vice versa.

According to this theory, then, every institution and every dynasty that ever exists possesses an inherent *raison d'être* and is of an inevitable nature. Whether the institution or dynasty comes into being by reason or by force is but a superficial moral problem. The fact that it exists proves that it is at once reasonable and inevitable. It exists by reason and force or—to transpose it—by the force of reason and the reason of force.

The Coming and Going of Institutions

Upon the metaphysical theory that what is reasonable is inevitable and what is inevitable is reasonable, Wang Fuchih constructs a systematic philosophy of history—of historical institutions and dynasties—which sounds strangely Hegelian.

Historical institutions, Wang thinks, do not come into being by accident, nor do they ever emerge as singular or isolated phenomena from societal vacuums. In every epoch there is a particular set of institutions which are structurally and functionally adjusted to one another in a particular historical situation. Furthermore, Wang believes that there are certain definite tendencies and processes in historical evolution. What is past cannot revive; what is present will not endure forever. The present inherits the past and modifies it, just as the future will inherit the present and modify it.

Contrary to most Chinese philosophers, including Huang Tsung-hsi the democrat, Wang Fuchih refuses to look backward to the golden age of antiquity. All the institutions of the ancient age have passed—and passed forever—beyond restoration. In his *Essays on*

General History, Wang discusses many institutions that have come and gone in historical evolution.

First he takes up the feudal system and the provincial and county system. The former existed in the ancient age, the latter has existed in the middle and modern ages. There are many philosophers in history who have either advocated the restoration of the feudal system or defended the provincial and county system. In Wang's opinion, such polemics are meaningless and fruitless. History changes and does not repeat itself. The feudal institution, while it lasted, had a *raison d'être* and was inevitable. Now the feudal system has gone, and the provincial and county system has come into being. This, too, must be reasonable and inevitable. One can no more restore the feudal system than turn back the march of time itself.

In the transformation of the feudal system into the provincial and county system Wang observes three inherent tendencies in historical evolution. In the first place, the principle of hereditary aristocracy is transformed into that of moral and intellectual aristocracy. Under the feudal system sons of lords were always lords, sons of gentlemen always gentlemen, sons of peasants always peasants; but under the provincial and county system magistrates and mayors were selected from among the virtuous and intelligent. In the second place, the principle of political division is transformed into that of political unity. Under the feudal system every dukedom, marquisdom, earldom, viscountcy, or barony was more or less an independent state, but under the provincial and county system the entire nation was a unified empire. Finally, the principle of feudal authority is transformed into that of imperial authority. In ancient times any feudal lord could raise an army or kill any subject within his domain, but now no county magistrate or mayor might have a private army or sentence any person to death contrary to imperial law. According to Wang, it is these three tendencies—which are both reasonable and inevitable in historical evolution—that account for the permanent disappearance of the feudal system and the coming into existence of the provincial and county system.

With the same historical insight Wang discusses another interesting pair of institutions—public ownership and private ownership of land. Many philosophers and statesmen have advocated the restoration of the ancient well-farm system, a system of public landownership, or have proposed a redivision or a restriction of private landownership. Wang is of the opinion that public ownership came to fulfill an historical mission but has gone forever, and that private ownership has come into existence and will not disappear immediately.

In the primitive stage, says Wang, there was no ownership. The earth belonged to none. As the struggle for existence entailed a great deal of bloodshed, sages arose to divide land into more or less equal squares and allot them to the people. The well-farm system therefore served a definite mission—that of establishing peace among the people. Now that the institution of private landownership has come into existence, it is no longer necessary, as it was in ancient times, for the government to allot farms to the people. Private ownership has come and is to stay until a time when it ceases to be reasonable and inevitable.

The feudal system and the public farm system, according to Wang, are structurally and functionally related to and dependent upon each other, as are the provincial and county system and the private farm system. Each set of institutions is reasonable and inevitable in a particular historical epoch. In the final volume of the *Essays on General History,* Wang declares: "The ancient institutions, which were necessary in the ancient age, cannot be revived as a means of governing the modern world. The existing institutions, which are products of the modern age, cannot be eternally useful in the future world. . . . Every age being a unique historical situation, the government should be liberal or rigorous, expansive or astringent, according as circumstances dictate."

The Rise and Fall of Dynasties

In interpreting the rise and fall of dynasties Wang reveals a keen insight into the evolutionary nature of human history. Against the weight of traditional philosophy—both Taoist and Confucian—he advances the theory that society progresses from a primitive bestial existence, through a barbarian stage, to a more or less civilized state, and finally to the existing state of high civilization.

The Taoist glorifies the prehistoric state of nature and the Confucian idealizes the ancient historic period. But Wang says: We have little knowledge of the prehistoric and ancient ages. Before the Nest-Builder and the Fire-Driller, mythical kings, taught people to construct shelters and to cook, men were not different from beasts. At the time of the Yellow Emperor men were barbarians. During the three ancient dynasties, Hsia, Shang, and Chou, human relations were gradually regularized. Even in Confucius' time society still suffered from the epidemic of regicide and patricide. The prehistoric and ancient ages could not have been such an utopian existence as the Taoist and Confucian imagined. To glorify the state of nature or idealize the ancient age is contrary to the fact of historical evolution.

Traditionally it is thought that the founders of the three ancient dynasties were sages, men of great virtue and wisdom, while those who established the dynasties in the middle and modern ages were merely men of ruthless courage or unusual competence. Against this view, Wang argues that the founders of the Han, the T'ang, and the Ming were as great in virtue and wisdom as those of the ancient dynasties.

Since antiquity, says Wang, the world has experienced many cycles—now a period of peace and order, then a period of war and chaos. Society is never unchanging. After a period of tranquillity society inevitably bursts asunder, and at the end of a period of disorder it naturally reintegrates itself. The Han, the T'ang, and the Ming each heralded a long period of peace and order. The Han

overthrew the despotic regime of the Ch'in, the T'ang that of the
Sui, and the Ming that of the Yüan. Each was a great dynasty
under which the people enjoyed the blessings of universal peace
for several centuries.

Furthermore, in Wang's opinion, the Han, the T'ang, and the
Ming are the most glorious periods in Chinese history. For the
Han successfully resisted the invasion of the Tartars; the T'ang
conquered the Hunnish and Turkistanish tribes; the Ming drove
out the Mongolian hordes who under Genghis Khan had overrun
Chinese territory. It is these dynasties that preserved the Chinese
race and culture and forged China into a nation. They are therefore at least as worthy and as illustrious as the three ancient dynasties.

The rise or fall of a dynasty is never accidental or incidental,
Wang observes. It is neither due to the virtue or evil of one single
man, however great, nor does it transpire in one night and day.
Before a new dynasty rises the old regime must be in the process
of deterioration and dissolution, and before a dynasty falls a new
force must be gathering strength. The founder of a great dynasty
is always a man who understands the trend of history and works
toward the fulfillment of historical destiny. No dynasty ever rises
contrary to what is reasonable, or falls contrary to what is inevitable.

The Philosophy of Nationalism

In Wang Fuchih's philosophic system, nationalism is the fundamental theme while the theory of institutions and dynasties is but
a subordinate issue. Wang is far more concerned with the preservation of the nation than with the coming and going of institutions
or the rise and fall of dynasties. Institutions may be allowed to
come and go, and dynasties to rise and fall, but the nation must
never be permitted to perish. Says Wang: Let there be wars of
revolution or succession, let there be internal disturbances, but

never let a foreign race divide the national house against itself!
Let despots reign, let evil institutions persist, but let not a foreign
ruler ever so much as set foot on Chinese soil!

Wang's philosophy of nationalism is a synthesis of three principles, heaven, earth, and man. The principle of heaven means
that men and animals, while both live, breathe, and have their
being, are to be separated, the former to overlord the latter. The
principle of earth means that civilized men and savages, although
having the same physiological structure, are to be segregated, the
former in the Middle Kingdom, the latter in the peripheral deserts
and wildernesses. The principle of man means that the civilized
race must protect itself against both animals and savages. These are
the basic assumptions in *Yellow Paper*.

Wang deplored the fact that the Chinese nation could not defend
itself against savages, nor even against beasts. "If we cannot an-
nihilate beasts, we violate the principle of heaven; if we cannot
resist the invasion of savages, we violate the principle of earth; if
we let ourselves perish, we violate the very principle of man."
That the Chinese race must rise again, must assert and safeguard
itself, Wang believes, is dictated by the fundamental principles of
heaven, earth, and man.

The concept of nationalism, in Wang's theory, is geographical,
racial, and cultural. A nation is a people of substantially a common
blood inhabiting a defined territory and having a common pattern
of culture.

Geography seems to have a determining influence. "The Chinese
and barbarians," says Wang, "are different, because they are born
in different lands. Lands being different, climates are different.
Climates being different, social habits and customs are different.
Social habits and customs being different, contents of knowledge
and patterns of behavior are different." Here once more Wang
sounds strangely Hegelian. In his *Philosophy of History,* Hegel surveys the entire earth to locate the abodes of states, suggesting the
deterministic influence of physical environments upon political

developments. Neither Wang nor Hegel, however, makes geography the creative force in the evolution of nations.

In the second place, the nation is a racial unit. Wang does not say that the Chinese race is pure. He thinks that the descendants of the Yellow Emperor constitute the essence of the Chinese race, and insists that the Chinese and the Manchus must never intermingle.

Wang opposed those who were preaching moral platitudes to the invader. In the preface to *Yellow Paper* he says: "The principle of benevolence means loving our own race, that of righteousness regulating social relations within our own race. . . . Now that our race cannot protect itself, why do we babble about benevolence and righteousness?"

In Wang's theory, more important than geography and race in determining the identity of a nation is culture. What distinguishes the Chinese nation is cultural uniformity and continuity rather than geographical fixity or racial homogeneity.

The geographical boundaries of the Chinese nation, Wang notes, have undergone many modifications. In ancient times the nation was confined to the Yellow River basin; later it expanded to the Yangtze valley; now it has extended to the South Sea. Says Wang: "Southern China was barbarian in ancient times but now it has become the center of Chinese culture. Northern China was civilized in ancient times but has now degenerated into barbarism"—under the influence of the Manchus. Here he seems to suggest that northern China had ceased to be part of the Chinese nation.

In the evolution of the Chinese nation, Wang notes, the Chinese race has assimilated and civilized many aboriginal tribes in the southeastern and southwestern provinces. These tribes have become integral parts of the Chinese nation although originally they were not Chinese.

Thus Wang shows that the geographical location and the racial composition of the Chinese nation may alter from time to time, and that whoever adopt the Chinese pattern of culture, wherever they are located, become members of the Chinese nation. Culture is therefore the final determining factor of a nation.

Wang is too good an anthropologist and ethnologist (having lived for forty years among the aborigines in southern China) to think that the Chinese race is pure or is superior to other races. In fact, he declares that the ancestors of the Chinese race were beasts and savages—a fact that few philosophers of nationalism are willing to admit. So imaginative and rational is Wang that he even advances the view that, when the Chinese were still beasts and savages, there must have been some nations, somewhere under the sun, whose civilizations had reached a high plane and from whom the Chinese were unable to learn because of the lack of communication. Chinese culture, in his opinion, is not the oldest in the world, nor is the Chinese race the most superior.

Of the peoples in East Asia, Wang thinks that the Chinese have achieved the highest civilization. He is proud of the fact that since the Han dynasty the Chinese have assimilated and civilized many kindred races and have thus expanded the Chinese nation. He is in favor of taking all the peoples of Greater China, excepting the Manchus, into common citizenship, by the process of civilization, not by the force of conquest.

Finally it must be stated that Wang never feared that the Chinese nation would perish from the face of the earth. He urged his people to rise again, to drive out the invader and re-establish a national state. For according to the nature of things it is both reasonable and inevitable that the Chinese nation is destined to be not only an independent nation but also a civilizing force in the world.

Wang's Place in History

It has often been said that Chinese nationalism is a new theory and a new movement, a resultant of China's contact and conflict with the West. This is an incorrect view. While Chinese national consciousness has certainly increased in recent decades, it began no less than twenty-five centuries ago, when Confucius paid a great tribute to Kuang Chung, premier of the Ch'i state, who "upheld the royal house and resisted the barbarians." Nationalism then was in the form of tribalism. When the First Emperor unified the feudal tribes, China succeeded in integrating herself into a large cosmopolitan nation, as Europe failed after the breakdown of the feudal system. Throughout the historical cycles, although China has been time and again invaded by nomadic tribes, Chinese nationalism has always been able to assert itself in the form of armed resistance, or territorial expansion, or racial and cultural assimilation. In no age has nationalism ever ceased to be a strong sentiment and a dynamic force.

Nationalism was particularly strong in the latter part of the seventeenth century when the Manchus invaded and conquered China. Wang Fuchih was the greatest spokesman of the Chinese nation at that time. Throughout the ensuing two and a half centuries of the Ch'ing regime nationalism had remained a strong underground movement, especially in southern China. Hundreds of literary societies and political clubs were organized in secret with the sole objective of overthrowing the alien regime. When Sun Yat-sen started the revolutionary movement, he relied heavily upon those secret nationalistic societies and clubs that had been in existence ever since the seventeenth century. In an historical sense, therefore, Wang Fuchih is the first father of modern nationalism in China.

In philosophy Wang is a kindred spirit with Hegel. Both employ the historical or evolutionary method in studying man and society and reach the conclusion that whatever is is both inevitable and rational. In developing the philosophy of nationalism Wang anticipates both Montesquieu and Herder. The influence of the environmental factors, such as climate and geography, upon the formation of national character is as clearly analyzed by Wang as by Montesquieu and Herder. While the French philosopher uses the ambiguous expression *esprit général,* and the German the romantic term *Volkgeist,* to convey the idea of national character, Wang simply adopts the term culture to denote the sum total of achievements of the Chinese nation.

15. K'ANG YUWEI: THE LAST
OF THE CONFUCIANS

The Great Sphinx

IN THE development of Confucianism as state doctrine two philosophers stand out prominently, Tung Chungshu of the Han dynasty and K'ang Yuwei of the Ch'ing. Some two thousand years ago Tung transformed Confucianism (then but one philosophy among several) into the official doctrine of the state and in recent times K'ang attempted to establish Confucianism as state religion. Tung was the first advocate, and K'ang the last defender, of Confucianism as the orthodox political creed of China.

K'ang Yuwei (1858-1927) lived at the time when the influence of Confucianism was beginning to wane and western science and philosophy and religion were making a tremendous impact upon the Chinese mind. While almost the entire nation was anxious to learn from the West the secret of power—political, military, and economic—K'ang discovered in Confucianism the great moral force that someday would bring about a universal commonwealth of nations.

Born of a scholarly family in Nanhai, near Canton, K'ang grew up under the tutorship of his grandfather. He was known as a child prodigy, for at seven he was an essayist and poet. He is said never to have forgotten any line he ever read. His demeanor in school was always severe and he seldom condescended to smile or talk. As a mere child he aspired to be a sage (like Confucius). His schoolmates dubbed him "Sage Yuwei," for whenever he opened his mouth he invariably began with "Confucius said."

Between eighteen and twenty-four he studied under Chu Chiu-chiang, a noted scholar, from whom he learned the fundamentals of philosophy and politics. During the next four years he lived in seclusion in a little cottage on Mount Hsichiao, losing himself completely in the study of philosophy and religion. On this mount at the age of twenty-seven he wrote the *Great Commonwealth* (*Tat'ung Shu*), a very extravagant and novel conception of a universal stateless society, based presumably on the teachings of Confucius.

When China ceded Formosa and Liaotung to Japan in 1895 at the conclusion of the first Sino-Japanese war, K'ang journeyed to Peking, then capital of the Empire, with the intention of forestalling the acceptance of the humiliating peace. He rallied over 1,300 students from different provinces to parade to the palace and present an 18,000-word memorial to the throne, urging refusal of the Japanese terms, removal of the capital to a place of safety, and political reform. (This event should be considered as the beginning of the modern youth movement in China.) Unfortunately, the memorial which came from the master pen of K'ang himself never reached the throne. However, he was undaunted, for in the next three years he presented five lengthy memorials, which one by one in turn were ignored. He became a subject of ridicule and scorn in the eyes of the scholars of the nation who thought him a paranoiac or lunatic. To every insult the "world of mediocres and imbeciles" could think of, he turned a deaf unheeding ear.

The year 1898 brought the greatest opportunity to K'ang. China bowed with repeated humiliations, the Emperor as a last resort invited K'ang, barely forty, to reform the government and adopt new policies with a view to strengthening the nation. Thereupon came the famous hundred-day reform. K'ang proposed to institute a constitutional monarchy and a parliament, to abolish the old eight-leg form of literary examination and establish a public school system, to dismiss incompetent officials, and to broaden the channels of public opinion. In a hundred days numerous reform edicts were issued by the Emperor at the instance of K'ang. Alarmed by the radical policy of K'ang, the Empress-Dowager seized the power of the throne and issued orders to arrest the reformers. K'ang escaped abroad, as did his student Liang Ch'ich'ao, but six of his friends, among whom was the young philosopher Tan Szut'ung, were executed. Had K'ang been in power for any length of time, he might have been a second Wang Anshih, a second "new dealer." His reform, however, was not a complete failure, for the spirit of the reform swept over the entire nation and stimulated new ideas and movements which eventually led to the downfall of the monarchy.

A radical thinker before forty, K'ang proved to be a most reactionary politician during the last thirty years of his life. At the turn of the present century, Sun Yat-sen was organizing a revolutionary party abroad, whose avowed purpose was to overthrow the Manchu monarchy and establish a Chinese republic. Though himself a political fugitive, K'ang organized a counter monarchical party. In 1913, a year after the overthrow of the monarchy, K'ang who had been a political exile for sixteen years returned to China and published numerous pamphlets and articles attacking the republican regime. He went so far as to instigate and participate in the restoration movement of 1917. Failing in this, he hid himself in the American Legation at Peking where he wrote *Three Essays on the Republic* (*Kungho P'ingi*), a scathing attack on the theory and practice of the revolutionary party. To the end of his life he remained a loyal subject of the Manchu dynasty.

K'ang is unquestionably the greatest scholar of modern China. Although he had a chequered political career, he found ample time for research in classics and history. In addition to the *Great Commonwealth,* he wrote *An Inquiry into the Spurious Classics* (*Hsinhsüeh Weiching K'ao*) and *An Inquiry Concerning How Confucius Formulated New Ideals in the Name of Antiquity* (*K'ungtzu Kaichi K'ao*), to mention only the most original works, which have exercised momentous influence upon recent classical and historical research.

Much as Confucius speaks in the name of antiquity, K'ang

attributes his own theory of the great commonwealth to Confucius. It is not unusual for him to interpret classical statements and historical facts in such a manner as to fit them into his own scheme of things and ideas. He usually first formulates a theory and then quotes in support extensively from ancient literature, as though "all the six classics were merely his footnotes." Thus extremely subjective and dogmatic was K'ang.

In recent politics K'ang was indeed a great sphinx. During the last decades of the nineteenth century when Chinese leaders were overwhelmingly conservative, K'ang proposed the most radical reform in Chinese political history—constitutional monarchy; but in the first decades of the twentieth century when the entire nation was turning to republicanism, he became the leader of the monarchist restoration movement. On the surface he appeared to have been a Janus whose faces always defied the world, but in reality he was by no means an inconsistent philosopher, for he held to the fixed belief that constitutional monarchy was the best form of government for China in the transitional period between absolute monarchy and pure democracy.

The Great Commonwealth

There are three inevitable stages in historical evolution, says K'ang Yuwei. First is the stage of war, second that of the minor peace, and third that of the great commonwealth. In the first stage every tribal state is at war with every other tribal state; during the second stage national states maintain an unstable peace by the balance of power; and when the final stage appears the entire world becomes one great commonwealth which transcends all racial, political, economic, and social boundaries. The ultimate goal of human evolution is the realization of the great commonwealth.

K'ang maintains that Confucius, who lived in the stage of war, visualized the stages of the minor peace and the great common-

wealth. Since Confucius the world has entered upon the stage of
the minor peace. Now that the distances between the continents
and the oceans have shrunken and all the civilizations and the
races of the world have established intimate contacts, the future
world will inevitably become a great commonwealth. This, says
K'ang, is all in accordance with the prophecy of Confucius the
great seer.

K'ang wrote the *Great Commonwealth* at the age of twenty-
seven when he was alone on a mountain cut off from human
reality. He was then a young dreamer, extremely imaginative and
romantic. The utopia he envisaged is the grandest and most perfect ever visualized by any Chinese philosopher or poet.

K'ang begins his rhapsodical extravaganza in the leitmotif of
Gautama the Buddha. Imagining that he descends upon the world
from nowhere, he finds that all is misery and sorrow; his heart is
sickened and his mind disturbed. After hours and days of medita-
tion, he arrives at the conclusion that the roots of all evils lie in
the nine boundaries or barriers which mankind has set up, the
boundaries between nation and nation, between class and class,
between race and race, between man and woman, between family
and family, between estate and estate, between territory and territory, between species and species, and between sorrow and sorrow.
Destroy these boundaries, says K'ang, and all will be well.

The existence of nations, says K'ang, is the first of all evils.
Where there are nations there must be wars. He surveys the wars
in world history and the numbers of innocent human beings
ruthlessly slaughtered, and concludes that the more civilized the
nations the greater the casualties. He proposes a world government under which all national states shall be abolished. The world
shall be divided into ten continents: Europe, East Asia, West Asia,
North Asia, South Asia, North America, Central America, South
America, Australia, and Africa. All men shall be world citizens,
not citizens of national states. There shall be a universal language,
a universal calendar (dating neither from Christ nor from Con-

fucius but from the inauguration of the great commonwealth), and universal standards of measurements. The word "nation" shall be deleted from the dictionary. All land and sea shall belong to the world government. K'ang is confident that such a world union is bound to come just as the national state has arisen from the union of tribal states.

The second great evil, K'ang says, is the distinction between class and class. All men are born equal and shall so remain. K'ang condemns the caste system in India and the feudal system in medieval Europe. He admires Abraham Lincoln who freed the black slaves in the United States. Above all, he thinks that the Confucian doctrine—all men are brothers—shall be the guiding principle of the future world.

In the third place, K'ang wishes to destroy the barrier between race and race in order to realize the ideal of the great commonwealth. The races on earth differ only in pigmentation and are basically equal in intelligence and worth. At present the "silver" race, which includes the Latins, the Teutons, and the Slavs, and the "golden" race, which includes the Chinese, the Japanese, and the Mongolians, are more progressive and populous, while the black and brown races are less so. They all, however, can merge as one great human family. The difference in color is a result of varying climatic and geographical conditions. The nearer to the tropic zone a people lives, the darker its color; the nearer to the polar zone, the lighter. K'ang believes that by fostering the processes of intercontinental migration and interracial marriage all people on earth will in the course of a thousand years become one great human race having more or less the same color, the same physique, and the same civilization.

In the fourth place, K'ang is in favor of obliterating the distinction between man and woman. To him the most unfair reality in the history of mankind is the domination of women by men, he declares. Since antiquity unknown millions of women have slaved and died under the domination of the man-made world; at present some eight hundred million women in the world are in misery and sorrow; but in the future females must not suffer the same fate at the hands of males. In most stringent terms K'ang condemns the old Chinese social and political system which barred women from becoming officials, scholars, legislators, and even citizens, denied them independence and freedom, and treated them virtually as prisoners, criminals, slaves, chattels, and toys. In reality, K'ang asserts, women and men are equal in intelligence and ability, possess the same human minds, ears, eyes, hands, and feet, can do the same things equally well, and therefore should be equally free and independent. He proposes that the marriage contract last not more than one year, at the end of which the parties may renew or dissolve the contract freely; that men and women dress alike, have the same education, and enjoy the same rights of citizenship and officialdom in the great commonwealth.

The barrier between family and family constitutes the fifth evil. Although the family system is a vital force of social solidarity, K'ang says, it is nevertheless an institution that breeds selfishness and acquisitiveness and much social struggle. The family system should be destroyed. Man and wife, father and son, brother and brother may live together as individuals in the great commonwealth. K'ang proposes a public child welfare system, a public education system, and a public old-age welfare system, to replace the family system. The public child welfare system consists of maternity hospitals, nurseries, and kindergartens, which will take care of children from birth to the age of six. The public education system consists of primary schools, secondary schools, and colleges, for boys and girls between the ages of six and twenty. The public old-age welfare system consists of homes, hospitals, and crematories for people above the age of sixty. Men and women between twenty and sixty, thus free from family ties and obligations, can devote themselves to the good of the great commonwealth.

In the sixth place, the boundary between estate and estate should be abolished completely, according to K'ang. There should be no private ownership in agriculture, industry, and commerce, but absolute economic equality. At present there are conflicts between peasant and landlord, between worker and capitalist, and between consumer and trader, which constitute a lethal disease in human society. K'ang proposes that all farms, factories, and business enterprises be owned and operated by the public. There should be a world ministry of agriculture, a world ministry of industry, and a world ministry of commerce, which separately and collectively will adjust the demand and supply of goods and services throughout the entire world. All people—men and women—should work for the great commonwealth and should enjoy the same right to goods and services.

The boundary between territory and territory is the seventh obstacle to the great commonwealth. K'ang proposes to section the globe into one hundred degrees both longitudinally and latitudinally. There will be a total of 10,000 square degrees on the globe and, excepting the surface of water, there will be some 3,000 square degrees for human habitation. The world will then fall into 3,000 administrative areas, each one square degree in size, each to be further divided into a number of autonomous units, all to be under the world government. All people are to be world citizens. They shall say that they are inhabitants of certain degrees north or south and east or west of the earth, not of China, America, or Europe. No man shall ever say: "This is my own, my native land."

The eighth boundary is that between species and species, says K'ang. When the age of the great commonwealth comes, man shall be vegetarian. He shall refrain from killing first horses and oxen, next chickens and geese, and finally fish, but shall exterminate all harmful animals. Of all animals, the monkey and the parrot are the most intelligent, and man shall teach them to speak. K'ang envisages a world in which birds will fly and sing freely in the air, elephants and deer roam unhindered over the earth, and fish swim unconcerned in the sea; they will know no fear of man.

Finally, K'ang thinks that man suffers from many forms of sorrow, material and spiritual. In the great commonwealth man will lack no material things as all natural resources will be scientifically developed. Spiritually man will be Prometheus unbound, knowing no fear of final judgment or of the supernatural power, and therefore eternally happy.

Such then is the perfect dream utopia of K'ang. He insists that it is a Confucian conception and ideal, for the great master said some twenty-five centuries ago: "When the great way prevails, the world is a common state."

Constitutional Monarchy

The proposal which K'ang made to transform the traditional absolute monarchy into a constitutional monarchy was indeed a very radical innovation in 1898. Although it has since been considered as a mild reformist measure, it was truly revolutionary in the light of the evolution of the Chinese body politic. For had the proposal been carried out, the historic system of monarchism would have been transformed into a new democratic regime sans revolution.

As K'ang intends them, the terms monarchy and republic denote two systems of government in a formal sense only. He contends that a monarchy can be democratic in operation while a republic may be a dictatorial regime in actual practice. The only valid criterion in politics, says K'ang, is not whether the state is monarchical or republican in structure, but whether it is a private possession of the one or a public institution of the many. He disapproves of the Platonic and Aristotelean formal definitions of monarchy, aristocracy, and democracy, and insists upon the soundness of the Confucian view that the state is a public institution when the great way prevails but a private institution when it does not. Regardless of form or structure, the state is democratic if it is a public institution of the many, but autocratic if it is a private institution of the one.

Although China had been under a monarchical system of government for two thousand years, K'ang declared, the Chinese people had enjoyed real equality and a great deal of liberty. Since the abolition of the feudal system, all citizens had been accorded equal opportunity to become officials and ministers or otherwise to rise to upper strata of social hierarchy, there having been no hereditary nobles nor permanent paupers. During those centuries the common people had seldom been deprived of the freedoms of person, property, profession, speech, press, and faith. All the rights of man which the western people had been struggling for in the last two centuries, K'ang asserted, the Chinese had possessed for twenty centuries. Therefore, a bloody revolution was not prerequisite to real democracy.

The real political issue, said K'ang, was not whether a monarch reigned or not, but whether the government was a private or a public institution. If this issue were understood, the difference between the revolutionary movement of Sun Yat-sen and the reformist movement of himself would not at all be an essential matter. He was a great admirer of the British constitutional system under which the king reigns but does not rule, while the Parliament exercises the real sovereign power. He hoped for a Chinese "Glorious Revolution" which would set up a parliament wherein the sovereign power resided but which would retain the nominal monarch as the symbol of the nation. To this end he proposed the creation of a constitutional monarchy.

The aims of the constitution K'ang proposed were to transfer the sovereign power from the throne to the parliament and to define the duties and rights of officials and citizens. He advanced the view that the *Spring and Autumn* which Confucius wrote was really a body of constitutional principles, which "rectified the names" and hence defined the status and functions of all grades of officials and citizens. During the Han dynasty, the text of the

Spring and Autumn was actually cited in the setting up of political institutions, the determination of national policies, and the decision of judicial cases. Therefore, K'ang declared, the *Spring and Autumn* was the Magna Charta of the Chinese Empire. He regretted that in recent centuries the monarchs had disregarded Confucian constitutional principles and become autocratic sovereigns.

K'ang proposed that a parliament should be instituted. It should consist of two houses in accordance with the Confucian dictum that the king should consult "officials and scholars" and "commoners." The establishment of the parliament, says K'ang, should be the first act of sound government, "for the parliament, being the assembly of the best talents of the country and representing the will of the people, is the proper legislative organ of the state. Whether the head of the state is a monarch or a president is inconsequential as long as the parliament is the sole organ wherein the sovereignty resides."

In organizing a constitutional system, K'ang thinks, there are three factors to be considered: the people, the nation, and the relations between them. From the point of view of the people, autonomy is the guiding principle. The people are to be considered as public citizens, not as private individuals or mere subjects of the monarch, and affairs in towns and villages are to be administered autonomously, not by officers appointed by the national government. From the point of view of the nation, centralization is the guiding principle. All matters of state are to be planned and carried out systematically on a national scale. As to the relations between the people and the nation, K'ang suggests that the country be divided into seventy circuits (instead of eighteen provinces) so that each circuit will have jurisdiction over only twenty to thirty counties (instead of sixty to a hundred). Circuit governors and county magistrates are to be appointed by the national government, while mayors of towns and villages are to be elected locally. Local autonomy, K'ang concludes, is the foundation of the nation, the national government is the superstructure, and the circuit and county governments constitute the channels between the people and the nation.

As indicated above, K'ang was a radical reformer prior to 1900. In one of his several memorials he urged the throne to effect immediate and complete change in the governmental system. "It is no longer possible to be conservative; it is imperative to change the laws. It is impossible to change them gradually; it is imperative to change them quickly. It is impossible to change them in part; it is imperative to change them totally." That impatient and aggressive was K'ang the radical reformer.

But after 1900 K'ang changed from a radical reformer to a reactionary politician. During his sixteen-year exile he attacked the revolutionary movement of Sun Yat-sen incessantly. In 1918 he published *Three Essays on the Republic,* in which he charged— not without reason—that the so-called Republic was worse than an absolute monarchy and had become a military dictatorship; that the draft constitution was drawn up not by the representatives of the people but by the personal delegates of the provincial war-lords; that civil liberties existed only on paper; and that without the unifying symbol in the person of a monarch the country had disintegrated into several warring states which would eventually perish from the face of the earth. The fundamental mistake of the revolutionary party, he declared, lay in the blind effort to adopt the republican systems of the United States and France wholesale with little regard to Chinese traditional democratic ideas and practices. He insisted that the Chinese Empire should be a constitutional monarchy, similar to the British and the Roman Empire. To the end of his days he regretted that his theory of constitutional monarchy was never given a fair trial.

Confucianism as State Religion

In the first year of the Republic when Confucianism was virtually abolished as the official doctrine of the state and the Confucian classics were no longer required subjects in schools, K'ang Yuwei "the sage" became truly alarmed. He feared that the abolition of Confucianism, which represented "the very soul of the nation," would eventually mean the destruction of Chinese culture and the disintegration of Chinese society. Whereupon in 1913 he made a formal proposal to the Parliament to establish Confucianism as state religion.

K'ang submitted that the constitution, which the Parliament was then drafting, should guarantee freedom of belief and worship to all citizens but simultaneously should establish Confucianism as state religion.

The principle of religious freedom, which the western people have won after centuries of struggle, is not a novel principle to the Chinese, says K'ang. Ever since ancient times the Chinese have always had freedom of faith. Even after the Han dynasty established Confucianism as the official doctrine of the state, no Chinese citizen, be he prime minister or humble peasant, has ever been prevented from becoming a Taoist, a Buddhist, a Mohammedan, or a Christian. Taoist and Buddhist temples have been established everywhere, so have Mohammedan mosques and Christian churches. As a matter of fact, many Confucians in history have been Taoists and Buddhists at the same time. Confucianism is a broad and tolerant doctrine and Confucius is not a jealous deity. That is why, says K'ang, although Confucianism has been the official doctrine for two thousand years, complete religious freedom has been preserved. This freedom has never been a problem in China, as it has in the West, because the Chinese have never been dogmatic or fanatic about personal faiths.

Confucianism is essentially a humanistic doctrine, different from supernatural Christianity and extramundane Buddhism, says K'ang.

It teaches the way of man; it teaches the principles of human relations. It is Confucianism that has held the Chinese people together as a nation. Had there been no Confucianism, the Chinese nation would have long been Balkanized (disintegrated) or Amerindianized (vanquished).

Although the western countries have won freedom of faith, yet they are not without state religions, says K'ang. Italy is a Roman Catholic country, Greece an Orthodox Catholic country. The coronation of the British King or Queen and the inauguration of the American President, though state functions, are both religious ceremonies. There is no necessary conflict between the principle of religious freedom and the practice of a national religion.

K'ang proposed that the Temple of Heaven in Peiping be made the center of reverence and worship. On state occasions the President of the Republic should lead the entire officialdom to the Temple of Heaven to offer sacrifice to Confucius. In every provincial capital, in every seat of county government, there should be a Confucian temple, where periodic services should be held. Students in all schools and colleges should study the Confucian classics, so that they might learn to know the crystallized experience of Chinese society and the essence of Chinese culture.

This proposal naturally aroused nation-wide debate. Old scholars and conservative politicians greeted it with wholehearted support and proceeded to organize Confucian societies throughout the country. But the revolutionary leaders in Parliament and out arose as one man to oppose what they considered a reactionary movement, although they did not oppose Confucianism as such. The proposal was quietly shelved by the Parliament.

Ironically, the writer who offered the soundest and most eloquent theoretical opposition was none other than Liang Ch'ich'ao, erstwhile disciple of K'ang and, second only to K'ang himself, the greatest Confucian scholar in modern China.

It is fitting to conclude this informal history of Chinese political thought by quoting Liang's view on Confucianism as state doctrine:

"In no other period in Chinese history has there been higher scholarship and more original thought than in the period of the Contending States. The reason is not far to seek. It is freedom of thought.

"When the First Emperor burned the works of ancient philosophers, freedom of thought was for the first time suppressed. When Emperor Wu of the Han dynasty extolled the Confucian classics and reproved the unorthodox schools at the instance of Tung Chungshu, freedom of thought was once again restricted. Since the Han, Confucianism has prevailed for two thousand years, and the dynastic houses have uniformly adopted the policy of extolling canonical schoolmen and reproving iconoclastic thinkers.

"There have been conflicts between the orthodox and the heterodox and between the ancient script school and the modern script school . . . each claiming to represent true Confucianism and attacking the other as non-Confucianism. . . .

"As a result, Confucius has undergone a series of transfigurations throughout these centuries. First, he became a Tung Chungshu and a Ho Shaokung; next, he appeared as a Ma Chich'eng and a Cheng K'angch'eng; then suddenly a Han Yu and a Ouyang Hsiu; then a Ch'eng Hsi and a Chu Hsi; again a Lu Chiuyuan and a Wang Yangming; and finally a Ku T'inglin and a Tai Tungyuan. All these schoolmen were obsessed by some aspects of Confucianism and unable to beat new paths of thought. . . . Such is the tragic consequence of two thousand years of Confucianism as state doctrine!"

EPILOGUE

EPILOGUE

WE HAVE come to the end of a long peregrination during the course of which we have witnessed one millennium of feudalism and twenty centuries of monarchism. Against the background of this long history the republican era—which has existed only three decades—is scarcely more than an iota in an infinity. It is extremely difficult to place the record of the last three decades in a proper historical perspective.

This much perhaps we may say: just as the feudal age existed one millennium before it disappeared, just as the monarchical age lasted twenty centuries before it finally passed away, the republican era will most probably endure a long time ere the Chinese invent a new form of government.

The Republic has lived thirty years. These have been troublous and difficult years. In the first decade the newborn Republic was threatened by two monarchist restoration movements; in the second the adolescent Republic had to fight against the reactionary forces of warlordism and provincialism; and in this third the young Republic has been struggling for its very survival. Through these years of trial it has been maturing in experience and growing in strength. Today there can scarcely be any doubt that it will not only survive the present crisis, but will also play a vital role in the free world of tomorrow.

Of the Republic Sun Yat-sen is both the ideological father and the real founder. He is the genius who interprets and symbolizes the spirit of the times. As K'ang Yuwei seals the omega of the monarchical age, Sun marks the alpha of the republican era.

Historians may well divide the formative years of the Republic into three stages. The First Republic, formally inaugurated in 1912, was an imitation of the British parliamentary system. The Second Republic, organized in Canton in 1925, was a variation of the Russian soviet system. Neither the parliamentary system nor the soviet, however, was a success. No nation can import a political system and make it work. It was not until 1928 that the Third Republic adopted the five-power constitutional system, a new but indigenous system conceived by Sun Yat-sen and brought into being by Chiang Kai-shek.

The ideal system of government, Sun thinks, is divided into five independent departments—legislative, executive, judicial, examination, and censorial—which can check and balance one another. Sun proposes the retention of the old examination and censorial departments in addition to the usual three departments, recommended by Montesquieu and sanctified in the Constitution of the United States. The examination department is to select civil servants, the censorial department to supervise the conduct of officials and the working of political machinery. This scheme of government, according to Sun, is a synthesis of the best features in the old scholastic empire and in the modern democratic constitutions.

The Chinese Republic is founded upon the Three Principles of the People (*San Min Chu I*)—the principle of national independence, the principle of political democracy, and the principle of social welfare. The three principles, says Sun, aim at establishing "a government of the people, by the people, and for the people." A government of the people means a government based upon the principle of national independence. A government by the people means one based upon the principle of political democracy. A government for the people means one based upon the principle of social welfare.

In explaining the principle of national independence Sun makes a distinction between nation and state. A nation is a body of people united by the general consciousness of a common blood, a common religion, a common language, and a common pattern of habits and customs. A state is a body of people politically organized to accomplish certain purposes, such as protection of rights and liberties, maintenance of public order, defense of national safety. A state may or may not be organized on a national basis.

The corporate sentiment that binds different national groups to a state is called patriotism. Sun was interested in promoting the corporate sentiment of patriotism among the Chinese. He was of the opinion that the Chinese had always shown loyalty to the family and the clan but had hitherto manifested little patriotism.

There are two aspects in the principle of national independence. In the first place, Sun says, China must maintain complete territorial and administrative integrity and must be free from foreign domination. In the second place, she must co-operate with all those nations that treat her on the basis of equality. Sun puts equal emphasis upon national independence and international co-operation. He wishes to see a China completely free and independent; at the same time he expresses the hope that all free nations will be organized into a great universal commonwealth.

In lecturing on the second principle Sun declares that democracy is the goal of political evolution. When the masses are unenlightened, he says, autocracy or aristocracy may be of considerable value. As civilization advances, people grow in intelligence and in reasoning power and develop a new consciousness of self-dependence and self-control. Democracy is the end-product in the process of civilization.

Sun makes a significant contribution to the theory of democracy in his emphasis upon the distinction between sovereignty and ability. Sovereignty, that is, control of public policy, should be vested in all citizens, while public administration should be undertaken by men of ability. "The government of a republic," says he, "must be built upon the rights of the people, but the administration of public affairs must be entrusted to experts."

The sovereign powers of the people, according to Sun, are four in number: election and recall of political officials, and direct legislation by means of initiative and referendum. With these four sovereign powers the people can control the government directly. It will then be safe, in Sun's opinion, to build a "high-powered strong government."

While the people enjoy four sovereign powers, the government, says Sun, must exercise five administrative powers, legislative, executive, judicial, examination, and censorial. Sun lays special emphasis upon the examination and censorial powers as means of securing men of competence and integrity to administer public affairs.

The principle of social welfare is a social policy the end of which, according to Sun, is that the needs of all are supplied by the efforts of all.

This principle sounds socialistic or communistic. Sun, however, turns a deaf ear to both utopian socialism and scientific communism. He thinks that the utopian socialists are "people who create a peaceful and happy world out of imagination." While he pays tribute to Marx, he flatly rejects the theory of historical materialism and the doctrine of class struggle.

The principle of social welfare is not a capitalistic principle. As China is to enter an era of industrialization, Sun thinks, she must prevent the gross inequalities and the chaotic business cycles that characterize laissez-faire capitalism.

Rejecting both anarchistic capitalism and rigorous communism, Sun proposes to follow the middle of the road. He proposes a new social policy, based upon two cardinal ideas: regulation of capital and equalization of landownership. First, the government should protect private interests in light industries but should own and operate enterprises that are monopolistic in nature. Second, the government should appropriate unearned increments in land values so that an equitable distribution of landownership may be brought about.

In historical perspective the three principles may be seen as the climax of a long series of nationalistic, democratic, and socialistic trends. Sun is more than a worthy successor of Wang Fuchih, the philosopher of nationalism, of Huang Tsunghsi, the philosopher of democracy, and of Wang Anshih, the new dealer. As an advocate of the great commonwealth Sun is heir and disciple of Confucius himself.

In terms of western political thought, the three principles represent a synthesis of the most important political ideals in modern times. The principle of national independence sustains the ideal of national unity and autonomy, which has inspired the modern nationalist movements in many lands. The principle of political democracy endorses the ideal of government by popular consent, which has inspired the democratic movements since the eighteenth century. The principle of social welfare expresses the ideal that the needs of all are supplied by the efforts of all, which has inspired the socialist movements in recent times.

While these three ideals are embodied in three distinct movements, they are integrated by Sun into a single system of revolutionary philosophy. The three principles are interdependent and inseparable. Sun's nationalism differs from imperialistic and jingoistic nationalism, for it is modified by the principles of democracy and socialism. His democratic ideal assumes national independence and serves ultimately the interests of the people. His socialistic ideal is predicated upon national independence and is to be realized through democratic processes. The three principles thus constitute in reality a unitarian revolutionary philosophy, upon which the Chinese Republic is founded.

In the light of this revolutionary philosophy, the war which China has been fighting against the Axis powers may be seen as a people's revolutionary war, a continuation of the war which Sun started at the turn of the present century. From China's point of view the aims of this war have long been defined in Sun's three principles. And from the point of view of the entire world the war may be said to be aiming at the establishment anywhere and everywhere of the principles of national independence, political democracy, and social welfare. Not to restore the *status quo,* nor to maintain the colonial or imperial system or the class system, must this war be fought, but to create a free world in which all men, regardless of color or status, may live as free beings. Even as the new war is dynamic and revolutionary, so the new peace that is to follow must be dynamic and revolutionary.

After ages of isolationism, symbolized by the Great Wall, the Chinese people have now found not only comrades-in-ideas but also comrades-in-arms in the western democratic countries. In the present five-ocean, six-continent, global war the Chinese people have been fighting stubbornly and courageously, hand in hand with the western democratic peoples, against the reactionary forces of aggression and tyranny. They are working toward the establishment at home of a government of the people, by the people, and for the people; and simultaneously they are looking forward to the creation of a United Nations of the World, a government at the world level, which will be able to maintain an ever enduring world peace, an ever expanding world economy, and an ever advancing world culture.

BIBLIOGRAPHY

BIBLIOGRAPHY

General References

Chang, Pingling. *Kuoku Lunheng (Critical Essays on Chinese Literature and Philosophy)*. Shanghai, 1920.

Ch'en, Kuyüan. *Chungkuo Fachi Shih (History of the Chinese Legal System)*. Shanghai, 1934.

Chiang, Weich'iao. *Chungkuo Chin Sanpainien Chehsüeh Shih (History of Modern Chinese Philosophy)*. Shanghai, 1932.

Ch'ien, Mu. *Chungkuo Chin Sanpainien Hsüehshu Shih (Chinese Intellectual History of the Recent Three Centuries)*. Shanghai, 1937.

Chin, Y. L. "On Political Thought," *T'ien Hsia Monthly*, IX (1939), 257-72.

Chou, Kuch'eng. *Chungkuo T'ungshih (A General History of China)*. 2 vols. Shanghai, 1939.

Fitzgerald, Charles P. *China: A Short Cultural History*. New York, 1938.

Fung, Yulan. *A History of Chinese Philosophy*, tr. by Derk Bodde. Peiping, 1937.

Granet, Marcel. *Chinese Civilization*. New York, 1930.

Hsiang, Linpin. *Chungkuo Chehsüeh Shih Kangyao (An Outline History of Chinese Philosophy)*. Shanghai, 1939.

Hsiao, Kungch'üan. "Chinese Theories of the Origin of Politics," *Tsing Hua Journal*, IX (1934), 535-48.

Hsü, Shihch'ang. *Ch'ing Ju Hsüehan (The Lives and Works of the Ch'ing Scholars)*. 208 vols. Peiping, 1939.

Hu, Shih. *Chungkuo Chehsüeh Shih Takang (History of Chinese Philosophy)*. Shanghai, 1919.

Huang, Tsunghsi. *Ming Ju Hsüehan (The Lives and Works of the Ming Scholars)*. 62 vols.

Huang, Tsunghsi, and Ch'üan, Hsiehshan. *Sung Yüan Hsüehan (The Lives and Works of the Sung and Yüan Scholars)*. 100 vols.

Ku, Chiehkang, and Lo, Kengtse (eds.). *Ku Shih Pien (Symposium on Ancient History)*. 6 vols. Peiping, 1926-39. Ku edited vols. i, ii, iii, and v; Lo edited vols. iv and vi.

Latourette, Kenneth Scott. *The Chinese: Their History and Culture*. New York, 1941.

Lee, J. S. "The Periodic Recurrence of Internecine Wars in China," *The China Journal of Science and Arts,* March and April, 1931.

Li, Maimai. *Chungkuo Kutai Chengchih Chehsüeh Pip'ing (Critical Studies on Chinese Ancient Political Philosophy)*. Shanghai, 1933.

Liang, Ch'ich'ao. *Ch'ingtai Hsüehshu Kailun (An Introduction to Ch'ing Dynasty Philosophy)*. Shanghai, 1921.

Liang, Ch'ich'ao. *History of Chinese Political Thought,* tr. by L. T. Ch'en. New York, 1930.

Lin, Yutang. *My Country and My People*. New York, 1935.

T'ang, Ch'ingtseng. *Chungkuo Chingchi Szuhsiang Shih (History of Chinese Economic Thought)*. Shanghai, 1936.

T'ao, Hsisheng. *Chungkuo Chengchih Szuhsiang Shih (History of Chinese Political Thought)*. 2 vols. Shanghai, 1932.

Ts'ai, Yüanp'ei. *Chungkuo Lunlihsüeh Shih (History of Chinese Ethics)*. Shanghai, 1920.

Waley, Arthur. *Three Ways of Thought in Ancient China*. London, 1939.

Wang, Lihsi (ed.). *Chungkuo Shehuishih Lunchan (Symposium on Chinese Social History)*. 4 vols. Shanghai, 1932-33.

Wang, Tungling. *Chungkuo Shih (Chinese History of Different Dynasties)*. 4 vols. Peiping, 1928.

Yang, Yuchiung. *Chungkuo Chengchih Szuhsiang Shih (A History of Chinese Political Thought)*. Shanghai, 1937.

PART I

Carus, P. (tr.). *Tao Teh Ching*. Chicago, 1913.

Dubs, Homer H. *Hsüntze, the Moulder of Ancient Confucianism*. London, 1927.

Dubs, Homer H. (tr.). *The Works of Hsüntze*. London, 1928.

Duyvendak, J. J. L. (tr.). *The Book of Lord Shang*. London, 1928.

Fung, Yulan. "The Origin of the Confucian and Mocian Schools," *Tsing Hua Journal*, X (1935), 279-310.

Fung, Yulan. "The Origin of the Logician, Legalist, Metaphysician, and Taoist Schools," *Tsing Hua Journal*, XI (1936), 279-82.

Giles, Herbert A. (tr.). *Chuang Tzu*. Shanghai, 1926.

Hu, Shih. "The Origin of the Confucian School," *Bulletin of the Institute of History and Philology, Academia Sinica*, IV (1934), 233-84.

Legge, James (tr.). *The Chinese Classics*. 5 vols. Oxford, 1865-95.

Legge, James (tr.). *The Texts of Taoism*. 2 vols. Oxford, 1891.

Liang, Ch'ich'ao. *Motzu Hsüehan (Philosophy of Mocius)*. Shanghai, 1925.

Liao, Wenkuei (tr.). *Han Fei Tzu*. London, 1939.

Lin, Mousheng. "Confucius on Interpersonal Relations," *Psychiatry*, II (1939), 475-81.

Lin, Yutang. *The Wisdom of Confucius*. New York, 1938.

Lyall, Leonard A. (tr.). *Mencius*. London, 1932.

Lyall, Leonard A. (tr.). "Yang Chu," *T'ien Hsia Monthly*, IX (1939), 189-204.

Mei, Yipao (tr.). *The Ethical and Political Works of Motse*. London, 1929.

Mei, Yipao. *Motse, the Neglected Rival of Confucius*. London, 1934.

Ssuma, Ch'ien. *Shih Chi (Historical Record)*. 130 vols. See the biographies of the ancient philosophers.

Waley, Arthur (tr.). *The Analects of Confucius*. London, 1938.

Wu, John C. H. (tr.). "Lao Tzu's *The Tao and Its Virtue*," *T'ien Hsia Monthly*, IX (1939), 401-23 and 498-521, and X (1940), 66-99.

Wu, John C. H. "The Real Confucius," *T'ien Hsia Monthly*, I (1935), 11-20 and 180-89.

Part II

Ch'en, Liang. *Lungch'uan Wenchi (Collected Works)*. 30 volumes.

Ch'i, Wenfu. *Ch'uanshan Chehsüeh (Philosophy of Wang Fuchih)*. Shanghai, 1936.

Holcombe, Arthur N. *The Chinese Revolution*. Cambridge, 1930.

Hu, Shih. "The Establishment of Confucianism as a State Religion during the Han Dynasty," *Journal of the Royal Asiatic Society, China Branch,* LX (1939), 20-41.

Hu, Shih. *Historical Foundations for a Democratic China.* University of Illinois, 1941.

Huang, Tsunghsi. *Mingi Taifang Lu (A Treatise on Political Science).*

K'ang, Yuwei. *Kuanchi Lun (On Government).* Shanghai, 1905.

K'ang, Yuwei. *Kungho P'ingi (Three Essays on the Republic).* Shanghai, 1918.

K'ang, Yuwei. *Ni Chunghua Minkuo Hsienfa Ch'aoan (A Draft Constitution of the Chinese Republic).* Shanghai, 1916.

K'ang, Yuwei. *Tat'ung Shu (The Great Commonwealth).* Shanghai, 1935.

Ke, Hung. *Chieh Pao (The Refutation of Pao),* being the 48th chapter of *Paopotzu.*

Liang, Ch'ich'ao. *K'ang Nanhai Chuan (Biography of K'ang Yuwei).* Shanghai, 1901.

Liang, Ch'ich'ao. *Wang Chingkung Chuan (Biography of Wang Anshih).* Shanghai, 1920.

Pan, Ku, et al. *Dynastic Histories.* See the biographies of the political thinkers.

Sun, Yatsen. *San Min Chu I,* tr. by Frank Price. Shanghai, 1928.

Tan, Szut'ung. *Jen Hsüeh (Theory of Humanity).*

Tung Chungshu. *Ch'unch'iu Fanglu (Interpretations of the Spring and Autumn).*

Wang, Anshih. *Wang Linch'uan Ch'üanchi (Complete Works).* 24 vols.

Wang, Fuchih. *Ch'uanshan Weishu (Works of Wang Fuchih).* 250 vols.

Williamson, Henry R. *Wang An Shih.* 2 vols. London, 1937.

Yüan, Chi. *Tajen Hsiensheng Chuan (Biography of the Great Man).*

INDEX

INDEX

A

Abdications of Yao and Shun, 17-18, 58, 108, 189

Agricultural adjustment act, of Wang Anshih, 165-66

Alexander the Great, 11, 77, 105, 123

Anarchism, Laotzu's, 66-70; Yangtzu's, 80-82; Mencius on Yangtzu's anarchism, 80; Chuangtzu's, 83-86; Yüan Chi's ideas of, 151; Pao Chingyen's, 153-58

Anti-new dealer, *see* Ssuma Kuang

Aristippus, 76

Aristocracy, moral and intellectual, Confucius' view, 36; Mencius' view, 52-53; Hsüntzu's view, 52-53; Tung Chungshu's view, 146-48

Aristotle, 4, 8, 11, 12, 28; cf. Confucius, 32, 42-43; cf. Hsüntzu, 44; concepts of royalty and tyranny, 54; cf. Hantzu, 105, 119, 142, 223

Axis powers, 237

B

Bacon, 4

Bakunin, 87

Balance of power, 219

Bamboo Grove, Seven Sages of, 151

Benevolent government, 54-56

Bentham, cf. Mocius, 92-93

Blitzkrieg, 184

Bodin, 4; cf. Hantzu, 113, 119-20

Bosanquet, Bernard, 25 note, 138 note

Bourgeoisie, 24, 145; *see* classes

Buddhism, 184, 227

C

Calvin, 51

Capitalism, Tung Chungshu's view, 145; Wang Anshih's opposition, 165-68; Sun Yat-sen's view, 236; *see* monopoly

Censorial system, imperial censor, 129; censorial power, 236

Chang I, 22

Chang T'aiyen, 114

Check and balance, T'ang dynasty, 128-29; Ch'en Liang's theory, 183; Sun Yat-sen's theory, 234

Ch'en Hsiang, 23

Ch'en Liang, 11, 13, 130; life, 174-77; synthesis of idealism and realism, 178-81; military and civil ways, 178-81; nationalism, 181-82; democratic idea, 182-83; military strategy, 183-84

Ch'eng Hsi, 229

Cheng K'angch'eng, 229

Chieh, 18, 57, 58, 107, 112, 115, 190, 191; *see* revolutions of T'ang Wang and Wu Wang

Ch'in dynasty, *see* First Empire

Ch'in, King of, *see* First Emperor

Ch'in Kuei, 174

Chinese history, *see* cycles in Chinese history, historical evolution

Chinese philosophy, nature of, 3-5

Chinese politics, promise of, 233-37

Ch'ing dynasty, 133, 186, 187, 200, 211

Chou, Duke of, 18, 36, 43, 57

Chou dynasty, 18-22, 143, 163, 180, 208

Chow, 18, 57, 58, 78, 107, 112, 115, 190, 191; *see* revolutions of T'ang Wang and Wu Wang

Christianity, 227

Index

R

Race, as a factor of nationalism, 210-11; K'ang Yuwei on, 220

Realism in politics, Hantzu, 103-20; Ch'en Liang's view, 178-81; *see* synthesis

Reason and force, Wang Fuchih's metaphysics, 203-05

Rectification of names, Confucius' doctrine, 3-4, 39-40; Hantzu's doctrine, 117-18

Reformism, of Wang Anshih, 162-64; of K'ang Yuwei, 216-17, 226

Religion, 227-28

Religious freedom, 227

Republic, Chinese, 233-34

Retrospective orientation, in thinking, 26, 43, 58-59, 70-71, 109, 179-80, 196; *see* prospective orientation

Revolution, Mencius' theory, 58; Hsüntzu's theory, 58; Huang Tsunghsi's theory, 190; Sun Yat-sen's theory, 237; *see* nationalist revolution

Revolutions of T'ang Wang and Wu Wang, 18, 58, 190

Ritual government, 54-56

Romantic pattern, *see* patterns of life

Rousseau, 4, 13, 28, 34; cf. Mencius, 49-51; cf. Laotzu, 66, 70, 71, 72; cf. Chuangtzu, 84, 86, 87; on China, 84, 145, 196

Royalty, views of Mencius, Hsüntzu, Plato, and Aristotle, 53-56

Rulership, Confucius' conception, 33, 40; Huang Tsunghsi's conception, 189-90

S

San Min Chu I, see Three Principles of the People

Santayana, 137

Science of political thought, 11-14

Sex equality, K'ang Yuwei on, 220-21

Shang dynasty, 18, 57, 58, 143, 163, 180, 208

Shang, Lord, 112

Shelley, 72

Shentzu, 112

Shun, 17, 57, 58, 78, 105, 106, 107, 108, 112, 115, 189; *see* abdications of Yao and Shun

Social analysis, 7-9

Social evolution, *see* historical evolution

Socialism, K'ang Yuwei's view, 222; Sun Yat-sen's view, 236; *see* new deal

Sociologic concept of the state, Pao Chingyen, 153-55

Socrates, 12, 25, 32, 76

Soldiers, regular and mysterious, 184

Solon, 43, 159

Son of Heaven, 18-20

Sophistic-Taoistic way of thinking, 70, 72

Southern pattern, *see* patterns of life

Sovereign, Mencius' view, 58; Hsüntzu's view, 58; Mocius' view, 96, 98; Hantzu's view, 113; Tung Chungshu's view, 140-41; Pao Chingyen's view, 155-56; Huang Tsunghsi's view, 189-90

Sovereignty, Hantzu's theory, 113; Huang Tsunghsi's idea of popular sovereignty, 189-90; Sun Yat-sen's theory of popular sovereignty, 235-36

Spring and Autumn, period of, 17, 21-22, 57, passim

Ssuma Kuang, anti-new dealer, 161-62, 165, 168, 170

State, as public or private property, 189-90, 223-24

State, Confucius' theory, 34-35; views of Mencius and Hsüntzu, 52-53; Laotzu's view, 66-70; Mocius' theory, 94-99; Hantzu's theory, 111-14; Tung Chungshu's metaphysical theory, 140-43; Pao Chingyen's sociologic concept, 153-55; Wang Anshih's view, 169;

Index